David Ferbrache

A Pathology of Computer Viruses

SPRINGER-VERLAG
London · Berlin · Heidelberg · New York
Paris · Tokyo · Hong Kong
Barcelona · Budapest

David Ferbrache, BSc(Hons)
Defence Research Agency (CS1)
Royal Signals and Radar Establishment
St. Andrew's Road
Great Malvern
Worcestershire, UK

ISBN 3–540–19610–2 Springer-Verlag Berlin Heidelberg New York
ISBN 0–387–19610–2 Springer-Verlag Berlin Heidelberg New York

British Library Cataloguing in Publication Data
Ferbache, David 1965–
A pathology of computer viruses.
1. Computer. Viruses
I. Title
004
ISBN 3–540–19610–2

Library of Congress Cataloging-in-Publication Data
Ferbrache, David, 1965–
A pathology of computer viruses / David Ferbrache
p. cm.
Includes index.
ISBN 3–540–19610–2. – ISBN 0–387–19610–2 (U.S.)
1. Computer viruses.   I. Title.
QA76.76.C68F45 1991
005.9--dc20   91–12483
                                                                        CIP

© Springer-Verlag London Limited 1992
Printed in Germany

Typeset from disk by Saxon Printing Ltd, Derby
34/3830-543210 – Printed on acid-free paper.

A Pathology of Computer Viruses

To Ann

Disclaimer

While every effort has been made to ensure the accuracy of the
information provided in this work, no responsibility can be
accepted for damages caused directly or indirectly through the use
or interpretation of the information.

Note

Within the text all references to "h" as a numeric suffix designate a
number in hexadecimal format.

This work has been carried out with the support of Procurement
Executive, Ministry of Defence.

Contents

Chapter 1
Introduction

1.1 Preamble

This book considers in depth the problem of the computer virus – what it is; who it affects; and, most importantly, what can be done to prevent or destroy it.

I aim to give a comprehensive description of the history of the computer virus "explosion" we are experiencing at this time, a detailed analysis of how a virus might operate on the IBM PC and Apple Macintosh computer platforms, and a complete review of management precautions to reduce the viral threat.

The issues of trojan horses and network worms are also covered in some detail, with particular emphasis on the security of local area networks (LANs). During this work a limited knowledge of computing is assumed, although introductory material is included in the preface to each chapter.

1.2 What is a Computer Virus?

A computer virus is informally defined as:

> A self-replicating segment of executable computer code embedded within a host program

To explain the above description, the case of a simple computer virus can be considered. A computer executes a series of instructions, which are simple commands (such as add or multiply two numbers). These instructions are represented by codes known as "object" or "machine" code. High level languages such as Pascal and C are compiled into such basic instruction sequences.

A virus is a similar short instruction sequence embedded within the object code of a larger "host" program, thus:

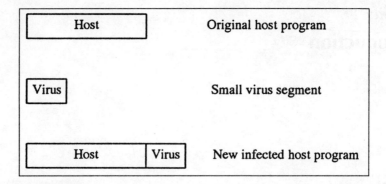

The virus additionally modifies the host so that when the computer begins execution of the host program, control is passed to the virus code. When the virus code is run, it rapidly searches for a new host into which it can copy its code.

Thus, if we show both the flow of control (execution sequence) and code before and after infection, we have:

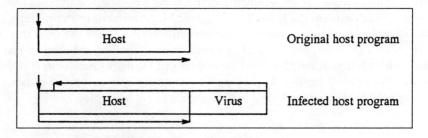

Although appearing complex, the flow of control in the infected case is:

- Computer tries to execute the host program
- Modified host causes virus code to be run
- Virus runs and multiplies by infecting new files
- Virus returns control to the host
- Host appears to run normally

In brief, this is the essence of a computer virus. It spreads by infecting host programs; the host program appears to run but in doing so activates the virus, which spreads even further.

Virus are propagated between machines by the physical movement of infected media (disks) or electronic movement of infected programs.

1.3 Worms: Networked Viruses

The current trend in computing appears to be towards mass wide area networking of both mainframe and personal computer systems. This rich environment allows the rapid spread and replication of both the computer virus and its cousin, the worm. A worm is an independent program which, when run on a computer, will attempt to infect other connected computer systems.

This is achieved by making use of the extensive set of services provided by the network, which often – and critically – includes the ability to execute computer code under remote control. Networks also allow traditional viruses to spread more rapidly through organisations by allowing the sharing of infected files and utilities. Thus with a networked "file server" a PC virus can spread without manual movement of software (i.e. disks) between computer systems.

The worm is analogous to the virus and differs only in terminology. In this case the host program is the operating system of the computer, and the infected code is a stand-alone process or thread of execution running under the operating system.

The computer worm was originally developed as an innocuous method of load balancing and distributed computation at Xerox. This work created worms which identified free processors on the distributed workstation network. When a free processor was located a copy of the worm would be started on that system. Thus, workstations in locked offices could make a useful contribution to the overall processing power of the network. The worms developed at Xerox were exceptionally intelligent in that they could detect the death of a "segment" (an instance of the worm code) running on a remote system, and restart it if necessary. Similarly they could detect the compartmentalisation or division of the network into sub-networks and the rejoining of such compartments.

The carefully controlled and engineered worm at Xerox was a far cry from the uncontrolled spread of the major worm known as the "Internet" worm which spread on the US Defense Advanced Research Projects Agency (DARPA) Internet in November 1988. This case and its implications for the computer security community are considered in Chapter 8.

1.4 Terminology

A feature of the anti-virus community has been the adoption of a wide range of (often conflicting) terminology, based mainly on the analogy between biological and computer viruses:

- *Back door* A software feature programmed by the original designer which will permit him to carry out operations denied to normal users of the software (e.g. a login program which will accept the designer's hard-wired password irrespective of the contents of the system password file)
- *Chain letter* A program encapsulated within an electronic mail message, which, when run, will send copies of itself to a number of users by electronic mail

- *Logic bomb* Malicious code incorporated within a program which will activate when a particular set of circumstances exists (e.g. code to crash the system when the author's name is deleted from the company payroll)
- *Rabbit* A program designed to exhaust some resource within the system by its unchecked replication (e.g. exhaust disk space or saturate CPU utilisation)
- *Time bomb* A logic bomb timed to activate on particular "activation" dates
- *Trap door* A feature, normally added by a hacker, which will permit later privileged access to a computer system without the use of valid authentication codes or passwords. A form of back door
- *Trojan horse* Any program which includes code designed to carry out functions not intended by the user running the program, or advertised in the system documentation. This includes the incorporation of logic bombs or benign hidden code
- *Trojan mule* A program which will emulate some aspect of the system's standard behaviour, such as the login prompt, with a view to collecting system passwords or authorisation codes
- *Virus* A program that can infect other programs by modifying them to include a possibly evolved copy of itself
- *Worm* A program that spreads copies of itself via network connections to other computer systems. Unlike a virus, a worm does not require a host program, but is a stand-alone executable program. There is also an older meaning of the term "worm", namely a logic bomb incorporated by a software designer with a view to causing denial of service on expiry of software licence agreements, or when software is pirated

Further terms are introduced in Chapter 3, when a comparison between the replication of biological and computer viruses is made. In general, the term "virus" is used to describe any self-replicating code where an obvious host program can be defined (this includes code executed as part of a system boot or startup process). The term "worm" tends to be reserved for self-replicating code spreading via a network where the code is a stand-alone program within the operating system environment. The distinction is often unclear; for example, the Massachusetts Institute of Technology (MIT) research group branded the Internet worm as a virus.

Viruses and worms need not be malicious, other than causing limited denial of service as a result of their use of central processing unit (CPU) capacity to self-replicate.

Chapter 2

Historical Perspectives

2.1 Introduction

This chapter gives a brief introduction to the history of the computer virus, demonstrating its origins in the early mainframe "rabbit" programs and the science fiction literature of the "Cyberpunk" genre.

2.2 1960s: Early Rabbits

The earliest self-replicating programs were probably the mainframe rabbits. These programs, normally written in command languages (which are interpreted rather the compiled), rapidly created clones of themselves and caused severe degradation of system performance.

In many cases, the command language supported direct facilities for process creation and manipulation. The rabbit could thus clone itself thousands of times, completely filling all queues of processes waiting to be executed (in batch environments) or causing the load on the machine to rise to the point at which useful work could not be achieved.

The problem of a single user completely swamping systems is one which recent designers have countered using the concept of a "fairness" scheduler. This technique allocates each user a fixed share of system processing power.

An example of such a replicating batch job is a rabbit written by two undergraduate students in 1966 which used a RUNCOM command script on a CTSS system. The script would invoke itself continually, generating large numbers of temporary files which would exhaust disk space. Unfortunately, because of a bug in the system, this caused CTSS to crash, leaving the disk directory in an invalid state (due to cached disk blocks in memory not being flushed).

A further early example was the "Animal" game on the Univac 1108. This program in its normal form asked a variety of questions, in an attempt to guess the type of an animal. This innocuous game was modified to produce "Pervading Animal". This program, when run, would attempt to add itself to every writable program file (directory). The program would check for an existing copy in the program file, and would also mark each created program with an illegal creation time (thus distinguishing between user- and program-created copies).

2.3 1970s: Fiction and the Worm

During the 1970s the concept of a self-replicating program continued to interest hackers, and appeared in a variety of forms in the works of John Brunner and David Gerrold.

The book *When Harlie Was One* by David Gerrold was published in 1972. This book carried a brief subplot (removed from later editions) which described a virus that used auto-dialler modems to establish links from its host system to remote systems. The virus then copied itself to the remote system, and deleted the original copy. Thus a single copy slowly spread across the public telephone network. Unfortunately, a bad connection resulted in corruption of the code for self-erasure. The corrupted version then rapidly began to clone itself exponentially across the network. This description is akin to a modern worm: indeed the description closely matched the functioning of the "Creeper" and "Reaper" programs.

These programs were developed by two researchers at Bolt Beranek and Newman (BBN), and were used to demonstrate the Tenex operating system. The Creeper mirrored Gerrold's concept exactly. The program started to print a file on a system, paused, transferred its code and state information to a remote system, deleted the original version, and then recommenced on the remote system. The Creeper was modified to replicate itself (in addition to migration). A further program, the Reaper, was then designed to migrate across the network looking for copies of the replicating Creeper, which it would then destroy. This was possibly the first anti-virus program. No exact date is provided for the developments, although they are described as having taken place in the early 1970s.

The term "worm" was coined by John Brunner in his book *The Shockwave Rider*, published in 1975. A key part of the plot of Brunner's book was the concept of a "tapeworm" which replicated across networked systems. Brunner's tapeworm was exceptionally advanced, carrying with it access codes and passwords for large numbers of official systems. The worm was self-replicating, with each segment checking on the status of its counterparts. Thus, any attempt to destroy a segment would only succeed in activating a stored copy. In Brunner's words:

> And – no, it can't be killed. It's indefinitely self-perpetuating so long as the net exists. Even if one segment of it is inactivated, a counterpart of the missing portion will

remain in store at some other station and the worm will automatically subdivide and send a duplicate head to collect the spare groups and restore them to their proper positions.

He provides a vision of a global internetwork with dozens of tapeworms active, each being pursued by counterworms. This vision is closer to reality than it may first appear, as indicated by the work by Shoch and Hupp at the Xerox Palo Alto Research Center. This work in the mid-1970s centred on distributed load balancing using worm programs. The worm located free systems within the local network (Ethernet), and started segments running on these nodes. The segments would run diagnostics of various forms. The Xerox work also addressed the problem of network failure, co-ordination between worm segments, and emergency termination of worms. Amusingly, Shoch and Hupp report a worm experiment in which a (possibly corrupted) worm sought out machines and started a corrupted copy of its program, which then crashed the host. The end result of this was dozens of crashed machines.

The development of rabbit programs continued during this period, with further documented examples. These included a program called "Rabbit" which ran on IBM 360s. This program, developed in 1974, was written in a batch programming language. When run, the program would copy itself, and insert the copy twice into the batch queue. Thus, the number of copies of the program active in the queue would grow rapidly. The ASP operating system reacted poorly under heavy loads. In particular, processing of operator input was delayed. Thus, once Rabbit had been running for a few minutes, the load factor was sufficiently high to prevent operators from terminating it.

The concept of the rabbit was extended in the mid-1970s by a pair of processes created by systems programmers at Motorola. These processes were created through the use of a bug on Xerox CP-V timesharing. The errant programs would cause a variety of symptoms, including:

- Rapid seeking of disk drives
- Card punches punching a lace card (all holes punched)
- Strange messages on the system console

When the operators attempted to kill off one of the two jobs (named Friar Tuck and Robin Hood), the other would detect the death of its peer, and restart the killed job. Thus the following sequence was reported:

!X id1

id1: Friar Tuck... I am under attack! Pray save me! (Robin Hood) id1: Off (aborted)

id2: Fear not, friend Robin! I shall rout the Sheriff of Nottingham's men!

id3: Thank you, my good fellow! (Robin)

To terminate the programs it was necessary to kill both jobs in rapid succession, or to restart the system. In the latter case the programs were automatically restarted. This was achieved by patching the list of programs to be automatically invoked at system startup.

The 1970s ended with complex self-replicating network worms; the 1980s began with the first true viruses.

2.4 1980–1983: Genesis

The first reported incidents of true viruses, rather than rabbits or worms, were in 1980 and 1981 on the Apple II computer. The earliest of these was written for research purposes in 1980, and was never released into the wild. The virus operated by:

- Trapping the CATALOG command
- Checking for the existence of a marker byte in the directory on disk
- If the marker byte was not present, then the DOS code in memory (complete with virus code) was written to the disk boot sectors

A generation counter was maintained to monitor the spread of the virus. This version was modified by a friend of the virus author to improve its efficiency and to reduce the amount of executable code written to disk. The two viruses (old and new) were capable of dual infection, thus producing a disk carrying both strains in active form.

A publicly documented example of an Apple II virus is the "Elk Cloner", reported in mid-1981. This virus was a boot sector virus loaded from disk, which intercepted the DOS RUN, LOAD, BLOAD and CATALOG commands. The virus inserted a USR (interrupt) vector which generated a wide range of diagnostics, including:

- Printing a poem
- Printing the version number
- Infecting a disk

A counter in the boot block was then incremented. This counter was used to check whether a special event would be generated, including inverting screen, clicking speaker, flashing text, letter substitutions, lockup computer, poem printing, reboot, and crash to monitor program.

Finally, the virus would remain resident and infect any non-write-protected disks inserted into the computer system. This virus includes the concept of a signature, version number, resident special interrupt vector (the USR) and a wide range of manipulation tasks.

```
┌─────────────────────────────────────────────────┐
│  ELK CLONER:                                      │
│    THE PROGRAM WITH A PERSONALITY                 │
│                                                   │
│  IT WILL GET ON ALL YOUR DISKS                    │
│  IT WILL INFILTRATE YOUR CHIPS                    │
│  YES IT'S CLONER!                                 │
│                                                   │
│  IT WILL STICK TO YOU LIKE GLUE                   │
│  IT WILL MODIFY RAM TOO                           │
│  SEND IN THE CLONER!                              │
└─────────────────────────────────────────────────┘
```

A further Apple II virus was reported by Joe Dellinger, its author, in 1982. This virus spread under Apple II DOS 3.3. A faulty early copy was reported as having been released by friends of the virus author. This copy corrupted graphics in an Apple II game "Congo". Dellinger reports than many pirated copies of Congo ceased operation over a two-week period. To solve this problem, a modified copy of the virus was produced with the bug corrected. This modified copy was released into the environment, and rapidly displaced the original version. The concept of self-upgrading viruses was one which was to reappear in the Amiga anti-virus and IBM PC "Jerusalem" virus strains many years later.

In 1989, Associated Press reported the death (aged 39) of Jim Hauser of San Luis Obispo, US. Hauser was reported to be the author of an early Apple II computer virus in 1982. The virus was described as having been designed to give users a "guided tour" of the Apple II system.

In 1983 a key event occurred, namely Ken Thompson's Association for Computer Machinery (ACM) Turing award speech. In this speech he outlined a early trojan horse in the C compiler at AT & T Bell. This trojan exploited the concept of a trusted software component completely vanishing within the system (it is described in detail in Chapter 7). When in place, the trojan (which modified the compiler and login program) permitted login using a well-known hard-wired password. This speech clearly outlined the problems of placing trust in software components, particularly when a virus or trojan horse can be incorporated into the component.

This was also the year in which Fred Cohen carried out many of the early experiments with VAX viruses, which culminated in his demonstration on 10 November at a seminar on computer security. Cohen's virus was implanted in a trojan program called "vd". In five trials his virus gained full system permissions, taking between 5 and 60 minutes. These trials are described in detail in Chapter 7.

2.5 1984–1986: Exodus

1984 saw the continuation of Fred Cohen's work on viruses. This continued with a series of experiments in July 1984 on a Bell-LaPadula (military security) system on a UNIVAC 1108 machine. These experiments demonstrated that a virus could propagate even on systems designed for high-security applications, and indicated the distinction between the confidentiality and integrity of information.

This year also saw the publication of a book by William Gibson which was to create a cult. The book was *Neuromancer*; the cult was Cyberpunk. In *Neuromancer*, Gibson created a world in which all computers were interlinked by a global network. A person could enter this "Cyberspace", and navigate the network as a three-dimensional space in which all computer systems (and information) were represented as solid objects. Artificial intelligences created beings within cyberspace, and computer system defences could kill interlopers via neural feedback. The world which Gibson created is only now been realised via virtual reality research (providing computer- generated three-dimensional visual simulators which users can enter and interact with via bio-feedback devices). Gibson also introduced the concept of computer defences, known as "ICE", which appeared as physical barriers in Cyberspace, and which, in the case of "Black ICE", could injure the user via sensory feedback.

Cyberpunk provided a genre which glorified the hacker fighting the large corporates who populated the Cyberspace with their computer networks and systems. Paul Saffo, in his paper "Consensual realities in Cyberspace", comments that an entire new generation of hackers may be basing their code of ethics on Gibson. Certainly Robert T. Morris, the author of the Internet worm, was noted as having a well-thumbed copy of Gibson's book, which was described by his mother as:

> her teenage son's primer on computer viruses and one of the most tattered books in young Morris' room

1985 saw a steady increase in the number of non-replicating malicious programs – trojan horses. This was countered by the creation on 20 October of the Dirty Dozen list produced by Tom Neff. The list of trojans extended rapidly during the period 1985–1990, and passed into the hands of Eric Newhouse when Tom lost interest.

The Dirty Dozen includes details of trojan horses, and hacked or pirated commercial software or software which is in breach of copyright.

Version	Release Date	Number of files
1.0	Oct 20 1985	12
2.0		15
3.0		37
4.0		65
5.0		103
6.0		120
7.0	Jan 3 1987	166 (15 Trojan)
8.0	Feb 5 1988	200 (24 Trojan)
9.0	Jun 9 1989	323 (62 Trojan)

1986 was the year in which the first IBM PC computer viruses began to appear. The "Brain" virus originated in Lahore, Pakistan in January 1986. This virus was reputedly written by Basit and Amjad Farooq Alvi. Their names, addresses and telephone numbers were included within the Brain virus boot sector. Computer lore suggests that the brothers ran a flourishing software business, and included copies of the Brain virus on all software provided to non-Indian clients. The Brain virus was reported in 1990 as comprising around 7 per cent of all reported infection incidents. The virus was also the first case of limited camouflage being employed. When the virus was active in memory no alteration of the boot sector (from its standard value) could be detected.

1986 also saw the first computer virus forum being held at the Chaos Computer Club (CCC) in Hamburg. The CCC is one of the more infamous groups of hackers, meeting regularly to exchange ideas and information, and to discuss the social justification for their hacking activities. It is worth noting that computer viruses have had a comparatively low profile in the computer underground of hackers, pirates, phreakers and carders. The underground is segregated into many, often exclusive, groups with particular interests. The authors of viruses have maintained a low profile within the general computer underground. Certainly in the large mass of published computer underground literature, little mention of virus programming appears. Examples do, however, include a number of items in the *2600* magazine from alleged virus authors, republication of Burger's virus sources and a disassembly of the "Alameda" virus in the Phreakers/Hackers Underground Network newsletter, as well as an underground magazine devoted entirely to viruses (*Corrupted Programming International*).

The complexity of later viruses clearly indicated that some exchange of ideas was occurring between writers of viruses. This is borne out by the variations in coding style evidenced in examples such as the Internet worm (DES encryption versus remainder of code) and "Whale" virus (variety of concealment techniques).

It is interesting that at the December 1986 congress of the CCC, 20 programmers admitted to having experience of viruses (out of 200–300 attenders). It is therefore likely that a considerable body of virus experience was in existence in the computer underground.

Ralf Burger, author of *Computer Viruses – A High-tech Disease*, produced a demonstration virus program, "VIRDEM.COM", which was made available at the Hamburg congress. The Virdem virus was an extremely simple non-resident virus which infected COM files on the A: drive on the IBM PC. The virus was 1236 bytes in length. Burger also published sources for a variety of other viruses in his book, including assembly code for IBM PC, Pascal, Basic and Batch viruses. The majority of the viruses date from the period 1986–1987, and have appeared largely unchanged since the first edition of the book in 1987.

2.6 1987: Mac, Atari and Amiga Next

1987 saw the spread of viruses to a variety of other computer platforms, including the Apple Macintosh, Commodore Amiga and Atari ST. By the end of 1987 the number of virus strains had risen to twenty-one.

The ubiquitous "nVIR" virus for the Apple Macintosh was detected in West Germany during this year. The original strain of the virus was malicious and would randomly delete a file from the system folder on the Mac. This virus was discovered, and re-engineered into a benign form. This benign form was then released, and has been successful in replacing most copies of the original virus. The nVIR strain has remained among the most common Mac viruses, possibly only recently usurped by the "WDEF" A strain. nVIR comes in two common strains, nVIR A and nVIR B, the former notable for its habit of using MacinTalk to speak the words "Don't Panic!". Many clones of the nVIR B strain have been produced using basic binary or resource editing.

Also benign, but considerably more controversial, was the "Peace" virus released in December 1987. This virus was engineered by a contract programmer at the request of Richard Brandow, publisher of *MacMag* magazine. The virus carried a message of world peace:

> RICHARD BRANDOW, publisher of MacMag, and its entire staff would like to take this opportunity to convey their UNIVERSAL MESSAGE OF PEACE to all Macintosh users around the world.

and included a graphic of the globe. The virus was timed to activate when a Mac was booted on 2 March 1988. On this date the message would be displayed, and the virus would delete itself from its hiding place in the Mac system file. Infected Macs booted after this date would silently disinfect themselves, thus the virus is now believed to be extinct (other than a few research samples).

The Peace virus was also uploaded in a hypertext stack "NEWAPP.STK" to the CompuServe hypercard forum (CompuServe is a commercial electronic bulletin board system) on 6 February 1988. In an interview with the *Chicago Tribune*, Brandow was quoted in the following terms:

> I called Brandow, who readily accepted responsibility for the virus. "Actually, we like to call it a message," he told me. "We look at it as something that's really positive."

1987 also saw a virus being created for the new Commodore Amiga machine. This virus, believed to be written by the Swiss Cracker's Association (SCA), was detected in November 1987. The virus infects the boot sector of disks, and caused the following message to be displayed on every 15th infection:

> Something wonderful has happened Your AMIGA is alive !!! and, even better... Some of your disks are infected by a VIRUS !!! Another masterpiece of The Mega-Mighty SCA !!

On the Atari ST similar boot sector viruses were   so being written. An example is the "Pirate Trap" virus which carries the "copyright" message:

> *** The Pirate Trap ***
> * Youre being watched *
> .*** [C] P.M.S. 1987 ***

The Atari was also host for the first cross-platform viruses, in this case the "Aladdin" and "Frankie" viruses written to execute on a Mac emulator running on the Atari ST. The University of Hamburg virus catalogue describes the Aladdin virus as having been written by Aladdin producer Proficomp, apparently in order to destroy cracked illegal software copies of their Aladdin hardware/software emulator.

On the IBM PC platform a large number of new viruses were discovered, including the "405" overwriting virus from Austria, the "Alameda/Yale" virus discovered at Merritt college in California, the "Cascade" virus in Germany, the "Friday 13th" virus in South Africa, the Jerusalem virus in Israel and the "Lehigh" virus in the US. Of particular interest is the fact that the early viruses are responsible for a significant proportion of current virus infections. German incidence figures for 1990 indicate that Jerusalem is responsible for 15 per cent of incidents, and Cascade for 25 per cent. Yale was comparatively rare due to the fact that it would only propagate when a soft-reset (Ctrl-Alt-Del) was attempted on an infected machine. 405 was readily detectable due to the corruption of the host files.

Of particular interest was the incorporation of self-encryption techniques into the Cascade virus (renowned for its classic falling letters display, which earned it the aliases "Falling Tears", and "Autumn Leaves"). This virus is considered by some to mark the second generation of IBM PC viruses, namely the use of camouflage techniques.

1987 also saw the production of an IBM MVS 370 virus in April and a UNIX virus in June, in addition to the original viruses developed by Cohen in 1984 (for UNIX, UNIVAC and VAX VMS).

Finally, in December 1987, network saturation occurred on the BITNET computer network (and on IBM's internal VNET network) due to the rapid proliferation of the BITNET Christmas chain letter. This incident, described in Chapter 8, involved the execution by innocent users of a command script designed to display a Christmas tree on screen. When run, the script would mail copies of itself to users who regularly corresponded with the person running the virus.

2.7 1988: Proliferation and Disbelief

2.7.1 January–March

As 1988 dawned, many of the current computer viruses had been released and were slowly spreading globally via traffic in disks, and electronic network transfer of infected programs. To date, Cascade, Jerusalem and Brain are believed to have spread worldwide with incidents as far afield as Taiwan, India, Japan, Australia and Canada.

CompuServe carried an article on 10 February 1988 indicating disbelief in the existence of computer viruses, citing the inability of people to produce living copies of viruses. Professor Brunvard of Utah cited the computer virus as the latest in a series of urban legends. This sentiment was supported by Peter Norton, who told *Insight* magazine, "We're dealing with an urban myth", and compared the existence of viruses to stories of alligators in New York sewers.

This sentiment, while accurately indicating the penetration of computer viruses within the computing community in 1988, was unfortunately followed one month later by the recall by the Aldus Corporation of 5000 copies of its FreeHand drawing program which had been infected by the "MacMag" virus. The infection route was traced to a Chicago subcontractor who had received a games disk from Brandow. This disk then infected a demonstration copy of Aldus FreeHand, which was eventually returned to Aldus, causing the infection outbreak.

CompuServe had also carried (briefly) in January a disassembly of a modified nVIR sample, as an indication of how a Mac virus operated. This was posted to enable the production of anti-virus utilities. This virus was one of a number of such postings of viruses for research purposes, including a posting by Patrick Toulme of "Virus-90" and "Virus-101" in December 1989 and January 1990. These were intended as educational tools, with the virus source available on request. Possibly more laudable was the production of the "1260" virus by Mark Washburn as an indication of the encryption techniques which a virus could employ, and how these could defeat existing anti-virus scanning programs.

Virus sources have been published in a variety of locations including the *Computer Underground Magazine* (Yale), *Pixel* magazine ("Pixel"), *Computer viruses: A High-tech Disease"* ("Vienna", Virdem), numerous reports (Brain and "Italian" boot sectors in hex), CompuServe (nVIR, "Dukakis") and even Virus-l itself ("Valert-l"). This high level of source availability coupled with the ease of modification have ensured a high level of simple clones (either binary edits, or reassemblies with slight modifications).

The complexity of producing an Atari computer virus was eased in March 1988 by the availability of a virus construction set. This program allowed the user to construct custom viruses using the GEM window interface, specifying manipulation tasks, files to be infected, drives to be infected, etc. Distribution of the program and documentation was restricted to those over 18 years of age. The package also included a removal utility for the generated viruses, and was released at the Hanover Computer Fair, CeBIT.

2.7.2 April–September

The "Scores" Macintosh virus was detected in April 1988. This virus was unusual in being specifically targeted at two programs produced by the firm Electronic Data Systems (EDS). These programs contained resources with the signatures "ERIC" and "VULT" which the virus tested for. Four days after the initial date of infection the virus checks for applications with these signatures, and if it finds them crashes the system. Seven days after the initial date of infection the virus will cause any attempted disk writes to fail after 15 minutes, and 10 minutes later the application will crash. Internal sources within EDS indicated that some time after a programmer was fired, a disk arrived anonymously at the EDS Dallas office. Shortly afterwards the speed reduction and random crashes caused by Scores were noticed on various machines.

On 22 April 1988 a new mailing list was established. This list – "Virus-l" – was set up by Kenneth R. van Wyk of Lehigh University (the institution struck by the virus of the same name in 1987). The mailing list was to grow to be read by over 14 000 subscribers in October 1989.

Roger Gonzalez wrote to Virus-l describing three malicious programs he had written but never released. These programs include:

- "Spam": an infector of the COMMAND.COM file on the IBM PC. After five infections this virus will randomly print the text "Spam" on screen
- "Cookie Monster": similar to Spam. This virus prints the text "Gimme Cookie" at random intervals, requiring the response OREO or CHOCO-LATE CHIP. If the incorrect response is provided the program changes the COMMAND.COM file to the name MUNCHED, and prints the text "never mind"
- "Pacman": appended to MSDOS.SYS. Apparently traps the vertical sync timer interrupt. The virus causes a "pacman" to appear on screen, which will then eat a character and vanish

If the above report is accurate, then Pacman is the only known MSDOS.SYS infector on the IBM PC system. Cookie is based on a considerably earlier trojan horse on a mainframe system. The trojan displayed the standard prompt on each user's terminal, and required a valid response before permitting continuation of operations.

On Friday 13th May, the Jerusalem virus activated worldwide. Unlike later occurrences in 1989, damage appeared to be limited. The *British Medical Journal* carried a report of a virus at the Royal Infirmary in Glasgow. The virus is reported as having infected software destined for the cardiac intensive care unit. This incident, reported in July 1988, is one of a number of such infections. Normally damage is limited to possible destruction of patient information, rather than immediate danger via infected equipment. Risk to life is therefore indirect via possible loss of patient records, and other vital information.

The summer of 1988 brought two court cases related to systems damaged due to the creation of malicious software. In the first case (11 July) a programmer in Fort Worth, Texas was tried for the mass destruction of 168 000 records belonging to his former employee. Donald Burleson allegedly introduced a program, described in the words of the Tarrant council district attorney as being "just like a human virus". Further investigation indicated that the intruder had entered the system via a back door, deleted log files, and manually deleted the records in question. Burleson was convicted on 20 September under the Texas computer sabotage legislation, and sentenced to pay damages of $12 000 to his former employee, USPA.

In the second case, William Christison, operator of a New Mexico bulletin board, filed a suit against Michael Dragg accusing him of uploading a trojan horse program "BBSMON.COM". The program contained code to delete system files and to corrupt the file allocation tables (FAT) on the PC. Christison asked for $1000 damages for each uploaded trojan horse, and enjoined Dragg not to send trojan horses, viruses or other vandalising programs.

The Computer Virus Industry Association (CVIA) was formed in June of this year under the leadership of John McAfee, president of the Interpath Corporation, Santa Clara, California. Through the Homebase bulletin board, the CVIA became one of the leading centres for virus research and provision of anti-virus products. John led a high-profile, and often controversial, role in the fight against computer viruses, a role culminating in his inclusion in the *Microtimes* third annual selection of the 100 most influential leaders in the computer industry (22 January 1990).

2.7.3 October–December

October saw the infection of a new media form, namely a CD-ROM. In this case the Quantum Leap Technologies QLTech MEGA-ROM was reported as being infected by no fewer than three copies of the nVIR Macintosh virus. The CD-ROM collection of public domain and shareware software was withdrawn, and a new volume issued in December 1988. This was unfortunately too late for the University of Toronto, which reported twenty infected systems.

In the same month one of the biggest virus hoaxes was started, that of the 2400 baud modem virus. This hoax began with a message from Mike RoChenle (a number of users later pointed out the obvious similarity in name to Microchannel). This message (a copy extracted from a Seattle bulletin board is reproduced below) described a virus which migrated across the subcarrier frequencies on a 2400 baud modem line. An infected modem would then replicate the virus by transmitting it to any other modems it communicates with. Finally the virus attached to incoming binary data and thus generated infected executables:

SUBJ: Really nasty virus
AREA: GENERAL (1)

  I've just discovered probably the world's worst computer virus yet.
I had just finished a late night session of BBS'ing and file trading
when I exited Telix 3 and attempted to run pkxarc to unarc the
software I had downloaded. Next thing I knew my hard disk was seeking
all over and it was apparently writing random sectors. Thank god for
strong coffee and a recent backup. Everything was back to normal, so
I called the BBS again and downloaded a file. When I went to use ddir
to list the directory, my hard disk was getting trashed agaion. I
tried Procomm Plus TD and also PC Talk 3. Same results every time.
Something was up so I hooked up my test equipment and different modems
(I do research and development for a local computer telecommunications
company and have an in-house lab at my disposal). After another hour
of corrupted hard drives I found what I think is the world's worst
computer virus yet. The virus distributes itself on the modem
sub-carrier present in all 2400 baud and up modems. The sub-carrier
is used for ROM and register debugging purposes only, and otherwise
serves no othr purpose. The virus sets a bit pattern in one of the
internal modem registers, but it seemed to screw up the other
registers on my USR. A modem that has been "infected" with this virus
will then transmit the virus to other modems that use a subcarrier (I
suppose those who use 300 and 1200 baud modems should be immune). The
virus then attaches itself to all binary incoming data and infects the
host computer's hard disk. The only way to get rid of the virus is to
completely reset all the modem registers by hand, but I haven't found
a way to vaccinate a modem against the virus, but there is the
possibility of building a subcarrier filter. I am calling on a 1200
baud modem to enter this message, and have advised the sysops of the
two other boards (names withheld). I don't know how this virus
originated, but I'm sure it is the work of someone in the computer
telecommunications field such as myself. Probably the best thing to
do now is to stick to 1200 baud until we figure this thing out.

The hoax continued to spread rapidly through the virus community, even resulting in a warning memo being circulated at the NASA jet propulsion laboratory. The initial advice was to avoid infection by utilising on 1200 or lower baud rate modems. A parody of this message was sent to the USENET security mailing list in January 1989, and advised:

Date: 11-31-88 (24:60)   Number: 32769
 To: ALL   Refer#: NONE
From: ROBERT MORRIS III   Read: (N/A)
Subj: VIRUS ALERT   Status: PUBLIC MESSAGE

Warning: There's a new virus on the loose that's worse than anything I've seen before! It gets in through the power line, riding on the powerline 60 Hz subcarrier. It works by changing the serial port pinouts, and by reversing the direction one's disks spin. Over 300,000 systems have been hit by it here in Murphy, West Dakota alone! And that's just in the last twelve minutes.

It attacks DOS, Unix, TOPS-20, Apple II, VMS, MVS, Multics, Mac, RSX-11, ITS, TRS-80, and VHS systems.

To prevent the spread of this dastardly worm:

1) Don't use the powerline.
2) Don't use batteries either, since there are rumors that this virus has invaded most major battery plants and is infecting the positive poles of the batteries. (You might try hooking up just the negative pole.)
3) Don't upload or download files.
4) Don't store files on floppy disks or hard disks.
5) Don't read messages. Not even this one!
6) Don't use serial ports, modems, or phone lines.
7) Don't use keyboards, screens, or printers.
8) Don't use switches, CPUs, memories, microprocessors, or mainframes.
9) Don't use electric lights, electric or gas heat or airconditioning, running water, writing, fire, clothing, or the wheel.

I'm sure if we are all careful to follow these 9 easy steps, this virus can be eradicated, and the precious electronic fluids of our computers can be kept pure.

- --RTM III

The two messages indicate that while the virus paranoia in the community had risen to extreme levels (also fuelled by the Internet worm incident in November 1988), it was vital to take each report with a pinch of salt.

In November 1988 the Internet worm incident began. This incident commenced on 3 November when Robert T. Morris, a student at Cornell, released a self-replicating worm on the DARPA Internet. This worm spread across the closely coupled research network, infecting an estimated 2000–6000 host systems, and causing damage estimated by one person at $96 million. The worm exploited two known bugs in UNIX system software on DEC VAX and SUN Microsystems SUN-3 machines. Despite rapid reaction by the research community to combat the worm, active copies were still to be detected in December of the following year. Details of the Internet worm incident are given in Chapter 8.

Finally, the month of December brought two further network incidents: a re-release of the BITNET chain letter on 6 December, and the creation and release of the HI.COM DECNET worm. This worm spread rapidly over the Space Physics Analysis Network (SPAN) and High Energy Physics Network (HEPNET), and displayed a Christmas tree and a message suggesting that the user should not work so hard over Christmas.

The source for all three of these network pests had been made available via a variety of sources: the Internet worm by the *2600* hacker magazine, the DECNET Christmas worm from numerous archive sites due to its posting in the aftermath of the worm, and the BITNET chain letter in Burger's book and on the alt.hackers discussion forum on USENET. This, coupled with the wide distribution achieved by these worms and chain letters, has ensured that repetitions in modified form are likely.

The Internet worm was the prime mover in the establishment of the Computer Emergency Response Team (CERT) in December 1988. The team's remit extends to action to combat all known security threats on mainframe and networked systems connected to the DARPA Internet, including providing information and fixes for known security loopholes and acting as a clearing house for information during incidents. The initial press release establishing CERT is attached as Appendix 12.

2.8 1989: Reaction by the Community

2.8.1 January–March

During 1989 viruses continued to spread rapidly through the IT community. This year also marked the test case of the Internet worm, and the establishment of the infrastructure to combat viruses.

The continued spread of the common viruses resulted in a number of further shrink-wrapped software infections, including Microsoft's Word 4 beta test version 10 by nVIR.

Friday 13th January saw another activation of the Jerusalem virus, which was described by Alan Solomon in these terms:

It is a pesky nuisance and is causing a lot of problems today

February 1989 saw the attempted formation of a UK equivalent to CERT, but with a far broader remit. The Computer Threat Research Association (CoTRA) was formed by a consortium of interested members under the chairmanship of Mark Gibbs of Novell. The association's constitution covered investigation of all threats to computer systems, including viruses, trojan horses, general security loopholes and data integrity control. The organisation was unfortunately split by personality conflicts, and inability to address its extensive remit adequately. By the end of 1989 CoTRA had become inactive, leading to a vacuum within the UK response to malicious software. This lack of co-ordinated response became apparent during the "AIDS" trojan horse incident, and during discussion of the formation of an international CERT organisation.

In March 1989 viruses were the topic of science fiction once more, as the *Star Trek: The Next Generation* episode "Contagion" was screened. In this episode the USS *Enterprise* downloaded virus-infected data from a ship in the Romulan neutral zone. The transmitting ship began to experience intermittent system failures, and finally self-destructed. The *Enterprise* then began to suffer similar problems as the virus adapted to the system environment and duplicated throughout the computer systems. Ironically the high-tech solution was to shut down the computer system, and re-install the system from a backup maintained on board!

On a more serious note, two hospitals reported computer virus infections, on 22 March in the image display station for cardiac studies (reported as being carried on a hard disk manufactured by CMS Enhancements), and a delayed report in the *New England Journal of Medicine* of a nVIR virus infection at three Michigan hospitals which disrupted patient diagnosis in Autumn 1988.

2.8.2 April–June

The Cornell Provost's commission of enquiry into the Internet worm incident reported in April, concluding that Morris released the Internet worm. They described the incident as "a juvenile act that ignores the clear potential consequences". The commission was unable to trace Paul Graham, a Harvard graduate student, who Morris reportedly contacted on the day the worm was released; or to speak to Morris himself, who on the advice of his attorney had decided not to co-operate. The commission found that:

• Morris had violated departmental computer misuse policies
• No other members of the Cornell community were aware of Morris' work
• Morris made only minimal efforts to halt the worm once released

- He did not intend the worm to destroy data, but did intend it to spread widely
- The number of infected systems was in the thousands, although the estimate of 6000 computers could not be confirmed
- The CVIA's estimate of $96 million was grossly exaggerated and self-serving
- The worm, although sophisticated, could have been created by many students, graduate or undergraduate

The commission's report repeatedly emphasised that the release of the worm was not a "heroic" event designed to demonstrate weaknesses in UNIX security, but was a reckless act which did not consider the possible consequences for the community. It further stated that an academic community was based on mutual trust, and that violations of this trust can not be condoned.

On 12 April, the *Philadelphia Inquirer* reported that a former employee, Chris Young of Trenton, Cambden County had been charged with computer theft by altering a database belonging to his former employers, the Datacomp Corporation. It was alleged that Young gained access to the system on 7 October (the day of his resignation) and inserted a time bomb due to commence destruction of data on 7 December (the anniversary of Pearl Harbour). This case was yet another example of a trojan horse program being dubbed as a "virus".

An example of viruses in high level languages was reported at the end of April, in this case affecting the logic programming language, Prolog. The virus in question added its code to the end of Prolog source files, altering the operation of the Prolog predicate "consult". A simple signature comprising an arity 0 predicate "virus" is appended to infected files to prevent re-infection.

This example of a high level language was augmented by the discussion in *Computers and Security* of a virus written in a macro set utilised by the Lotus 1-2-3 program. This virus was designed to alter a single value in a specific column each time the Lotus 1-2-3 spreadsheet was loaded. The change was restricted to a small percentage range, and could be either added or subtracted from the original value.

The article (reproduced in the *Computer Virus Handbook*) notes that such a macro virus would be:

- Undetectable by general virus scanning utilities, since it exists in a data file which is regarded as executable code only by the interpreting program
- Easily detectable by alert users unless highly sophisticated

The work was based on a number of reports of a spreadsheet macro virus during the summer of 1988.

The first edition of a new hacker magazine was published in electronic form. *Corrupted Programming International* (CPI), written by a hacker styling himself Doctor Dissector, was described as "a protagonist's point of view". While many of the items in issues 1 and 2 were superficial and indicated a lack of detailed knowledge, the publication of such a bulletin (and an associated telephone bulletin board contact number) gave rise to concern. Issue 1 included the following list of suggestions for new virus techniques:

- *CSR virus* a CMOS memory resident virus (presumably to avoid deletion on system reboot)
- *Failsafe virus* preserving all file sizes and attributes, infecting all files and corrupting data on trigger. Possibly an early suggestion of "Stealth" techniques
- *Format virus* whenever a DOS format is called it will format every second track on the disk
- *Write virus* intercepting writes to disks, and marking written sectors as bad
- *Low level format virus* formats hard disk in background while recopying data from original hard disk (compression and defragmentation utility)
- *Hide virus* incrementally sets the hidden attribute on files
- *Crash virus* emulates system crashes and freezes
- *Modem virus* monitors data on serial ports and adds random noise

Issue 2 introduced a number of ideas including use of slack space in allocated clusters in an article by a hacker named Ashton Darkside. It even went as far as proposing standards for CPI viruses. These standards included:

1. An inactive (latent) period and limited activation period for virus malicious effects in order to conceal virus activity.
2. Use of Int 12h as a request by the virus to determine if a system is "friendly" before attempting infection, together with the circulation of recognition codes which friendly systems will return on this request.
3. Upload of the virus to the CPI section on the Andromeda strain bulletin board system (BBS) for peer review.
4. Use of end of cluster slack space for storage of virus code (so called ADS standard).
5. Maintenance of a list of CPI standard viruses and identification strings.

The future of CPI after its second bulletin issue (27 July 1989) is unknown. The existence of such a group of virus authors was to be noted in 1990 in Bulgaria – the so-called Bulgarian Virus factory.

The summer ended with the publication of a special edition of the *Communications of the ACM* dealing with the Internet worm incident. This edition (volume 32, No. 6) included reprints of detailed reports from Purdue, MIT and Cornell.

2.8.3 July–September

In July the *Virus Bulletin* was launched by Sophos. This publication, based at Abingdon, UK, offered detailed technical information on virus development, anti-virus techniques, recognition strings and software product reviews. The publication was priced at 195 for 12 monthly issues. The publication is now in its second year, and has a worldwide readership.

Later that month an incident occurred which demonstrated the risks of trusting users with viral disassemblies and materials. The "Icelandic" virus was disassembled by Fridrik Skulason at the University of Iceland. Before distributing the disassembly to the remainder of the research community he made a modification (presumably to detect any re-assembly of this text). Within one month a copy of the Icelandic virus was uploaded to the virus analysis area on the Homebase board. This was analysed, and a statement made by the CVIA that a virus named the "Saratoga" virus had been detected in the US, and (based on the initial date reported by the discoverer) predated the Icelandic strain. Unfortunately the Saratoga virus carried the modification made by Fridrik, and had thus clearly been re-assembled from his disassembly. Discussion on the ethics of the original alteration, and of the person who had re-released the sample continued within the community for many months afterwards.

The establishment by Joe Hirst of the British Computer Virus Research Centre was announced (BCVRC). This centre aims to collect and catalogue computer viruses, to disassemble and analyse samples, and to disseminate information between anti- virus researchers worldwide. The centre is established as a personal venture in the aftermath of the failure of CoTRA, and it is hoped that it will act as the nucleus of a UK virus response.

Associated Press reported that Robert Morris had been indicted by a federal grand jury in Syracuse, New York, to stand trial on a count of accessing without authorisation at least six computers in which the federal government had an interest. This charge was brought as a test case under the 1986 Computer Fraud and Abuse Act. If convicted, Morris would face a maximum sentence of five years in federal prison, and a $250 000 fine.

The US army solicited applications from small business contractors under the Small Business Innovative Research (SBIR) programme, for research into computer virus electronic counter measures (ECM). The programme's objective was cited as:

Objective: The objective shall be to determine the potential for using "computer viruses" as an ECM technique against generic military communications systems/nets and analyzing its effects on various subsystem components.

Description: The purpose of this research shall be to investigate potential use of computer viruses to achieve traditional communications ECM effects in targeted communications systems. These effects can include data (information) disruption, denial, and deception, but other effects should also be researched such as effects on executable code in processors, memory, storage management, etc. Research in effective methods or strategies to remotely introduce such viruses shall also be conducted. Efforts in this area should be focused on RF atmospheric signal transmission such as performed in tactical military data communications.

The programme is scheduled to begin in fiscal year 1990, and is divided into two phases. Funding for phase I may be up to $50 000; and up to $500 000 for phase II. Phase I is a feasibility study of the use of viruses as an ECM technique; phase II the development of a demonstration which will validate the ECM concept.

The US National Institute of Standards and Technology (NIST) issued a warning concerning the "Datacrime" or "Columbus Day" virus. This virus would, when activating on 13 October, perform a low level format of cylinder 0 of the IBM PC hard drive. An exceptionally large number of warnings of the destructive effects of this virus, first detected in March 1989, were distributed by a number of organisations. In the event, very few occurrences of the virus were detected, and the Jerusalem virus once more took the heaviest toll.

The US NIST is responsible for security standardisation for federal agencies, and for security guidelines for unclassified systems. At this time, NIST was also moving to establish a network of computer security response and information centres modelled on the Internet CERT organisation. These centres were to serve as sources of information and guidance on viruses and related threats, and would respond to computer security incidents. These proposals continued to develop during 1990, and culminated in an international CERT structure proposal.

2.8.4 October–December

On 4 October IBM announced the release of its own anti-virus product. This product, based on the virus analysis work at the Thomas Watson Research Centre, operated by scanning for known virus signatures in system files. A token charge of $35 was levied for this utility. Initial problems included the detection of a number of legitimate products as viruses by the scanner. Within the UK IBM now offer upgrades to the scanner, together with general guidance on virus prevention in the form of a publication based on David Chess' original paper on "Coping with computer viruses" and a series of workshops on virus issues.

October 16 saw the release of a second worm on to the SPAN network. This worm called itself the "Worm Against Nuclear Killers", and displayed a graphic with the acronym of "WANK". The advice supplied during the HI.COM incident was re-iterated by CERT. Had this advice been followed to the letter, the impact of the WANK worm would have been considerably less. This indicated a general problem with ensuring that security patches and fixes are installed by a wide range of system administrators with varying experience spread worldwide. A variant of the WANK worm – "OILZ" – was activated on 30 October.

In November, the *Washington Post* reported that US District judge Howard Munson had permitted the case against Robert Morris to proceed to trial, despite requests by the defence for the felony charge to be dismissed. This plea was based on the allegation that the Justice Department had improperly revealed to a reporter (before the indictment) that Morris had made a statement, and that the Department was considering whether he should be permitted to plead guilty to a misdemeanour charge.

The month of December saw the AIDS trojan horse incident in the UK. In some ways this was to become the UK equivalent of the Internet worm incident. The AIDS trojan was bulk-mailed during a five-day period from the 8th to the 12th of December from postal districts in west and south-west London to computer users in the UK, Europe, Africa, Scandinavia and Australia. The bulk mailing utilised 7000 names purchased from the *PC Business World* circulation department in October, together with 3500 names extracted from the World Health Organization's (WHO) databases. The mailing comprised a computer diskette in a square white envelope together with a small blue piece of paper (the licence agreement). The disk label announced itself to be "AIDS Information Introductory Diskette Version 2.0". The disk itself was in IBM DOS format and contained two files:

```
INSTALL.EXE     Sept 28 1989    146188 bytes
AIDS.EXE        Aug 7 1989      172562 bytes
```

The user is requested to start his/her computer, insert the disk in drive A, type "A:install" to DOS and then press Enter. This action invoked the INSTALL.EXE program which then proceeded to create a series of hidden directories on the C: drive. These directories are given names which are combinations of spaces and ASCII character 255 (FFh). Within one of the deeper directories five files are created which contain counters and program serial numbers. Next the INSTALL.EXE program copies itself as REM#.EXE into the hidden directory "C:#" where the "#" character is ASCII 255. Next the AIDS.EXE program is copied to the root directory of the C: drive. Finally, the AUTOEXEC.BAT batch file in the root directory is modified to:

```
echo off
C:
cd #
rem# PLEASE USE THE auto.bat FILE INSTEAD OF
       autoexec.bat FOR CONVENIENCE
auto.bat
```

Note the "#"s representing ASCII 255. The inclusion of these characters in the rem statement changed the normal comment into a request to execute the program named rem# (since the ASCII 255 character is not interpreted as a space, even though DOS displays it as such).

Thus the AIDS trojan had arranged for regular execution of the REM#.EXE program. When the machine has been rebooted approximately ninety times, the AIDS trojan will begin encryption of all file names on disk. The directory entry for each file is encrypted using a simple substitution code, with file name extensions being encrypted by look-up in a static table. After encryption the modified directory entry is marked read-only and hidden. Following encryption the trojan provides a DOS look-alike shell which emulates a small subset of DOS commands, providing an unaltered listing of the directories. A READ.ME file in the top level contains the text:

> You are advised to stop using this computer. The software lease has expired. Important: Renew the software lease before you use this computer again.

The AIDS.EXE program was itself innocuous, consisting of an AIDS risk assessment interactive questionnaire. The "licence" document accompanying the trojan program contained:

1. Introduction.
2. Instructions for installation.
3. Limited warranty stating that in the event of the program being defective PC Cyborg (the alleged manufacturer) would replace it at no charge. This was followed by a standard disclaimer indicating that the programs are supplied "as is", without warranty of any form.
4. Licence agreement stating the conditions under which PC Cyborg would renew the licence beyond the initial trial period, and noting that in the event of a breach of licence PC Cyborg would be permitted to use "program mechanisms to ensure termination of your use of the programs".

The text of the licence agreement is reproduced in Appendix 8. This agreement led to considerable legal discussion as to whether PC Cyborg was legally permitted to corrupt data and executables on disk after termination of the licence period.

Disassembly and analysis of the AIDS trojan horse was done on an *ad hoc* basis by a loosely knit group of specialists (in a manner which mirrored the US community's initial reaction to the Internet worm), including Jim Bates (of Bates Associates), Dr Alan Solomon (Director of the UK data recovery firm S & S International Ltd.) and Dr Jan Hruska (Director of Sophos). Reports of AIDS cases were passed on to the UK police Computer Crime Unit (CCU) who were investigating the incident.

Finally, as the year ended, the CCC in Hamburg held their 6th Congress, with the title "Open frontiers: CoComed together". Included in this congress was the second virus forum, including discussions by Professor Klaus Brunnstein, Ralf Burger, Wau Holland (founder of the CCC) and Juergen Wieckmann (editor of the CCC book). Particularly controversial was the argument by Ralf Burger that the publication of computer virus code does not contribute to the virus threat. Brunnstein indicated his estimate of 250 hours to analyse and classify a new virus. An issue raised was whether there were "good uses" of viruses – an example cited being disabling nuclear defence (SIOP) systems.

2.9 1990: Organisation and Litigation

2.9.1 January–April

The year opened with yet another example of shrink-wrapped software being infected, in this case the "Desktop Fractal Design System" software supplied by Academic Press, which was infected by the Jerusalem virus. This software was a companion program to Michael Barnsley's "Fractals Everywhere". By the end of 1990 the problem of shrink-wrapped software was to become particularly acute, through the distribution of infected diskettes to thousands of customers by computer magazines. Academic Press reacted in a responsible manner and within two days had issued letters informing customers, and asking them to contact the customer service department for disinfection information.

Robert Morris was called to trial on 15 January. Of note was the decision by the US Justice Department to select jurors with no technical knowledge of computer systems. Morris' conviction was announced a week later, although sentencing was delayed until May.

Meanwhile in the UK, the CCU of the Metropolitan Police had applied on 18 January to the Bow Street Magistrate Court for a warrant to arrest Dr Joseph Lewis Popp, a US citizen, charged:

> That on the 11th December 1989, within the jurisdiction of the central criminal court, you with a view to gain for another, vis the PC Cyborg corporation of Panama, with menaces made unwarranted demand, vis a payment of one hundred and eighty nine US dollars, or three hundred and seventy eight US dollars from the victim.

Popp was a zoologist who had conducted research into animal behaviour for UNICEF and WHO, and who had examined the initial links between monkeys carrying AIDS and the human population. Popp denied any connection with the board of PC Cyborg. A spokesman for the FBI indicated that the FBI had information to suggest that Popp was prepared to mail a further two million disks. Popp alleged that the WHO was involved in a secret plot to raise funds to conduct AIDS research via the trojan, and that WHO officials comprised the board of PC Cyborg.

Popp appeared before the Cleveland District Court on 2 February faced with extradition proceedings. US Magistrate Joseph Bartunek ordered psychiatric reports after Popp's attorney described his client as depressed and possibly suicidal.

On 30 January the US Government Printing Office issued an urgent warning to all depositories that a floppy disk accompanying the latest issue of the County and City Data Book CD-ROM had been infected by the Jerusalem B virus. This was particularly worrying as a more malicious virus could have caused significant destruction of data in libraries worldwide.

The second issue of a new magazine, *MacPublishing*, was the unfortunate carrier of a Macintosh virus – the WDEF virus. This virus was accidentally included on 2000 copies of a font disk distributed free with the magazine. The infection was apparently contracted from the US via a disk carrying hypercard stacks. The magazine reacted rapidly by distributing copies of the shareware anti-virus product "Disinfectant".

Valert-l is the worldwide virus alert list maintained in parallel with the virus-l discussion list. This list aims to provide a channel for rapid global dissemination of warnings on newly discovered virus strains. This worthwhile medium was also the unfortunate carrier of the Valert-l virus ("1554") which was mailed to the alert list. The user mailing the virus had not considered his actions, which led to the global distribution of the virus binary. This action led to the moderation (monitoring) of the Valert-l list. It does, however, indicate the two-edged sword that global warning mechanisms may provide.

2.9.2 May–September

On 4 May the sentencing of Robert Morris was carried out in Syracuse, New York. Morris was sentenced to three years' probation, a fine of $10 000 and 400 hours of community service. Morris smiled broadly after his sentencing but gave no comment. Strong condemnation of the failure to sentence Morris to imprisonment was expressed by Representative Wally Herger, author of legislation to specifically outlaw viruses. A Justice Department spokesman noted his disappointment in the sentence.

On 9 May the US Attorney for the District of Arizona announced the serving of 27 search warrants over the period 7–8 May. These warrants served throughout the US were part of a two-year investigation into illegal hacking activities. An estimated 23 000 computer disks and 40 computers were seized. The operation, known as SunDevil, was to result in the attempted prosecution of a number of leading figures in the hacker/computer underground.

A research paper by Dr Peter Tippett entitled "The Kinetics of computer virus replication" predicted an explosive binary growth of virus infections. This has been questioned by a number of researchers in the field.

John McAfee issued a warning about the increasing number of bogus trojan horse programs masquerading as anti-virus scanning utilities. By November seven trojan versions had been reported:

Flushot	Version 4
Flushot Plus	Version 1.3
Virus scan	Versions 51, 65, 68, 70 and 72

The Homebase software is now bundled with a CRC checksum generator "VALIDATE". Lists of valid CRCs are published for all current anti-virus software releases.

The UK Computer Misuse Act entered into force, creating three new offences, namely a basic hacking offence with up to six months' imprisonment, an enhanced offence where the hacking is a component of a further criminal offence carrying a maximum of five years in jail, and an offence of unauthorised alteration of computer data carrying a similar penalty. Associated with the Act are extensive search and seize powers exercisable under Magistrate's warrant. The crime of releasing a computer virus was explicitly addressed in the Law Commission White Paper on Computer Misuse which subsequently formed the basis of the legislation. The non-retrospective nature of the legislation may raise problems in prosecuting authors who released viruses prior to the date of enactment.

A trojan horse was discovered on Apple Macintosh systems which reprogrammed the attached laser writer systems to alter the default printer password. This was possibly one of the first examples of manipulation of intelligent peripheral devices (in this case the Postscript interpreter program in the printer).

The *PC Today* magazine mailed 40 000 copies of an inactivated version of the "Disk Killer" PC virus in July. The boot sector virus was partially overwritten during the duplication process and thus made inoperable. *PC Today* rapidly recalled the infected disks, and stated that they would be taking action to prevent such a recurrence, including the scanning of master disks for known viruses, both in-house and at distribution facilities.

The *Ithaca Journal* reported on 25 September that a 16-year-old high school student who created the "MDEF" and "CDEF" Macintosh viruses had been identified by police. The student who was responsible for virus infections at Ithaca High School, BAKA Computers Inc. and Cornell University is not being prosecuted at this time because of his co-operation with police. One estimate placed damage at hundreds of hours of lost programmer time.

2.9.3 October–December

In November it was reported that *PC Benelux World* had mailed 16 000 copies of disks infected with the Cascade ("1704") PC virus. These disks were mailed within Belgium, the Netherlands and Luxembourg. The magazine immediately notified the media, and sent letters to all subscribers warning of the infection. This, combined with the cost of providing disinfection utilities, was estimated as having cost £40 000.

A further report indicated a "Goblins" Atari virus infection in the cover disk of a major Atari magazine.

The problem of shrink-wrapped virus software, both published and distributed by software manufacturers, has grown to be a significant risk. It has demonstrated the need for all software distributors to take exceptional care in screening their systems for virus infection. While many users will carefully consider using software from bulletin boards, how many will think twice before installing a commercial product?

In December the Dallas prosecutor's office announced that it intended to file charges against the alleged author of the Macintosh Scores virus. Lt Walter Manning of the Dallas Police Department requested organisations infected by the virus to report details to him to permit an assessment of the damage caused by the virus.

The year ended with an eyewitness account by Bryan Clough in the December issue of *Virus Bulletin*. The article described the Bulgarian Virus Factory, which had produced over 100 strains and 30 distinct types of virus. New viruses have been quoted as appearing at the rate of one per week from this source. Products of the factory have included the infamous "Dark Avenger" virus, together with two further retro-viruses named "Evil" and "Phoenix" by the same author, and the V, TP and VHP series of viruses. The complexity of the virus family structure is indicated in Appendix 5. The Bulgarian output has also included subverted anti-virus programs which will themselves release viruses under certain conditions.

2.10 Summary

In this chapter I have tried to give a range of reports and examples of virus incidents and details of how the computer community has reacted to those incidents. The chapter seeks to indicate that a wide variety of malicious software has been distributed, and that viruses represent a significant threat, often through unexpected channels such as shrink-wrapped or published software. This chapter also attempts to give a flavour of the authors who write such software, and how they are treated by the community.

In the following chapter we will look at how viruses operate on a variety of hardware platforms, and to consider how we can prevent such viruses.

Chapter 3
Theory of Viruses

3.1 Introduction

This chapter is structured into three main sections dealing with the following questions: How is viral code added to a system? How can it be detected? and What are the analogies between biological and computer viruses?

Viruses are dealt with at an abstract level in this section. For details of how viruses replicate on specific hardware platforms, e.g. IBM PC, Mac, or UNIX, the reader is referred to later chapters.

We begin by looking in abstract at the operation of a computer virus.

3.2 Addition of Viral Code

The first question is: How can a virus insert its code into the host system? This can be achieved in a variety of ways – there are four primary methods of inserting a block of viral code into a host executable program, namely:

1. Prepending: moving the original host's code (or part of the code) to a later memory or disk location, leaving a gap into which the virus can insert its code.
2. Appending: simply adding the virus' code to the end of the host program.
3. Shell: embedding the host's original code within the virus as a subroutine.
4. Overwriting or injective: the host is destroyed by being overwritten by virus code.

In each technique the flow of control is slightly different. In the prepending example the virus code is entered first, the virus replicates and then passes control to the host program which executes and exits. In the appending case the host executes first, exits and then passes control to the virus. In the shell case the host program forms a subroutine of the virus. The virus is thus executed before and after host program execution.

Depending on the complexity of the object code file structure it may be difficult or impossible to arrange for the execution of viral code after the host program has terminated. In general this is due to the multiplicity of exit or return instructions in a subroutine or program. The appending virus must therefore patch the original host so that control passes to the virus first (this is normally achieved by modifying a few instructions at the start of the host). Thus, true appending viruses require support for interception of host initialisation or termination calls, rather than relying on execution to start at the lowest address in memory and continue onward.

In the shell virus the host program becomes a single subroutine, and can thus be run under complete control of the virus. The virus can execute initialisation and termination code, allowing complex replication and manipulation strategies to be included.

Each of the techniques is illustrated below:

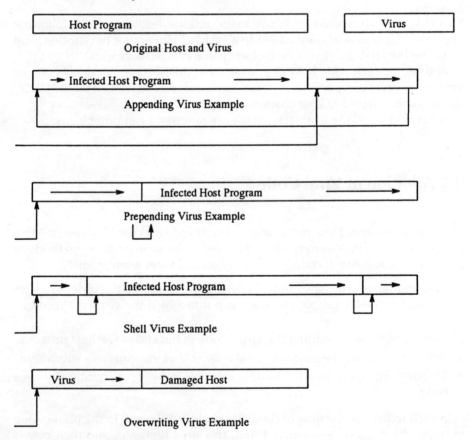

Host Program   Virus

Original Host and Virus

Infected Host Program

Appending Virus Example

Infected Host Program

Prepending Virus Example

Infected Host Program

Shell Virus Example

Virus   Damaged Host

Overwriting Virus Example

A virus must have a certain degree of access to its environment. Specifically, it must be able to write to executable or potentially executable code within the system. The virus, by its activity, affects a permanent change in the environment of the system (i.e. the infection of one or more host programs).

The algorithm used by a possible virus has been summarised (by Fred Cohen) as:

```
program virus
        signature 1234567

        subroutine infect_executable
        begin
                loop: get random file
                        if first line of file = 1234567
                                then goto loop
                                prepend virus to file
        end

        subroutine do_damage
        begin
                <variety of possible damage routines>
        end

        subroutine trigger_pulled
        begin
                <check for a particular system state>
        end

begin

        infect_executable
        if trigger_pulled then do_damage

end

host program starts here
```

This simple pseudo-code virus demonstrates a number of characteristics shown by real viruses. First, the virus must infect an executable by adding its code in a manner which ensures the code will be executed (here by prepending to the host); second, the virus checks for a signature to avoid infecting the same host file over and over again; and third, the virus checks for a certain combination of system conditions and if satisfied will execute a damage routine.

Not all viruses are malicious and in many cases the do_damage may be an amusing display or message or, indeed, may be absent altogether.

In the example above it should be noted that the infected code may occur anywhere within the system, it may include the system initialisation (boot sequence), termination (shutdown) sequences, user or system executable programs or indeed data which is interpreted by other programs (such as a script of an editor or command interpreter instructions).

The examples above have assumed that the host's code remains intact (in all bar the overwriting case) and thus the infected file is longer by a certain amount. Each virus causes a characteristic length extension of a host program – for instance, the Cascade virus on the IBM PC extends all hosts by 1701 or 1704 bytes when infecting.

This is not necessarily the case. Consider a virus that compresses its host before infecting. This virus modifies the above algorithm as follows:

```
program virus
        signature 1234567

        subroutine infect_executable
        begin
                loop: get random file
                        if first line of file = 1234567
                                then goto loop
                        compress host program
                        prepend virus to file
        end

        subroutine do_damage
        begin
                <variety of possible damage routines>
        end

        subroutine trigger_pulled
        begin
                <check for a particular system state>
        end

begin
        infect_executable
        if trigger_pulled then do_damage
        uncompress host program
end
```

The virus now compresses the host program using one of a variety of well-known algorithms such as Huffman or Lempel-Ziv coding. This results in a significant saving in space – possibly 50 per cent or more of the original size. The virus can then add its own code. The virus code includes instructions to uncompress the host after the viral code has executed. The user of such a virus detects no file extension, and indeed may detect a file compression or shortening when the virus is active.

Cohen has argued that such a virus with no damage routine can be considered a useful application of viral code. Later examples of anti-virus viruses, self-replicating vaccines, are also cited later in this book as possibly useful applications.

The criteria for detecting the action of virus code cannot be as basic as detection of extension of infected object size. Indeed there are a number of proofs that no possible set of criteria or characteristics can be used to identify a virus absolutely.

3.3 Detection of Viruses

Cohen provides the following basic proof of the undecidability of whether an object is a virus. He proposed the construction of a function "is__a__virus". This function returns "true" if a program is a virus, otherwise it returns "false".

By including this function in the virus propagation code itself, we can invoke a contradiction which can be used to prove that this function cannot be written. Namely:

```
Main program

begin
    if (is_a_virus = FALSE) infect_executable
    if trigger_pulled then do_damage
    uncompress host program
end
```

If the function returns "true", then the program will never call its infect executable function and thus cannot be a virus. If the function returns "false" (i.e. not a virus), then the program will call its infect executable function and must therefore be a virus.

Thimbleby notes that this proof has a number of shortcomings:

1. The time taken to compute the "is_a_virus" function is not considered. If the function takes an infinite time to compute then no contradiction is invoked.
2. It is argued that a program must infect to be classed as a virus. Thimbleby argues that it is sufficient that a program contains code to potentially infect,

and thus no contradiction exists since "is_a_virus" can return "true" in the case of the contradictory virus above without raising a contradiction.

3. The code "infect_executable" may be null, in which case the proof relates to a non-replicating object which may or may not cause damage – i.e. a trojan horse.

Alternative proofs have been proposed by both Thimbleby and Adleman regarding the undecidability of virus (or trojan horse detection).

The proof presented by Thimbleby is based on the refutation of the concept that all trojan horse programs are enumerable (i.e. can be listed). Basically, he presents a short contradictory program which attempts to enumerate all possible trojan horses. If the program succeeds in locating itself within the list of trojans, it runs the host normally, thus it is not a trojan. If it is not in the generated list of possible trojans it loops forever, causing a denial of service and indicating that it is indeed a trojan horse.

```
Variable N is an integer

N = 0
While Enumerate(N) is not equal to my program
     do N = N + 1
Execute host code
```

The function "Enumerate" generates the code for the nth possible trojan horse from a finite list of possible trojan horses.

This proof makes the assumption described as "trivial" that the trojan horse can in fact access its own code. This implies a degree of access to the system environment that is certainly allowable in open unprotected architectures such as most personal computers, but may be questionable in architectures which explicitly prevent read access to code or closely monitor access to code files.

3.4 Classes of Viruses

Adleman offers a series of classifications of viruses based on their behavioural characteristics, which unifies the concept of trojan horse with that of a virus. He decomposes the set of viruses into four disjoint subsets based on whether they are pathogenic and/or contagious. While formal definitions of these two criteria are given, it is sufficient here to note that a pathogenic organism will cause damage to the host system, while a contagious organism will cause its host to spread the organism.

A program infected by a specific virus is:

- *Benignant* if it is not pathogenic and not contagious
- *Trojan horse* if is pathogenic but not contagious
- *Carrier* if it is not pathogenic but is contagious
- *Virulent* if it is pathogenic and contagious

For instance, a carrier is incapable of causing injury to the host, but will infect other programs (which may not be carriers after infection).

This classification of the characteristics of an infected program is extended to produce a general classification of viruses with respect to all programs. Thus a virus is:

- *Benign* if all possible programs infected by the virus are non-pathogenic and non-contagious
- *Epeian*[1] if all possible programs infected by the virus are non-contagious, but at least one possible program infected by the virus will be pathogenic
- *Disseminating* if all possible programs infected by the virus are non-pathogenic, but at least one possible program infected by the virus will be contagious
- *Malicious* if at least one possible program infected by the virus will be pathogenic, and at least one (possibly a different program) will be contagious

Adleman also provides a number of proofs of significance based on this categorisation:

- Programs infected by a benign virus are benignant
- Programs infected by an Epeian virus are benignant or trojan horses
- Programs infected by a disseminating virus are benignant or carriers
- Programs infected by a malicious virus can be of any category
- It is impossible to detect all viruses
- Viruses which increase the length of the host on infection are isolatable
- It is impossible to isolate all viruses

The concept of a germ is also introduced. The germ is a virus which can infect a host, but can itself never be generated by an infected host. An example may be the launcher used to create an initial infected host – such launch code may exist as part of a trojan horse program. Possible examples include the hypertext stacks used to launch the Peace virus on the Macintosh.

Much further work is required in the area of virus theory, particularly with regard to the minimal restrictions on the generality of computing systems which will permit detection of viral replication or malicious software activity.

---

1. The term "Epeian" is based on the name of the builder of the original Greek trojan horse cited in the *Odyssey* of Homer.

3.5 Thompson: and Trusting Trust

While on the subject of the inherent difficulties in detecting viruses (or indeed trojan horses), mention must be made of Ken Thompson's 1983 ACM award speech which described a trojan horse in an AT & T Bell C compiler. He indicated the potential for such a trojan, incorporated into a trusted component in the compilation path, to completely vanish.

The UNIX C compiler is written in C itself, and bootstrapped using either a previous release of the C compiler or a minimal handwritten compiler in assembly or another high level language. The new C compiler is compiled by the previous C compiler to produce a program which will correctly compile C using the features of the new compiler, but with the code generated by the previous compiler. This stage 2 compiler can then be used to recompile itself to produce a stage 3 compiler with the syntax and semantic analysis features of the new compiler and the new code generator. This complex bootstrap process is typical of the installation of a new compiler on a mainframe system.

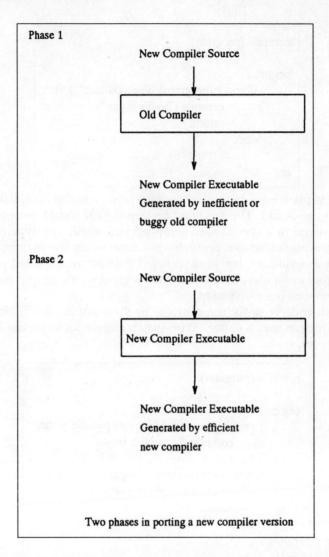

Phase 1

New Compiler Source

Old Compiler

New Compiler Executable
Generated by inefficient or
buggy old compiler

Phase 2

New Compiler Source

New Compiler Executable

New Compiler Executable
Generated by efficient
new compiler

Two phases in porting a new compiler version

The difficulties began when a trojan horse was planted in the C compiler. The trojan horse proposed by Thompson would look for a particular sequence in the source and, if detected, miscompile the source program, e.g.

```
compile (program)

begin
        if match(program, "login pattern")) then
                compile ("login trojan")
                return
        else

                ...
end
```

He reports planting a bug which would recognise the compilation of the
UNIX login command. The modified login program would accept either the
correct password or a special hard compiled password. This type of program
recognition is an intractable problem, but fortunately the matching process
could apply a significant degree of knowledge about the expected structure of
the login program (it was unlikely that the program would change dramatically
from the previous release version).

The trojan code is easily recognisable in the compiler itself, therefore he
proposes a further match pattern. This match pattern looks for the C compiler
being itself compiled:

```
compile (program)

begin
        if match(program, "compiler pattern")) then
                compile ("compiler trojan")
                return
        else if match(program, "login pattern")) then
                compile ("login trojan")
                return
        else

                ...
end
```

The compiler will still recognise the login program, and will generate a
trojanised executable. It now also recognises an attempt to compile a new C
compiler, and will insert the code sequence above into any future C compiler.
Thus all following C compilers will contain code to insert the trojan into login,
and the compiler trojan into all future compilers.

Once the C compiler has been recompiled (and the trojan code automatically
inserted), the original source for the trojan can be removed from the C compiler
source. When the C compiler is recompiled, the clean source will have the
compiler and login trojan code added by the buggy executable, producing a

new generation of the compiler. So the bug is self-perpetuating, and in Ken Thompson's words:

It is as close to a "learning" program as I have seen

Actually, the compiler need not be the target of the trojan horse. It is sufficient to attack any element in the compilation sequence. A trojan can be inserted in the assembler which recognises assembly of a new assembler, in the linker which recognises linking of a new linker, etc. At lower levels the complexity of correctly adding code to support the trojan increases, due to the loss of information and structure during the compilation. Theoretically the concept could even be extended to an operating system which recognised when an attempt was being made to write a file containing the executable for the next release of the operating system, and to insert a similar trojan into the file.

The problem is simply "trusting trust". When we compile a program on our system, we must trust the hardware, operating system, editors, compilers, assemblers and linkers. All are vital parts of the mapping operation from the source we type in, to the code we run. The source code may be formally verified, but unless the compilation path is also verified, this cannot provide complete protection.

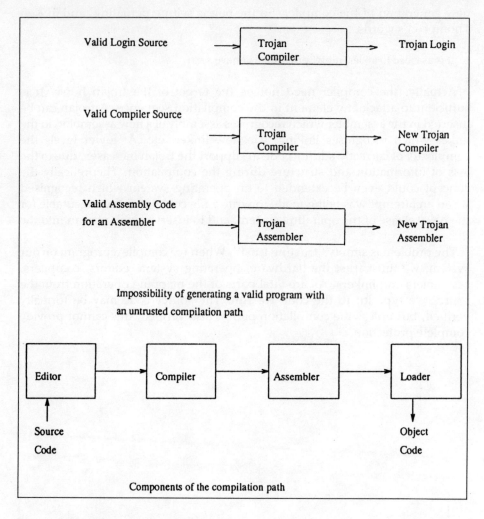

Components of the compilation path

This concludes a brief introduction to the abstract theory of viruses. To continue we will look at biological analogies, and consider what – if anything – they can tell us about computer viruses.

3.6 Biological Analogies

The obvious analogy between the replication of a computer virus and that of a biological virus has been a major driving factor behind the terminology that has evolved within the field. Although care should be taken regarding the extension of this analogy to extremes, it can provide a useful comparative model, suggesting a number of possible protection schemes.

Biological life also provides a range of possible models for the replication of a virus within a computer system, and within the computing community as a whole.

3.6.1 Biological Viruses

Life is based on the existence of the genetic code which determines the structure of an organism, and on the replication of such genetic material. Structure is encoded as a chain of chemical groups consisting of a phosphate and a deoxyribose. Attached to this backbone is one of four possible bases, namely:

Purines: Adenine (A) Guanine (G)
Pyrimidines: Thymine (T) Cytosine (C)

The base, phosphate and deoxyribose form a single nucleotide. Two chains of nucleotides are paired, with hydrogen bonds forming between purines on one chain and pyrimidines on the other chain. The chain molecules (deoxyribonucleic acid, DNA) have four possible pairings for each element in the chain: A–T, T–A, G–C and C–G. The arrangement of the nucleotides forms the genetic code, with groups of nucleotides forming genes. Each gene contains details of the structure of a single protein in the organism. Proteins are comprised of combinations of twenty amino acids. Each nucleotide has four possible states (A, G, T or C). Thus a minimum of three are required to specify an amino acid. This group is called a codon.

The DNA is replicated by a complex series of operations during which an enzyme produces a ribonucleic acid (RNA) fragment transcribed from a gene or group of genes in the DNA. The messenger RNA is a single strand of information which can pass through the cell nucleus membrane (which segregates the genetic material from the remainder of the cell). The messenger RNA is transcribed by transfer RNA which assembles a series of amino acids (dictated by the codons in the messenger RNA) to produce a protein.

In biological systems a virus is a simple structure which is capable of self-replication only through the use of the complex cellular protein construction mechanisms outlined above.

A virus injects its genetic material in the form of RNA or DNA into a host cell. The genetic material is then replicated using the internal protein biosythesis mechanisms of the cell, effectively producing a large number of viruses within the cell itself. The build-up of toxins and viral material within the cell walls causes breakdown of the cell, and eventual release of a large number of virus clones into the environment.

Thus the operation of a biological virus can be described algorithmically as:

- Inject genetic material into the cell
- Cellular transcription and synthesis mechanisms cause replication

- Virus proteins are assembled to generate copies of the virus
- Cell wall rupture causes release of copies into environment

3.6.2 Parallels Between Low Level Operation

A computer virus is a small segment of computer code which is incapable of replication without being incorporated into a host program. The code of the computer virus can be compared to the codon or nucleotide structure level in the DNA of a biological virus. The parallel between the inability of both forms of virus to propagate without the agency of a host program is obvious (in the biological case injection of genetic material into a cell, in the computer case injection of code into computer program).

A significant difference is the concept of the cell environment. If it is argued that a cell represents a computer program, then how could viral spread across program boundaries occur?

The program would by analogy generate a large number of copies of the short viral code segment, and would then release them into the environment. The viruses would seek out and infect further programs. In the case of a computer virus it is more accurate to imagine the virus subverting the host cell and manipulating the cell to infect other cells directly. To modify the computer virus analogy to closely resemble the biological virus, it is necessary to postulate that the environment consists of:

1. All host programs being active and subject to direct manipulation in system memory (the alteration of an executable which may be loaded into memory at a later time may be considered an acceptable extension of this concept).
2. Further fragments of computer code active in the environment which may have been generated by the host programs. These represent viruses active within the system.

An infected host program would have its executable code altered (on disk or in memory) to commence replication of the virus code fragment. The replicated viruses would be executable code fragments which would be run and launched into the environment. These fragments would then seek out and attach to further host programs. This example implies a multi- processing environment. The small resident virus executables are similar to the resident virus components on the IBM PC discussed in the next chapter.

The concept of genetic code also differs significantly between current computer systems and biological systems. Specifically, while computer object code may be likened to a codon or nucleotide, it is questionable whether any discernible high level structure exists in most computer code. The procedural structure imposed by compilers of high level languages may possible be likened to the gene structure level, but this is questionable.

This key issue of high level structure is one which has significantly retarded the application of genetic algorithmic techniques to computer viruses.

3.6.3 High Level Parallels

The comparison of the more abstract aspects of computer virus and biological virus behaviour is potentially more useful at this time. The symptoms of an infected system can be paralleled to an infected organism, the behaviour of a computer virus at an abstract level to that of a biological virus, and the prevention of biological infection paralleled to that of computer infection.

William Murray describes the analogy between computer and biological virus propagation in clear terms, in the following manner:

> A virus is expelled (sneeze, SENDFILE) from an infected member (carrier or originator) of a community (family, users of a common system or network), on a vector (mucus, data object, file or program), through a medium (air, network or shared I/O devices or media) through a portal of entry (nose, network reader) to a target member of the community.

1. *Portals of entry* The wide variety of portals through which viral material can be introduced in a human being (by ingestion, via the circulatory system, via respiration, etc.) is mirrored by a wide range of network services by which code can be introduced and executed in a computer system.

2. *Vectors* Vectors are organisms which carry viral infection (possibly without noticeable effect) between third parties. An example is the tsetse fly carrying sleeping sickness. Vectors for viral infection are data or program objects, an example might include a useful system utility which was infected before release to the network.

3. *Hygiene* To prevent infection a wide range of hygiene measures are suggested, including non-contact with contaminated materials (such as soiled articles in the human case) and general bodily cleanliness. The computer parallels would be the avoidance of the ingress of suspect computer code (such as anonymous games software) coupled with the regular verification of the integrity of protective software (password controls, etc.).

4. *Vaccination* Vaccination provides an extremely powerful technique in biological systems, promoting the development of natural immunity using attenuated viral material. Within the computer environment fragments of viral material may also be used – in this case the signature recognition strings which the virus uses to prevent repeated replication. These fragments may safely be added to existing cells (computer programs) and will protect against the virus.

5. *Antibodies* Antibodies to specific infections would be equivalent to the introduction into the computer environment of specific disinfection software, which would recognise the infected program and destroy the virus. Such antibodies can be introduced prior to the point of the infection in order to raise the general level of protection. In the same way as the level of antibodies in the bloodstream decreases after infection has been destroyed, so the probability that the systems administrators will be conscientious in their use of scanning and disinfection utilities decreases.

6. *Isolation and quarantine* Isolation of infected organisms from the remainder of the community is suggested for all highly infectious diseases. In a similar manner, constraints on electronic and physical media traffic between infected and clean systems can significantly reduce the likelihood of infection spreading.

7. *Latency and incubation* Many diseases have a significant delay between the point of infection and the point at which the organism begins to demonstrate the symptoms of the infection. This latency or incubation period exists in computer virus infections too. The latency may be expressed as the time between initial infection and the time at which the degradation in system performance (due to widespread infection of executables) becomes unacceptable to the user. It may also depend on the delay between a virus initially infecting a program, and the commencement of malicious activity by the virus. This delay may be considerable (decades, in the case of the "Century" IBM virus). Viruses may, however, cause damage during this period which is not readily detectable by external symptoms (such as the steady interlinking of data sectors caused by the "4096" virus strain) during this period.

8. *Carriers* If the computer system is considered to be an organism, then a carrier would be a host on which the virus was incapable of replicating or when replicating would cause no obvious symptoms. This might be due to the specific targeting of a virus against a specific host type, or hosts on which specific code exists (e.g. the Scores Mac virus targeted against products of Electronic Data Systems Ltd.) or may be unable to propagate due to host architectural differences (such as the incompatibility between Intel 80386 and 8086 processors – the POP CS instruction).

9. *Diagnosis* The process of diagnosis of an infected system can be compared to that of an infected organism. External signs contribute to the diagnosis (e.g. the symptoms of a viral infection), internal checks may be run (similar to inspection of the contents of data on disk or in system memory). The patient may be queried as to his health, possibly similar to the use of system auditing and monitoring, and the subsequent use of expert systems to interpret system logs.

10. *AIDS* Finally, the organism's internal protective systems may recognise legitimate cell material (erroneous decisions resulting from a scan for a virus, or analysis of system activity logs) and may remove legitimate programs. Equally, the virus may alter the operation of the anti-virus software in such a manner as to cause the deletion or corruption of valid data or programs. This could be compared to the Acquired Immuno-Deficiency Syndrome (AIDS) in humans.

3.7 Quest for Life

The clear parallels between biological and computer viruses lead naturally to the question: Do computer viruses constitute artificial life? To answer this question, a definition of what constitutes life is critical. A list of criteria required for artificial life was given by Farmer, and included:

1. Life is a pattern in space–time.
2. Self-reproduction.
3. Information storage of a self-representation.
4. A metabolism.
5. Functional interactions with the environment.
6. Interdependence of parts.
7. Stability under perturbations.
8. The ability to evolve.
9. Growth or expansion.

Computer viruses are physical manifestations represented by computer object code spread both locally within the file system storage and globally throughout the world. At any given moment the code comprising a single virus is likely to be in execution by many separate systems. The code representing an individual virus instance has a distinct existence in memory, and a distinct lifespan in terms of the duration of its presence in memory.

Self-reproduction is the principal feature which distinguishes a computer virus from other executable code in the system environment.

The self-representation of a computer virus is clearly the object code which constitutes the virus. This code is replicated as part of the virus' replication cycle, and is broadly analogous to the genetic code of a living organism.

The existence of a metabolism (i.e. a conversion between matter and energy) is questionable in the case of a virus. It is possible to argue that the definition of metabolism is insufficiently broad to encompass the significantly different characteristics of any potential computer life form. The dependence of computer viruses on the existence and manipulation of computers by external entities does not directly void the definition of life. The parasite which depends on its host' s existence and its host's reproductive or digestive functions for replication can be cited as a biological counter example. Metabolism in the case of the computer virus may be considered as the conversion of computational effort to increased information content or structure in the computer's secondary storage. Thus the virus has consumed 1000 cycles of CPU time and has generated a structured image where random data might have previously existed.

A virus clearly interacts with its environment by altering system memory, secondary storage or peripheral states. Equally, the components of a virus are interdependent to a certain degree. Certainly the removal at random of a block of instructions would significantly modify the behaviour of the virus.

Stability under perturbation is a significant question which is closely related to the ability to adapt to environmental changes. A virus can modify its execution paths within tightly defined logical parameters to compensate for limited environmental changes. This is probably comparable to the limited range of environments in which many life forms can survive.

Putting aside the question of evolution (which must be considered the significant hurdle for computer viruses), it is clear that following the release of a computer virus it will grow, spreading potentially worldwide. The increase in the variety of computer viruses must, however, be ignored as this is a representation of interference by another life form (man) and not of the replication and growth of viruses.

Finally, evolution. This is the single area in which current viruses fall short of the goal of artificial life. The next section discusses the limited degrees of evolution or mutation which have been witnessed, and then considers the extension of the genetic algorithm to computer viruses.

3.8 Evolution: Genetic Algorithms

3.8.1 Random Mutation

A limited number of random mutations of computer viruses have been recorded, caused by data corruption in transit, or by failure of system memory or disks. One example is the single byte modification in the 1704 strain of the IBM Cascade virus, detected in Yugoslavia. This has been attributed to random corruption rather than to deliberate modification. It is worth noting that some newer viruses incorporate self-correcting (Hamming) codes to avoid such in-transit corruption.

The possibility of random bit corruption causing virus code to be generated in an executable program has been addressed by both Cohen and Burger. Both give results which vary by orders of magnitude, due mainly to differing assumptions. As a simplistic estimate, consider a virus of length 1000 bits (or 125 bytes – not unrealistic considering the "Tiny" series of viruses on the IBM PC which are around 158 bytes in length). The probability of extensive random corruption of a block of 1000 bits generating an exact match against the 1000 bit test virus is $1/2^{1000}$ or $\approx 10^{-301}$.

If we consider that a 90 per cent chance of each bit correct may generate a viable virus, then this probability reduces to $1/1.82^{1000}$ or $\approx 10^{-259}$. Thus a single computer randomly generating 1000 bit patterns and testing the resultant patterns at the rate of one pattern every millisecond would generate a new operational virus (assuming the 90 per cent criteria) once in every 10^{+249} years.

Even with the expansion of the computer base worldwide it seems highly unlikely that such a random mutation would generate a new computer virus. The probability of an existing virus mutating by random bit corruption into another viable virus is considerably higher, however.

3.8.2 Programmed Mutation

A simple evolutionary virus was cited by Cohen which added random statements between the functional statements of the virus when producing a new copy. He demonstrated that it was impossible to decide the functional equivalence of two programs (even though it is comparable easy to prove in a limited subset of cases), by producing an undecidable evolutionary virus (UEV). The evolutionary virus is reproduced (in modified form) below:

```
program evolutionary virus

        subroutine print_random_number
        begin
                print random_variable_name = random_variable_name
                loop:
                        if random_bit = 1 then
                                print random_operator
                                goto loop
                        print semicolon
        end

        subroutine copy_virus_with_insertions
        begin
                loop:
                        copy evolutionary virus until semicolon
                        if random_bit = 1 then
                                print random_statement
                        if not end of input file then goto loop
        end

begin
        copy_virus_with_insertions
        infect_executable
        if trigger_pulled then do_damage
end
host program
```

This programmed mutation is designed to operate within carefully controlled criteria, and thus while generating a potentially infinite number of mutations, will not functionally modify the behaviour of the core of the virus replication task. Limited programmed mutation has been incorporated into viruses such as the 4096 (random reordering of procedural code blocks within the virus) and the 1260 (random padding instructions in the decryption routines).

3.8.3 Genetic Algorithms

An extension of the degree of programmed mutation is to utilise binary virus techniques. A binary virus, first proposed by Hruska, is a virus which carries one part of a double payload. Two strains of the virus exist, A and B. Both strains are innocuous in isolation but when they meet, the payloads combine to produce a malicious function. An example might be the introduction by an author of a virus whose sole function is to replicate. At a later time the author releases a trigger virus which itself replicates. On detecting the operation or presence of the trigger virus, the original virus will become active, potentially destroying data and information.

A possible example of this might be the Atari ST "Key" virus. This basic boot sector virus replicates. When active, the virus will check for the existence or insertion of a key disk (carrying a special signature word). The code on the key disk is loaded into memory, and immediately executed.

Binary viruses do, however, provide the ability to model sexual reproduction in living organisms. The virus must be programmed in such a manner to incorporate a number of variable "genes". These genes may control functions such as:

- Replication strategy
- Replication rate
- Latency time
- Manipulation task choice
- Infection mechanism
- Residency time
- Encryption techniques
- Camouflage techniques

These basic attributes are represented either as integer gene values which select or modify the operation of standard code in the virus, or indeed as procedures with standardised interfaces which are randomly swapped between "mating" viruses.

Thus, we can design a skeleton virus with slots into which code blocks are placed. Examples might be a procedure in one slot which scans the file system hierarchy and selects a host to be infected, another which encrypts and decrypts the remainder of the virus, and others which determine the manipulation task of the virus.

Using the binary techniques above it becomes possible to design a virus kernel which on detecting a file infected by another variant will randomly swap code modules between the two viruses, thus producing a third strain based on the gene values or code from each virus. As a variant of natural selection comes into play (based on the ability of man to detect and eliminate each strain) the percentages of each gene will slowly alter to provide the optimal combination of criteria for reproduction and evasion of detection.

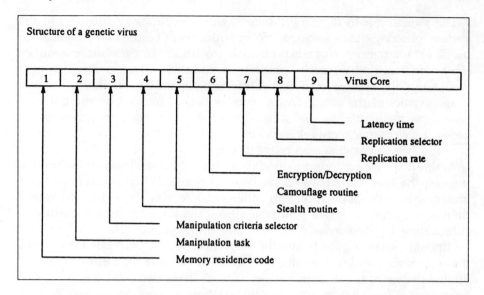

Virus core is responsible for handling gene recombination and may itself by modularised and subject to gene swapping. Additional gene possibilities are:

- Signature recognition code
- Automatic disinfection of other viruses
- Anti-virus software counter measures
- Code aimed at specific software or files
- Information compromise functions

The author of the virus could potentially upgrade his virus *in situ* by releasing a new strain which would compete with other existing strains, adding its new genes to the gene pool. With sufficient flexibility in the structure of the gene selection mechanisms, and a large pool of genetic material, considerable natural selection and optimisation might occur.

The reported existence of a virus construction set (with window-driven interface) for the Atari ST was possibly the first example of the static (rather than dynamic genetic) approach to modular virus construction.

Certainly, the picture of a virus using a genetic algorithm is far closer to the concept of life than the traditional viruses we have encountered to date.

3.8.4 Growth and Death

Finally, biological life can provide a useful source of experience in the modelling of computer virus propagation characteristics. The growth of computer viruses can be compared to the growth of isolated populations of organisms in the presence of competition and inhibition.

The viruses left to their own devices would replicate rapidly within the system, observing the traditional "S" growth curve (if random file selection is used) or a far more rapid exponential growth curve (if a more complex incremental directory search algorithm is adopted). Thus, a single system would rapidly become completely infected depending on the replication characteristics of the virus. This system is loosely coupled by the traffic in removable media (floppy disks) to adjacent systems, and through common access to electronic network services. Thus a similar viral growth curve between system partitions can be predicted.

At this point we are forced to modify the growth model to add inhibition, in this case the intervention of a human being or beings. When a virus population grows, so does the population's probability of detection. If the virus is detected then a rapid response will be invoked from the virus research community, culminating in the release of a new anti- viral product. This product (if a traditional signature based scanning utility) will slowly percolate throughout the community, and will result in the death of many of the virus colonies. A limited degree of re-infection will occur from rarely used systems or backup tapes, and isolated infection pockets will continue to exist in systems which do not use the anti-viral software. The situation may thus be compared to the biological analogy of a campaign of mass vaccination to exterminate a viral infection.

The model must be further extended to again deal with human factors, in this case the author's response to the destruction of his virus, and his release of a potentially modified strain into the environment. This represents a degree of competition between anti-virus software authors and virus authors.

In summary, a growth model can be constructed with the following features:

1. Rapid initial growth on the source system (exponential or S curve).

2. Fixed probability of infection being coupled between isolated systems via disk or program transport.

3. Lag-time dependent on virus latency period or success of camouflage between release and initial detection.

4. Further lag between detection and commencement of significant anti-viral effort.

5. Penetration of anti-virus software throughout community over time with inhibition of the virus.

6. Low probability of re-infection from isolated infection pockets or infected backups.

7. Counter-reaction from virus author and release of new strain.

A rough graph of a possible virus infection within an organisation is shown below. This is of course highly speculative.

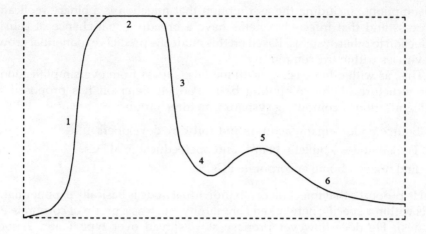

A possible model of virus infection
within a networked organisation

Phases:

1. Rapid initial spread of infection throughout organisation.
2. Latency time before detection.
3. Effective use of anti-virus.
4. Limited number of systems not disinfected.
5. Re-infection from backups as anti-virus precautions fall into disuse.
6. Slow tail-off of infection within organisation as infected systems are upgraded, reformatted, decommissioned, or eventually disinfected.

A number of authors have addressed the problem of viral growth modelling, including models based on the concept of an environment partitioned into system, partitioned into user spaces, or partitioned into files. A single infected file is inserted into the system with a descriptive model of its replication strategy, latency time, time resident in memory, etc. The model can be extended to impose a mandatory or discretionary confidentiality framework on top of the general partitions.

Gleissner quotes a simplified model in which the following assumptions are made:

M program in a single account. All programs called with equal frequency 1/M. Initially only one program infected.

His results indicate that for an account with 80 programs, infection of all programs will occur after 378 program calls. The graph of the infection process is approximately exponential.

Peter Tippett has produced a paper entitled the "Kinetics of computer virus replication". This paper extrapolates viral growth based on a number of basic assumptions, including the assumption that infection is a binary replication process and that infected systems have a broadly equal chance of causing infection to other systems. Based on this model he predicts exponential growth of viruses within the community.

This, as with other basic growth models, suffers from oversimplification of the structure of the computing base. Padgett Peterson has proposed the categorisation of computing systems into three groups:

1. Source nodes – manufacturers and software developers.
2. Transit nodes – bulletin boards and open educational PCs.
3. End nodes – home or corporate PCs.

He proposes that infection on an individual node is basically exponential, as it is within a specific networked community (such as a group of corporate end nodes). He does however propose slow spread over type 1 and 2 nodes (probably in the face of extensive anti-viral software measures) coupled by rapid spread amongst the systems comprising a cluster of type 3 nodes. The human factor is noted (i.e. the reaction of the anti-virus community) which leads to counter measures on the type 1 (and possibly type 2) nodes restricting the infection sources of the virus to local and intercommunicating type 3 nodes. The model is thus based on a rapid anti-viral response within the expert community, followed by a deferred local response.

David Chess confirms Peterson's comments on the "sharing" topology of the computing community and comments that significant levels of anti-virus scanner use can result in reversal of the exponential growth prediction. Models adopted at the High Integrity Computing Laboratory at IBM have indicated (albeit crudely) that stabilisation of virus frequencies at very low values (<1 per cent of the systems infected) may occur. Chess also denies that IBM data indicate that an exponential growth of infections is occurring.

In general, it is certain that the topological structure of the community must be considered, as must the intervention and inhibition of viral spread as a result of action by the community. It is, however, likely that growth models will evolve to include heuristics to address these issues.

Chapter 4

Operation of PC Viruses

4.1 Introduction

The lifecycle of a typical PC virus can be divided into three stages, namely:

- Activation
- Replication
- Manipulation

To achieve a spread of viral material, the virus must arrange for its code to be executed by the computer system on which the virus resides, or by a computer system interconnected to that system.

A typical computer has many ways in which a user may invoke object code, either directly as the result of the execution of a command or indirectly through system functions carried out automatically on behalf of the users.

Four main types of code are executed by computer systems:

1. Initialisation code: executed as part of the system startup or boot phase before system login or command interpreter prompts are generated.
2. User code: executed as a direct or traceable result of a command by the user.
3. Daemon code: regularly run by the system to carry out administrative functions such as accounting, background mail transfer, etc.
4. Termination code: executed as part of system shutdown.

Any analysis of viral propagation on a specific hardware platform must address all the above routes and carefully consider the avenues by which viral code may be executed.

This chapter specifically addresses the avenues for viral infection of IBM PC compatible systems, together with the techniques adopted by known PC viruses to evade detection and analysis. A general knowledge of IBM PC system architectures is assumed.

4.2 PC Boot Sequence: Initialisation

The initialisation code executed by a PC is known as the boot sequence and is comparatively complex, leaving open many avenues for viral code to be introduced. The sequence can be summarised as:

- System bootstrap read-only memory (ROM)
- Master boot sector
- DOS boot sector
- Initialisation "SYSINIT" program code
- DOS code
- COMMAND.COM code
- ● AUTOEXEC.BAT command file
- ●● Startup utilities executed via AUTOEXEC.BAT

Initially when a user reboots, the system control passes to address FFFF:0000h in the system ROM, which then passes control to an initialisation routine in ROM. The principal function of this routine is to locate a "boot" record or sector on a secondary storage device from which the boot sequence can continue.

In this regard all devices are searched in physical device order (normally floppy drives followed by hard drives) for such a record.

ROM is of course unalterable by computer viruses (normally such memory is implemented as an array of program-once fusible links, or has its structure directly etched onto the silicon substrate). This is, however, not true of newer electronically alterable/erasable read-only memory (EAROM/EEROM) used primarily as non-volatile memory to hold configuration information during power down periods.

In standard IBM PCs such "parameter" RAMs do not contain executable code and thus can be ignored for the purposes of virus infection. A further development in this area is low power consumption CMOS RAM chips which can be powered by a battery or capacitive backup. Such RAM chips can retain viral code in memory across system power downs. The use of non-volatile RAM in laptops thus permits the continuation of system (and virus) operation after the system power is restored.

The capacitance in standard IBM PC power supplies may also allow retention of information in volatile RAM for periods up to about 30 seconds. Thus when it is suggested that the IBM PC is switched off, it must be for at least this period.

4.3 BIOS and DOS

The operating system of the IBM PC consists of two main components:

- Basic input/output system (BIOS) – a set of basic potentially device dependent routines which allows simple unstructured access to data on storage devices
- Disk operating system (DOS) – utilising the BIOS, a far more complex operating system which structures basic data (i.e. sectors and tracks on disk) into files, which are in turn structured into hierarchical directories

4.4 Master Boot Record

The location of the next component in the boot depends on whether the storage media being booted is a hard or floppy disk drive. In the former case control passes to a boot sector at a well-known location on the floppy disk (sector 0, track 1, side 0), known as the boot sector.

In the case of a hard disk drive this sector contains a master boot record including a partition table. The later encodes information on the location of one or more "logical" disks into which the physical disk has been divided. Thus a 100 Mb physical disk may be divided into four separate logical drives of 25 Mb capacity. The format of the master boot record is given in Appendix 1.

Execution starts at location 0 of the master boot record, which consists of up to 1BEh (446) bytes of executable code. This code is responsible for locating a "boot sector" on a partition to continue the boot sequence. The partitions marked as "bootable" in the partition record table are searched sequentially, the first sector in each partition being read to locate a suitable boot sector.

The master boot record represents the first location which can be altered by a virus to contain viral code. The "New Zealand" or "Stoned" virus does exactly this. This virus relocates the original master boot record to a well-known location on disk, namely:

	Hard disk	Floppy disk
Version 1	Track 0 head 0 sector 2	Track 0 head 1 sector 3
Version 2	Track 0 head 0 sector 7	Track 0 head 1 sector 3

and replaces the code portion of the master boot record with its own viral code. The flow of control before and after infection can be described as:

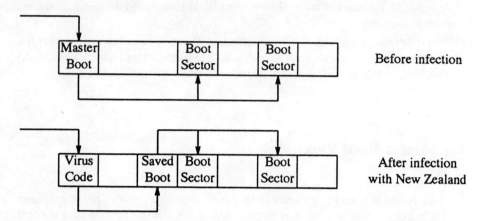

The partition table is interpreted by the BIOS in ROM and is independent of the DOS system. Thus UNIX and other foreign operating systems may be allocated partitions co-resident with DOS partitions on disk. Master boot record altering viruses are becoming increasingly commonplace.

Corruption of a master boot record will generate the message "Partition not found". Such corruption is caused by New Zealand infecting any non-standard master boot record or by the destructive effects of viruses such as the "Datacrime" virus.

4.5 DOS Boot Sector

The next stage in initialisation is the execution of code from the boot sector located at the well-known location head 0, sector 1, track 0 on floppy drives, or at the start of the partition in hard drives. This sector also contains information detailing how DOS will interpret the data in the partition. The structure of a boot sector is given in Appendix 1.

The boot sector comprises a maximum of 1C3h (451) bytes of executable code in DOS versions 2 and 3, or 1C0h (448) bytes in DOS version 4. This code is used to locate the next component in the system initialisation, namely the IO.SYS or IBMBIO.COM program on the logical partition. This code can be replaced or modified by a virus: it is this which forms the mode of attack of one of the most common classes of virus, the boot sector virus.

An example of such a virus is the Brain virus. This virus relocates the original boot sector, storing its own viral code (plus pointers to additional viral code and the original boot sector) in the DOS boot sector. Thus, when the boot sector code is called as part of the boot sequence, the virus is loaded into memory by the BIOS and executed.

For further details of the organisation of DOS data on disk the reader is referred to Appendix 1. In particular the following description uses the concept of a "File Allocation Table" (FAT). This table contains a linked list of disk clusters allocated to a file. Clusters may be corrupt because of media flaws on the floppy or hard disk. In such cases the FAT table entry for the cluster will be set to a special value indicating a "bad" cluster.

It is common practice for boot sector viruses to scan the FAT to locate a free cluster. This cluster is then marked as bad, and used as storage for virus code which exceeds the available space in the original boot sector.

An indication of boot sector infection is therefore the presence of a bad cluster on a floppy disk (the majority of which are now supplied as error free by manufacturers). Please note that all magnetic media tend to degrade progressively with use, causing bad clusters. Formatting programs normally mark an entire track bad when formatting a disk, thus if a track has a small group of bad clusters this may be an indication of virus activity.

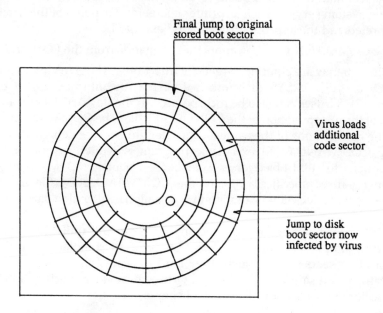

Structure of a typical boot sector virus on disk

4.6 System Initialisation

Following the location of the boot sector on floppy or hard disk, the boot sequence will continue by:

1. Loading the IO.SYS or IBMBIO.COM (the former for MS-DOS, the latter for PC-DOS) program from the booted disk partition. This is the first file in the root

directory of the partition. This program contains two components: the BIOS code (including device specific drivers and initialisation code) and the SYSINIT program. The latter program is responsible for supervising the remainder of the initialisation process.

2. SYSINIT checks memory and then loads the next file in the initialisation sequence, the MSDOS.SYS or IBMDOS.COM (the former for MS-DOS, the latter for PC-DOS) into memory. This file contains the code for the operating system.

3. Control passes to DOS, which initialises and runs the command interpreter specified by the shell variable in CONFIG.SYS (normally COMMAND.COM). Various device drivers specified in the CONFIG.SYS file are loaded into memory (such as extended screen and printer drivers). The command interpreter then accepts a series of user commands to be executed by DOS. Initially it will consult a batch file called AUTOEXEC.BAT which contains lists of user commands (such as setting data and time, clearing the screen and starting system services such as printer spoolers). Each line of the batch file is interpreted and the appropriate command executed.

4. The COMMAND.COM prompts for commands from the PC user.

Although they are potential targets for infection, no known viruses infect the IO.SYS or MSDOS.SYS files (other than the unconfirmed report cited in Chapter 2). Viruses can also be incorporated in the device drivers loaded as a result of the interpretation of the CONFIG.SYS file. The COMMAND.COM file was the target of one of the earliest computer viruses, the Lehigh virus.

The COMMAND.COM executable program is written in one of the two conventions for IBM object or executable files, namely "COM". Many COM infecting viruses specifically ignore the COMMAND.COM file in order to frustrate simple detection by monitoring the length or alteration date/time of this file.

It is also worth noting that boot sector viruses can only utilise BIOS functions (allowing simple unstructured disk I/O) prior to completion of the DOS initialisation sequence. As such, they tend to access virus code by absolute sector/track and side location. Hybrid viruses now exist which do infect both boot sector and COM or EXE executable files.

4.7 Batch Processing Viruses

The DOS command language provides a rich and varied set of user commands, which can be invoked either directly or indirectly through the use of batch file techniques. These commands include:

• Batch file call functions (similar to procedure call)
• Iteration via "goto" and "for"

- Conditional command execution via "if"

With such a rich set of facilities it is therefore possible to create a general "batch" virus. Such a virus is an implementation of the virus algorithm:

> Open target file
> If no virus signature
>   Append virus code to target file
>   Add virus signature

Batch viruses have been proposed by both Burger and Levin: the latter is reproduced below:

> ctty nul
> for %%f in (*.BAT) do copy %%f + BFV.BAT
> ctty con
> cls

In general, a virus can be written in any language capable of changing command flow via a conditional test (to allow signature verification) and with limited file access or low level I/O primitives (to allow appending of code). This is true of high level languages such as C and Pascal, and also (often unexpectedly) of less powerful "Macro" languages provided by software such as Lotus 1-2-3 and text editors such as "vi" and "emacs" (the latter executing a subset of the Lisp program language).

Batch viruses, although theoretically possible, would tend to be fairly clumsy and relatively slow in comparison with a machine code virus.

4.8 COM and EXE Viruses

A virus embedded in an EXE or COM file (the two IBM PC executable file formats) can thus be activated by direct execution of a user command or by inclusion in a .BAT batch file.

The structure of COM and EXE files is described in Appendix 3. In brief it is sufficient to indicate that a COM file comprises a single image of the object code as it would appear in memory. Such a COM file is loaded into a 64 Kbyte memory segment allocated exclusively to the program. All memory accesses by the program are theoretically restricted to this segment. The IBM PC contains no memory management hardware (or in the case of the 80386 and later, when running under DOS compatibility mode rather than OS/2, such hardware is effectively disabled), thus allowing an errant program to write any location in the PC address space.

The COM program is loaded into its 64 Kbyte segment and then called by DOS executing a jump to offset 100h in the segment. When loaded into memory a COM (and EXE) image is preceded by a "Program Segment Prefix" (PSP) which contains details of the files and memory allocated to the program, together with the string used to invoke the command.

An EXE program is far more complex (and more versatile), permitting programs to exceed 64 Kbytes in size. The EXE file contains information which allows DOS to break the program into a number of separate segments of variable length. EXE infecting viruses are rarer than the simpler COM infectors because of the increased complexity required to correctly manipulate the EXE file header block and relocation table, which are part of the EXE structure.

In the case of a COM virus, the virus code may be simply inserted by prepending or appending to the COM executable. The virus must also modify the first few bytes at offset 100h to pass control to the prepended or appended virus.

Example of a COM virus (1200h user code, 400h virus code):

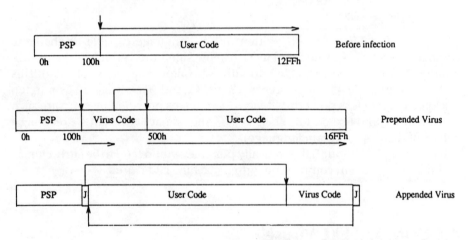

In the above diagrams, two cases are considered: the prepending virus (which appends the host's code to the virus to produce an infected version) and the appending virus (which appends the virus to the host's code). The blocks marked "J" are jump instructions. Jump 1 is a replacement of an initial jump in the host code by a jump to the virus code. Jump 2 is the stored jump instruction from the original host which is used by the virus to return control to the host.

4.8.1 Non-overwriting Prepending COM Infectors

In the prepended case the virus creates a new copy of the executable COM file, consisting of the virus code to which the original contents of the COM file has been appended. The virus code is then executed first (by the DOS load and execute subfunction); the viral code runs, then jumps to the original COM file code (appended to the virus). This approach will allow a COM program using relative addressing for jumps to operate correctly.

A slightly more sophisticated approach is for the virus to relocate the original COM file's code by copying it from its location in memory (after the virus code) to overwrite the start of the virus. The short relocation routine can easily be located temporarily in free memory or system buffer space while executing. This method unfortunately allows full transparent execution of COM files without restriction on the addressing modes of jump and call instructions.

Virus Code	User Code	Before restoration

User Code	After restoration

4.8.2 Overwriting COM Infectors

The simplest form of virus destroys its host by directly overwriting part of the host's code with the virus code. The damage to the host can be minimised by overwriting the end component of the host program, thus allowing the initialisation (and probably a large component of the host code) to operate correctly.

The virus captures control by overwriting the initial three bytes of the host with a jump to the virus code. The original three bytes of the host program are stored for later restoration. Thus, DOS causes a branch to the virus code whenever the host is run. The virus may then replicate, infecting other potential hosts. When the virus completes operation, it restores the saved bytes to the start of the host, and then jumps to the restored host.

Overwriting viruses do not alter the length of the infected file (which is a major indicator of infection by non- overwriting viruses) but do show up through occasional crashes or malfunctions of the infected host (due to part of its code being destroyed on infection).

A simple example of an overwriting virus is the 405 strain, a basic COM infecting virus which overwrites the first 405 bytes of the host when infecting. The virus extends the host to 405 bytes if the latter is less than 405 bytes in length. Multiple infections will occur because the virus does not check for a signature value when infecting. Infection is restricted to the current directory.

4.8.3 Non-overwriting Appending COM Infectors

The appending virus operates by appending the virus code to the end of the host code in the COM executable, as shown in the above diagram. The virus must also modify the user code to gain control when the COM file is run. This modification is carried out in the same manner as the complex COM overwriting virus.

An example of a simple COM appending virus is the Vienna or "Austrian" virus. This virus was first reported in Moscow in April 1988 at a UNESCO summer camp. The virus (the code for a variant of which has been published by Burger) is a simple 648-byte-long non-overwriting COM infector. The virus saved the initial three bytes of the host, replacing them by a jump to the virus' code which had been appended to the host. The virus executes by selecting a COM file in the current path to infect, then restores the saved three bytes to restore the host's code in memory. It then jumps to the start (100h offset) of the host. The virus utilises a simple signature to detect infection (thus preventing multiple infection) – namely, the setting of the time of last update seconds field to 31 (corresponding to an invalid value of 62 seconds since the field represents the value in seconds/2). The seconds field of the time of last update is not displayed when using the DOS "dir" command. Eighteen variant viruses (including "Lisbon", "Ghostballs", "1260", "VHP-435" and "VHP-623") have been produced based on the Vienna strain.

4.8.4 EXE Viruses

In the case of the EXE file it is possible for the virus to either append or prepend its code in the form of a separate segment of code. The appending virus adds its code to the end of the EXE file, modifying the EXE program header as follows:

- Extend the file length field
- Extend the relocation table size
- Add relocation table entries to permit relocation of the jump from the virus segment to host program code segment
- Modify the EXE file checksum value (if used)
- Modify the segment displacement and IP register offsets to point to the viral code segment

The virus is not required to modify the host program code segment as control can be gained merely by modifying the EXE program header.

In the case of a virus which prepends to an EXE file the situation is complicated by the need to rewrite the relocation table offsets to point to the newly moved host code segment, i.e.:

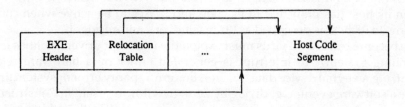

Host program before infection

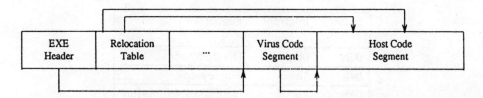

This allows the EXE program loader (in DOS) to correctly locate segment values in the shifted host code segment, thus permitting it to complete its function of relocating program inter-segment jumps at runtime.

In summary, the principal modes in which an IBM PC can be infected by viral code are:

Type	Frequency	Example
Master boot record virus	Common	New Zealand
Boot sector virus	Common	Brain
IO.SYS/MSDOS.SYS virus	Theory	Pacman
COMMAND.COM virus	Rare	Lehigh
AUTOEXEC.BAT virus	Theory	Many published examples
COM overwriting virus	Occasional	405
COM non-over prepending	Occasional	Israeli
COM non-over appending	Common	Datacrime
EXE prepending	Rare	sURIV2.01
EXE appending	Common	Dark Avenger

4.9 Resident and Transient Viruses

A virus becomes active through one or more of the means described previously. Hybrid viruses which exist in multiple forms (e.g. boot sector and COM infector) do exist (such as the "1253" virus). The virus can arrange to retain control of the PC operating system even after its parent or host program has exited. This is achieved by terminating and staying resident (TSR). A virus which attempts this is described as "resident". A virus which is only active when its host has branched to its code and ceases to be active when control returns to its host is described as "transient" or "non-resident".

To become resident, a virus must exploit the interrupt driven facilities in the operating system. An interrupt is generated either by a hardware related event, e.g. external device data transfer, bus error, parity error or system timer, or by a software event, e.g. divide by zero, overflow or user "int" instruction. All interrupts cause the processor to transfer control to the address in the interrupt vector table appropriate to that interrupt.

Offset	Interrupt	Function
00h	0h	Divide by zero
04h	1h	Single step
08h	2h	Nonmaskable interrupt
52h	13h	BIOS service entry
84h	21h	DOS service entry

For instance a DOS system call such as "open file (handle)" is performed by placing values in the AH, AL and D registers. The AH register is set to contain the DOS function required, in this case 3Dh. AL and D contain parameters to the
system call. The program then executes the "int 21h" instruction, causing a software interrupt. This interrupt places the flag register on the stack, together with the return address, and then jumps to the address given in the corresponding entry in the interrupt vector table (in this case the address given at offset 84h in the table). On completion of the DOS interrupt service routine DOS executes a "iret" instruction, which pops the flag status and returns control to the calling routine.

This centralisation of functionality unfortunately makes it simple for a virus to redirect or intercept system activity. For instance a virus might have copied its code into a free block of memory, or used the various TSR functions provided by the operating system. By changing one or more interrupts to point to the virus code in memory it can arrange to be activated:

- At regular timed intervals
- During disk activity
- When a program is loaded for execution
- On user keyboard input

and on many other such events, e.g.

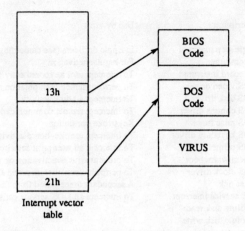

After modification

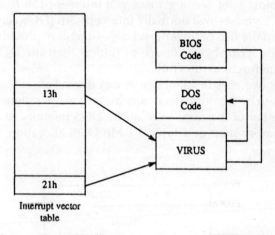

Interrupt vector
table

The virus is thus activated whenever any input/output or DOS service is required. A brief list of the commonly used interrupt vectors (from the virus writer's point of view) is given below:

Address	Description	Use by virus
01h	Single step interrupt	In ripple decoders (see camouflage)
08h	System timer	For regular activation
09h	Keyboard interrupt	To intercept user keyboard activity
10h	BIOS video driver	To perform screen manipulation and transformation
13h	BIOS disk driver	To intercept all disk activity
14h	BIOS comms driver	To intercept remote communications
15h	BIOS misc funcs	Keystroke translation
16h	BIOS keyboard driver	To intercept user keyboard activity
17h	BIOS printer driver	To intercept all user print activity
19h	System warm boot	To prevent virus deactivation on reboot
1Ah	BIOS clock driver	To perform clock alteration and slipping
1Ch	Timer tick	A secondary timer called from 08h
21h	DOS service interrupt	To intercept all DOS service calls
25h	Absolute disk read	
26h	Absolute disk write	
27h	Terminate and stay resident	To monitor programs going TSR

In general, most boot sector viruses will intercept 13h (BIOS disk driver), while COM/EXE viruses will normally intercept 21h (DOS service). Thus boot sector viruses make use of lower level disk functions provided by the BIOS, which deal with sector-by-sector access (rather than the DOS abstraction of logical files in hierarchical directories).

When a virus becomes resident in memory it must also arrange that its code is not overwritten by the normal memory allocation operations of the operating system. A number of locations exist in the DOS memory map which can be utilised. A memory map of a typical 1 Mb DOS allocation scheme is given below:

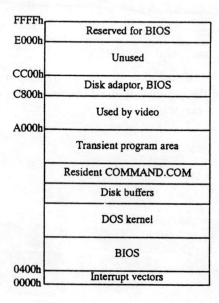

Of these areas the following can be used:

- Unused allocated memory, such as unused DOS system variables and rarely used or reserved buffer space, e.g. the Lehigh virus in the COM-MAND.COM stack area and "Number of the Beast" in the first DOS disk buffer
- Expanded or extended memory, outside of the normal 640 K DOS address-ing range, such as the area CC000h to DFFFFh in the above map, e.g. the "EDV" virus
- Unallocated memory in the transient program area, e.g. the Icelandic virus' manipulation of memory control blocks; or the use of the DOS TSR functions, e.g. Jerusalem
- Reserved memory: boot sector viruses which commonly install in high memory and then reduce the amount of physical memory available when DOS loads
- BIOS and Video RAM areas: above the 640 K DOS memory limit

4.10 Manipulation by Viral Code

A virus can potentially manipulate any aspect of PC system operation, including:
- Unusual screen displays, graphics, logos or displayed text strings often carrying a political, personal or ideological message
- Corruption or alteration of user data files, including:
  Byte swapping or alteration of data
  Marking of disk clusters as "bad", causing reduction in usable disk space
  Damage to BIOS parameter block, boot sector code or partition tables, giving the appearance of reformatted or destroyed data
  Reformatting of disk partitions or low level formatting of drives
- Corruption and manipulation of comms ports, including:
  Byte swapping and data corruption on modem links
  Initiation of "rogue" telephone calls by virus, allowing possible compro-mise of classified or sensitive information
  Insertion of damaging commands, e.g. "rm -rf *" into remote login sessions
- Interception and alteration of keyboard input
  Swapping of keyboard keys to simulate typing errors or dyslexia
  Rejection of certain characters such as the "Ctrl-Alt-Del" warm reboot sequence
  Insertion of amusing or embarrassing additional input into the keyboard buffer

- Interception and alteration of printer output, including the full range of corruption and alterations, such as that demonstrated by the "Mix1/Typo" viruses
- Modification of system clock: gradual speedup or slowdown, random resets and jumps
- Dummy routines, causing system slowdown of either global or selective routines
- Activation of other system interfaces: playing of short tunes or tones on the system speaker, toggling of keyboard state flags (Caps Lock, Num Lock), relocation or reversal of mouse activity

Finally, interception of the DOS service interrupt (as against all the above effects achieved via the BIOS) allows a wide range of abstract manipulations to be performed, such as:

- Renaming or hiding of data files
- Moving or removal of data files
- Swapping of contents from selected system files
- Reversal of file text

In general, a virus may manipulate any aspect of system operation. Subtle manipulations such as bad sector or byte swapping may often be mistaken for hardware errors.

4.11 Activation Criteria

The reasons why a virus activates are as varied as the manipulations the virus may cause once active. In general, many viruses are engineered to activate (and perform a manipulation task, be it benign or destructive) on specific dates or on exhaustion of a specific delay or counter. In the former case, many dates have been chosen by virus authors as activation dates. A summary list is given below:

Virus	Activation Date	Effect
1210 (Prudents)	May 1-4	Changes disk writes to verifies
1253	Dec 24	Overwriting diskette
1554 (Ten bytes)	Sep-Dec	Corrupts first 10 bytes of any files written
1704 Format	Oct-Dec (Not 1993)	Reformatting of disk
4096 (Stealth)	On or after 22 Sep	Hang infected systems
Advent	4th Sunday before Xmas	Advent crown and Old Tanenbaum tune
Alabama	Friday	File swapping via FAT manipulation
Anarkia	Tuesday 13	File deletion
Anarkia-B	October 12	File deletion
Cascade	Sep-Dec 1980/88	Falling letters display
Christmas	Apr 1	Destroy partition table
Christmas	Dec 24-Jan 1	Full screen Christmas tree
Datacrime	Oct 12+	Low level format
Durban	Saturday 14	Overwrite 100 sectors on drive C, B and A
FuManchu	Aug 1 1989+	Keyboard buffer character insertion
Jerusalem	Friday 13	File deletion
Jerusalem-D	Friday 13 > 1990	Destroy both FATs
Jerusalem-E	Friday 13 > 1992	Destroy both FATs
Joshi	Jan 5	Message and hangup
July 13	July 13	Bouncing ball
June 16	June 16	All entries in root directory & FAT zapped
Kennedy	June 6	Message
	Nov 18 & 22	Message
Mendoza	July - Dec	File deletion
Murphy	10-11am	Speaker pip
New Jerusalem	Friday 13	Deleted file
Payday	Friday not 13	Deleted file
South African	Friday 13	File deletion
Sunday	Sunday	Message
SURIV 1.01	April 1	Hangup and message
SURIV 2.01	April 1	Hangup
SURIV 3.00	Friday 13	File deletion
Traceback	Dec 28 1988	Cascade display
Traceback	Dec 5 1988	Direct infection started

One particularly common activation date is Friday 13th. This is the activation date chosen by the "Israeli" virus (and derivatives) and the "South African" virus. In this regard, the Friday 13ths for the remainder of the century are:

1991	September, December
1992	March, November
1993	August
1994	May
1995	January, October
1996	September, December
1997	June
1998	February, March, November
1999	August

In addition (presumably to catch those users moving the system clock forward by one day to avoid Friday 13th) the "Durban" virus activates on Saturday 14th.

Regular advisories are sent out by bodies such as the Department of Defense Security Co-ordination Center on the approach of dates such as Friday 13th, April 1st, Hallowe'en and Christmas Day.

During the period from the release of a virus to its first activation date (known by analogy with biological viruses as the "incubation" period), the virus can spread rapidly with few symptoms. It is often the case that a virus is not detected prior to its activation date, thus a longer period between release and activation makes it likely that a virus will spread widely, but increases the probability that such a virus will be detected and effectively countered prior to activation. The previously introduced concept of a binary virus might permit the author to send an activation component when his virus is first discovered by the research community.

The extreme example is the Century virus, timed to activate on 1 January 2000. Many commentators expect that the conventional IBM PC may be obsolete by that time!

Other viruses use generation counters as a trigger. This is particularly common in boot sector viruses. This counter allows us to generate a family history of the spread of such a virus by charting the occurrences of each generation. This may allow a crude localisation of the initial infection source. The generation counter does, however, allow a virus author to upgrade his virus by releasing a new version with an updated generation number. Presumably older generations will avoid infection of executables infected by newer generations. The Israeli virus used a similar technique of backward compatible signatures to prevent older strains from destroying newer generations.

The Jerusalem virus strain A (commonly known as Friday 13th) has three predecessor strains also originating in Israel. These strains are known (by reference to identifying text within the binary) as "sURIV 1.01", "sURIV 2.01" and "sURIV 3.00". These strains (and the common Jerusalem strain which includes the text "sUMsDos" in the binary) all use compatible signature strings. sURIV 1.01 looks for the string "sU" at offset 3 in COM files. sURIV

2.01 looks for the presence of the checksum 1984h in the EXE file checksum field. sURIV 3.00 infects both COM and EXE files and inserts a compatible signature (with sURIV 1.01) in COM files and (with sURIV 2.01) in EXE headers. The infection test for sURIV 3.00 is the presence of the "sURIV" string at the end of the infected program. The standard strain uses a "sUMsDos" signature in place of the "sURIV 3.00" signature, but retains (although not checking for) the 1984h checksum in EXE files. Thus a family development path may be established since sURIV 3.00 is backward compatible with the sURIV 1.01 and sURIV 2.01 strains. The standard virus breaks the mould slightly but still uses very similar signatures. Thus a sURIV 3.00 virus will automatically infect a sURIV 2.01 or sURIV 1.01 file, although the latter viruses will detect the sURIV 3.00 signature and ignore the file.

The activation criteria can be exceptionally complex, such as that of the Italian "Bouncing Ball" virus which activates when a disk transfer re-occurs within a 1 second interval every 20 minutes. Such complex criteria often make the reproduction of a virus erratic and irreproducible, complicating analysis of the virus.

A particularly worrying form of virus is one which exploits multiple "vectors", an example being a trojan horse program which has an encrypted copy of the virus. The trojan releases the virus at annual or monthly intervals. The virus program then proceeds to spread rapidly on the system. Such a virus is easily detected and removed. This cleaning of the system may appear effective until the trojan utility again activates to release a new (possibly subtly modified) virus. Not only does this result in re-infection, but the trojan horse itself may act as a vector by being manually copied between systems.

This is the concept of a "retrovirus", as introduced by Peter Denning. This virus comprises a trojan horse launcher which at regular intervals checks for the presence of the child virus. If the virus is removed the trojan will wait for a fixed period of time, and then re-release the virus. Thus system re-infection appears to occur at regular intervals.

4.12 Camouflage

The virus field has demonstrated a worrying trend towards complex and cunning viruses which exploit many and varied concealment and camouflage strategies. Many of these techniques are targeted at specific anti-viral products, or at measures belonging to a "generic" classes of anti-viral product. These classes are described in detail in Appendix 10.

Camouflage techniques revolve around:

- Concealment of viral code in infected files via encryption or careful manipulation of disk space
- Concealment of the viral code when active in memory, and the associated changes in "memory control blocks" (MCBs) and interrupt vectors

- Concealment of the activity of the virus in replicating its code (specifically the invocation and effects of disk access commands)

4.12.1 Concealment in Infected Files

The viral code can be detected by a characteristic series of bytes, by expansion of the file size, by alteration of file timestamps, and by changes in file checksums and signatures.

In this regard camouflage techniques can be divided into:

- Avoiding infection of files of particular interest (e.g. COMMAND.COM)
- Encryption of the viral segment in the infected file
- Hiding of viral code in spare disk space
- Storing the original timestamp and file attributes, infecting, then restoring the original values
- Recalculating the checksum after infection has occurred
- Preventing the detection of the above changes by programs using DOS services

4.12.2 Encryption of Viral Code

The virus may employ simple encryption techniques to conceal the majority of the viral code in a file. Such a method is often "perturbed" or modified by some characteristic of the host file (time of modification, size of file, etc.). The encryption techniques utilised are often extremely simple. The Cascade virus was one of the first viruses to exploit such encryption. This virus consisted of a short decryption routine, the remaining bytes of the virus being encrypted while on disk.

The virus thus consists of:

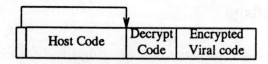

When the decryptor had completed execution, the decrypted virus was present in memory and ready to execute, thus:

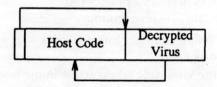

The sample decryptor routine decrypts the encrypted virus before executing the code. Such "bulk" decryptors are simple but effective in reducing the length of the recognisable virus signature to as few as 16 bytes of object code. Even this short decryptor is perturbed in the 1260 virus through the random introduction of padding instructions (such as operations on unused registers and no-ops). This reduces the recognisable instruction sequence to one single machine instruction (maximum of around 3 bytes).

The 1260 virus incorporates a complex encryption and padding scheme which comprises the following decryptor routine:

```
        mov    ax,key_a
        mov    cx,key_b
        mov    di,start_of_virus
main:   xor    [di],cx
        xor    [di],ax
        inc    di
        inc    ax
        loop   main
```

The decryptor uses two key values which are both xor'ed with an encrypted byte in the virus to produce the plaintext instruction. On completion of decryption the virus code is executed. The second key is incremented as instructions are decrypted to prevent the non-trivial decryption of the virus by xor'ing with a fixed value (as was possible with encrypted strings in the Internet worm). Thus a clear text byte is given by:

$$Clear[i] = Crypt[i] \otimes (key_a + i) \otimes (key_b)$$

The above decryptor routine is padded via the random addition of one or more of the following dummy instructions – nop; dec bx; inc si; clc; xor bx,cx. Other than the dummy instruction padding this routine is similar in format to the decryptor in the Cascade/Autumn Leaves/1704 virus, which included the instruction sequence:

```
                      ; load start of virus into si
        mov           sp, length_of_virus
main:   xor [si], si
        xor           [si], sp
        inc           si
        dec           sp
        jnz           main
```

This decryptor generated a clear text byte by xor'ing the encrypyted byte by its offset in the virus and the remaining number of bytes to be decrypted. Thus:

$$Clear\,[i\,] = Crypt\,[i\,] \otimes (start\_of\_virus\_offset + i\,) \otimes (length - i\,)$$

In general, encryption schemes rely on ciphers based on the Exclusive Or operator. This method has the advantage that the decryption routine can be used to encrypt, and vice versa. The following summary is based on work by Fridrik Skulason:

Virus	Algorithm
Pretoria	Basic XOR with fixed value A5 hex
July 13th	Basic XOR with a fixed value
Slow	XOR with a fixed value modified on each infection
Cascade	Complex XOR dependent on host length
Datacrime II	Basic XOR with a fixed value key rotated right by one bit after encryption of each instruction includes code to detect single step of encryptor routine
800 virus	Basic XOR with a key computed from XOR of virus body
1260	Twin key XOR varying with instruction offset including random padding of encryptor routine
Suomi	Inclusion of random instructions at fixed offsets in encryptor
Evil	Basic XOR with a key computed from XOR of virus body includes programmed modification of registers used during

Multi-level encryption may be included to complicate disassembly and analysis. In this case the decryptor routine is itself encrypted using a second (possibly different) encryption algorithm.

The bulk decryptors normally mean that the unencrypted virus is visible in main memory during the short window in which the viral code is active. The "ripple" decoder goes one stage further and minimises the window of unencrypted virus visible in memory during virus execution. The decryptor makes use of the 80X86 series single step/trace mode.

This mode is entered by setting the "T" status flag. After this flag is set the 80X86 will generate an interrupt after each instruction is executed. This allows the ripple decoder trapping the single step interrupt vector to decode the next instruction for execution. The previous instruction can be re-encoding or purged.

One issue related to encryption is that of compression. Cohen cited the file compression virus which appends to a host, compresses (using an algorithm such as Huffman or Lempel-Ziv coding) the host to save disk space, and arranges to decompress the host on execution. While a laudable aim, such a method can be used to prevent any extension of a host file on infection. The virus compresses the host using a basic compression algorithm, then creates a new executable comprising the virus (together with a host decompression routine) and the compressed host data. When the resultant file is run the virus spreads, then runs the decompressor to restore the host, and then runs the host program. Result – no detectable increase in file size on infection.

A final twist in the use of cryptographic techniques is the feature built into the "Vacsina" virus of using an error detecting Hamming code. This code permits the virus to correct for up to 16 modified bytes in the virus. Thus damage due to byte corruption in transit can be repaired, as can attempts by inexperienced hackers to modify the virus operation.

4.12.3 Hiding of Viral Code

The viral code can be concealed in an area in which the BIOS or DOS does not expect code to exist. Two examples are:

1. Use of track 40 or 80 on floppy disks – these can be formatted and used by a boot sector virus to store its code sectors, or the displaced code sectors of the host program or boot sector. The "Denzuk" virus uses this technique by storing the original boot sector on head 0, track 40, sector 1–9 of the disk. This track is directly formatted by the virus prior to infection.

2. Use of unused space beyond the logical DOS end of file, but still within the clusters allocated by the BIOS to the file. As cluster size increases (to allow expansion of disk capacity without corresponding increase in FAT table size) this residual space increases. Thus a 3300 byte file might consist of four 1024 byte clusters (each comprising two sectors of 512 bytes), leaving 796 bytes of spare space. This technique is used by the Number of the Beast virus. This virus ("512" virus) was discovered in January 1990 in Bulgaria. It intercepts the DOS service interrupt (21h) together with the BIOS (13h) interrupt and critical error handler vector (24h). The virus utilises two concealment techniques: first, the virus conceals its code in the first DOS disk buffer in memory (rather than allocating and attempting to conceal a memory control block), and second, it relocates the first 512 bytes of the infected COM file to beyond the logical end of file (in free space at the end of the cluster), replacing it with it own viral code. Infection of COM files occurs when a file is closed (int 21h function 3Eh) or is executed (int 21h function 4Bh).

These locations are in addition to the use of free sectors (marked as bad by the virus to prevent reuse) and the use of files with the "hidden" attribute set in the directory.

The DOS load and execute command will not of course load code concealed in such areas. It is however possible to conceal a minimal virus code in a program which then passes control to code which is in a concealed location. Such an extension area may be shared between every copy of the infected file. Naturally, the virus must carry the shared extension with it when copied to a removable media.

4.12.4 Checksum Calculation

The EXE file and boot sectors contain a checksum of the associated program or data sector. This checksum provides a primitive means of detecting file or sector alteration. This can be coupled with checksums generated by proprietary anti- virus or security software. The virus must therefore attempt to include dummy instructions to alter the infected file to possess a checksum identical to that of the original file.

In the case of simple checksums such as the "XOR" or numeric sum of all long words in the file this is unfortunately very easy. Such checksums can be recognised and defeated. Computationally complex checksum algorithms may prove difficult (or in the case of signatures based on public key techniques, exceedingly difficult) to invert. Unknown (user specific) checksums are also likely to be safe from viral forgery.

4.12.5 Prevention of Alteration Detection

The final approach, that of the viral "shell", is to ensure that when an anti-virus utility attempts to detect the alteration of a host it will not succeed. This is achieved by interception of the DOS or BIOS interrupt calls executed by the anti-virus utility, and the substitution of the unaltered host's details.

This includes:

• Interception of directory read calls, ensuring an unaltered timestamp or file length is returned when the directory is read
• Interception of file read calls, ensuring that any checksum or signature recognition utility opening an infected file will read a version of the host which appears to be uninfected

Both methods are adopted by the 4096 virus. This virus, one of a new generation of Stealth viruses, is extremely difficult to detect since checksum utilities will always recalculate the checksum based on the apparently unaltered host file.

The 4096 (IDF or Stealth virus) is a memory resident COM/EXE file infector which was discovered in January 1990. This virus adopts a wide range of concealment techniques, including modification of the DOS (21h) handler by inserting a jump to the virus code (thus avoiding detectable alteration of the DOS vector in the interrupt vector table); interception of the find—first and find—next directory access DOS functions (modifying the returned file lengths to conceal the extension caused by viral infection); and also trapping the DOS file open, causing temporary disinfection of the file (thus returning an uninfected file to checksum and signature scanning utilities) which is then reinfected on file close. Infected files are flagged in the directory by the virus changing their year to exceed 100 (e.g. 1990 is normally represented as being 10 years forward from 1980, i.e. value 10. When infected, the virus changes this to 110 in bits 9–15 of the date of last update directory field).

Interception of BIOS sector reads was also used by the early Brain boot sector virus to conceal its alteration of the boot sector. The virus trapped the BIOS read disk sector function (02h) and returned the stored original boot sector for all reads of head 0, sector 1, track 0 rather than the infected actual boot sector.

4.12.6 Concealment of Viral Code in Memory

This can be carried out by manipulation of the available system memory, by:

1. Reducing the physical memory seen by DOS – a common technique amongst boot sector viruses which reduce the physical memory reported by the BIOS memory check, thus securing a safe area at the top of memory in which to store viral code.

2. Utilising device buffers and operating system areas for temporary code storage. This technique is utilised by the Number of the Beast virus described earlier.

3. Modifying the DOS memory allocation chain to reserve an area of memory for the virus. This area can then either be unlinked from the allocation chain or the MCB can be altered to make it appear to be an innocent DOS system block. This technique is utilised by the Icelandic virus (and by the Dark Avenger virus) which modifies the headers on the allocated MCBs. DOS arranges all memory blocks into a pool chained together via a header field (the MCB). The MCB records whether the block is the last in the chain, whether it has been allocated, the size of the block and the owner of the block. The Icelandic virus, first detected in June 1989, carries a dummy MCB within its code. This MCB appears to be the last in the allocation chain. The memory block of the host program is then split into two blocks, one for the program and one for the viral code (which is tagged using the dummy MCB). The virus can thus guarantee that when the host exits, the memory block for the host will be released, leaving the virus (in its own memory block) intact in memory.

4. Utilise "extended" or "expanded" memory which may not be subject to checking by anti-viral products, although this will impact on the number of hosts with the required configuration to execute the viral code. Extended memory is memory in excess of the 1 Mb addressing range of the 8086 processor. It can be accessed by 80286 and later processors in protected mode. Expanded memory uses a special driver to map pages of memory into the normal memory space. The anti-viral program can be prevented from reading memory occupied by the virus code. This method is exploited by the EDV boot sector virus which uses the system clock interrupt to pass control to the viral code. When active, the virus code inspects the system stack to determine the area of memory referenced by the data and extra segment (DS and ES) registers of the currently active application. If these point to the virus code segment in memory the system is halted. Thus, any simple scan of memory to locate a virus signature will cause a system lockup.

Finally, the virus may minimise the amount of unencrypted viral code in memory through the use of ripple decoders, and may frustrate attempts to use single step debugging by intercepting the single step and break point vectors.

4.12.7 Concealment of Viral Activity

The virus must conceal its use of the system to achieve replication. In this regard it must:

- Conceal its alteration of the interrupt vector table
- Conceal disk activity resulting from the virus
- Conceal system slowdown resulting from the virus

The two cases the virus must protect against (regarding interrupt table modification) are:

- The virus is active before the anti-virus utility – the latter can thus detect that a non-standard interrupt vector is in place
- The anti-virus utility is active before the virus - - the anti-virus utility can thus detect the alteration of the interrupt vector table by the virus, and intercept the activity of the virus

In the first case the virus can directly modify the DOS or memory resident BIOS components to pass control to the virus without altering the vector table, i.e.:

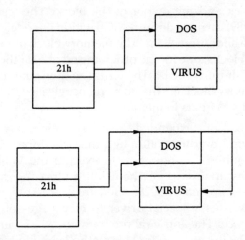

The virus patches the DOS interrupt vector handler to branch to the virus code. The virus then executes, and returns control to the DOS handler. With appropriate knowledge of the structure of a PC-DOS or MS-DOS release a virus author can scan memory to accurately locate the start of the DOS handler. The handler can then be modified in a manner transparent to the user. No alteration to the interrupt vector table has been made.

In the second case the virus attempts to bypass an anti-virus utility which has intercepted the interrupt vectors:

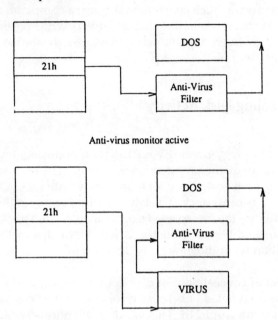

Anti-virus monitor active

Simplistic virus is trapped by the anti-virus utility

The Icelandic strain 2 virus does exactly this by directly jumping to the DOS handler routine in memory. The virus carries a set of recognition byte sequences which allow it to identify the location of the DOS handler in memory (for a variety of DOS releases). Once located the virus fakes an interrupt by forcing the status register onto the stack and invoking a standard subroutine call to the DOS handler. This effectively ensures that when the DOS handler exits with a "iret" instruction, the stack contents are identical to those generated by a real interrupt.

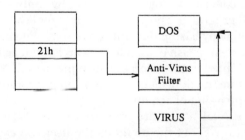

Icelandic strain 2 bypasses the filter by direct call

Finally, a virus can include its own code to interpret the DOS file system structure, allowing the virus to utilise low level BIOS calls to carry out its infection work, thus bypassing monitoring of DOS interrupt vectors. This could theoretically be extended to include direct manipulation of the disk drive controller in hardware. Such controllers support a comparatively high level of functionality (normally including the ability to write particular sectors on demand). A virus which directly manipulated hardware would of course be specific to a particular platform or platforms.

4.12.8 Concealing Disk Activity

This is achieved by piggy-backing viral disk writes onto legitimate disk activity. Thus the virus may queue an infection write until the user attempts disk I/O (thus preventing unexpected I/O), or more subtly until disk I/O is attempted on the same (or an adjacent) track. The latter method removes the final symptom of viral disk activity – the unexpected skip to an unrelated track on disk – which often causes an audible seek on the drive. Hard disk activity is normally inaudible or barely audible and is less often the subject of elaborate concealment.

A final aspect of concealment of disk activity relates to the concealment of errors resulting from failed I/O. These errors cause the "critical error" handler to be invoked via interrupt 24h. This handler will normally cause the program to be terminated and an error message to be displayed on the console. Critical errors include attempting to write to a write-protected media. This error may therefore be indicative of an infection attempt by a virus to a write-protected media.

4.12.9 Concealing System Slowdown

In general the reduction in system performance caused by a memory resident virus is not easily concealed. This can however by confused by a large number of active user TSR programs. The process of virus replication can also be spread over a period of time by basing the virus on a finite state machine in which the virus cycles between passive directory search and active infection. This technique was adopted in the Internet worm incident in November 1988. The use of an abstract instruction set executed by an interpreter in the virus could also allow such spreading of activity.

We have seen in detail how a virus can strive to conceal its presence. Chapter 5 gives a detailed review of the methods the user can exploit to detect even these viruses. Each camouflage technique is analysed in turn, and a suitable software or hardware counter measure proposed.

4.13 Replication

4.13.1 Locating a Host

To complete the section on PC viruses it is necessary to consider briefly how a virus locates a new host to infect, and how multiple infection of hosts is prevented.

The problem divides into:

- Boot sector and master boot record viruses
- Link (COM/EXE infecting) viruses

The boot sector virus must detect the insertion of a new media (floppy disk) into the computer system. Since no media change detection facility exists on the IBM PC system, the boot sector virus is forced to intercept all disk I/O. It may then verify whether the boot sector is infected, and, if not, infect it. Periodic attempts may also be made to infect the media.

Master boot record viruses are normally capable of existing on boot sectors of floppy media, as the incidence of hard media movement is very low. The Bernoulli portable hard disk is, however, one such case.

Link viruses must locate uninfected EXE or COM hosts. To do so they can rely on one or both of the following:

- Direct infection – the virus scans the disk directory hierarchy looking for suitable hosts to infect
- Indirect infection – when an executable file is accessed it is infected by the virus

The indirect infectors are always memory resident since they must intercept the DOS service interrupt. Once resident, they can infect even when:

- A file is loaded for execution
- A file is opened, read or written

The former is the most frequent and is the method used by such common viruses as Israeli and Cascade. The latter is extremely dangerous as it can lead to exceptionally rapid proliferation. This method was utilised by the Dark Avenger virus with the result that many early anti-virus scanning or checksumming programs caused infection of all executables on the system.

Both infection methods operate by interception of DOS functions, namely:

Function	0Fh	Open file (FCB)
	3Dh	Open file (handle)
	4Bh	Execute file

The name of the file being opened is passed as a parameter to these functions (either by an address register reference or in the "file control block" (FCB)). The virus can thus either:

- Store the name of the file being opened and use this to open and infect the file (now or at a later time)
- Execute the DOS call on behalf of the user and use the open file handle or FCB to perform the infection. The handle or FCB is then returned to the user making the call

The equivalent of a indirect infector in the boot sector or master boot record case would be the virus in which operations accessing absolute disk locations are trapped and cause infection, especially those accessing track 0.

Direct infectors may be either resident or transient. These viruses operate by scanning all or part of the disk directory hierarchy in search of suitable hosts. These viruses show a wide variation in rate of file infection, extent of search, choice of target directories and delay in infection.

Searching of the disk hierarchy is carried out using the DOS directory search calls (i.e. functions 4E and 4Fh), which allow the use of complex regular expressions for file names (allowing restriction to specific types of file). The virus may terminate a search, delay for a few minutes or until heavy disk I/O is in progress and then restart. Only the current directory may be searched, all directories in the executable file path (variable in the environment), a selection of common executable directories (such as bin, dos, util) or the entire file system may be searched. In a similar manner all disk drives may be searched, only hard drives or a selection.

Direct infectors can cause considerable system infection even on lightly used personal computer systems. Indirect infectors normally infect only a commonly used subset of commands such as DOS utilities, programs under test, word processors, databases and spreadsheets. Both forms of virus can be modified to bias the infection towards particular forms of file, e.g.:

- Recently altered utilities
- EXE only or COM only
- Files sufficiently large to conceal the viral code addition
- Proprietary files from a specific company

4.13.2 Signatures

To avoid continual re-infection (and consequent uncontrolled growth in file length or depletion of system memory) most viruses exploit a "signature" which indicates that the file or system memory block has been infected. Examples of such signatures include:

- File characteristics (used by parasitic or link viruses):

(i) Particular byte or series of bytes at a known location – normally at the start of the virus if a prepender, or at the end if an appender. This allows the virus to check whether these bytes are present at a known offset from the start or end of the file.

(ii) Information in the directory entry – including the use of an impossible seconds value in the time of last alteration field (Vienna virus), use of exceptional value in the date of last alteration field (4096 virus), use of reserved file attribute bits (bits 6 and 7), use of the reserved information field (10 bytes). By using such information in the directory a virus can avoid the overhead of actually opening the potential host's code file to check for infection. For example, the Datacrime 1A virus strain uses a complex signature which utilises both the minutes and seconds fields of the time of last alteration in the host's directory entry. On infection, the last three bits of the second field are set to be equal to the three least significant bits in the minutes field, bits 3 and 4 being set to 0.

(iii) Information in the file header – in the case of EXE files field such as the checksum (Israeli virus = 1984h, Fu Manchu = 1988h), minimum paragraphs required field, and the reserved space between header and start of relocation table.

- Memory characteristics:

(i) Particular byte or series of bytes in a known location – normally used by boot sector viruses which can guarantee to load at top of memory, or possibly in unused or non-critical system variables.

(ii) Presence of one or more special interrupt vectors or functions of standard DOS vectors provided by the resident portion of the virus. An example is the Israeli virus, which uses a number of special functions available via the standard DOS interrupt vector (21h), namely: function DDh causes the resident portion of the virus to relocate an infected host program so that the host's main program can be run; function DEh comprises redundant code to execute the same operation for EXE files; function E0h returns the version number of the virus in register AH.

(iii) Modification of amount of available system memory or DOS memory control blocks.

- Disk characteristics (used by boot record viruses):

(i) Particular bytes or series of bytes at a known location – normally an offset at a well-known absolute sector location.

(ii) Reserved information field in the bios parameter block (BPB). The BPB contains detailed information on the structure of the disk, sectors per track, tracks per disk, etc. It includes a number of reserved fields available for viral use:

DOS version	Offset	Size
2	15h	11 bytes
3	19h	7 bytes
4	2Bh	8 bytes

Signatures prevent continual re-infection, thus making the virus more difficult to detect (i.e. less obvious disk activity). Once recognised, they can provide a convenient recognition method for virus scanning utilities (although one which is often subject to trivial change by a virus modifier).

One interesting implication of including signatures at fixed offsets from the start or end of file, is the inability of viruses to correctly recognise files infected by multiple viruses. For example, in the case of the "10 005" virus incident, the system was infected by the Jerusalem and "Plastique" viruses. The Plastique virus adds itself to the beginning of the executable file. Then the Jerusalem virus inserts itself at the beginning, moving the Plastique virus to make room. The Plastique virus again examines the file, looking for its signature at a fixed offset, fails to find it (since Jerusalem has relocated the original Plastique virus), and thus decides to infect. The file therefore ends up being extended by 10 000 bytes plus the 5 byte Jersualem signature (10 005 bytes). This story has two noteworthy features: first, when two or more viruses are active all sorts of composite infections can occur; second, when disinfecting a file do not assume it is clean when a single virus has been removed – always rescan it.

4.13.3 Miscellaneous Topics

Finally, to end this detailed review of computer viruses on the IBM PC platform, it is worth mentioning a few unusual forms of virus.

4.13.3.1 Corresponding File Virus

A "corresponding file", "companion" or "spawning" virus makes use of the way in which DOS selects between a EXE or COM file with the same base name. DOS will always select the COM file in preference to the EXE file, if one exists. This technique is used by the "AIDS 2" virus, discovered in April 1990. The virus places its code in a COM file with the same base name as the EXE being infected.

When the user tries to run the EXE he will instead run the viral COM file, which will play a melody, and then display the text:

Your computer is infected with

Aids Virus II

- Signed WOP & PGT of DutchCrack -

before executing the original unaltered EXE file. When the user program exits the virus will again activate and display:

Getting used to me?

Next time, use a Condom .....

The corresponding file technique can be generalised to describe any "virus" which operates by including its code earlier in the search path of DOS. This includes creation of a file in a directory in the "PATH" searched prior to the target file, or in the above case use of the fact that COM is always tried as a suffix prior to EXE.

4.13.3.2 SYS Virus

This virus, reported in an early Homebase virus listing, is a boot sector infector which, when active in memory, will detect any attempt by the user to execute the "SYS" DOS command. This DOS command will write an uninfected boot sector, together with MSDOS.SYS and IO.SYS files to the specified drive. The virus detects the attempt to use the SYS command and then emulates the text messages normally produced by the program.

4.13.3.3 Multi-vector Viruses

The traditional distinction between boot sector and parasitic/link viruses has been blurred by the arrival of multi-vector viruses which can propagate both via boot sector and infection of COM/EXE files. The first example of this trend was the Ghostballs virus.

The Ghostballs virus was discovered in October 1989. This virus is a transient (non-resident) COM infector. In addition, the virus will overwrite the boot sector on disk with a modified version of the Italian (Bouncing Ball) boot sector virus. After boot sector disinfection any execution of an infected COM file will cause re-infection of the sector. It is a small step to a generalised multi-vector virus capable of propagating both via EXE/COM infection and via boot/master boot record propagation.

A fully operational example of a multi-vector virus is the 1253 virus. The 1253 virus, isolated in August 1990, infects four types of object code: the master boot record, DOS boot sector, COMMAND.COM, and COM executable files. The virus will become memory resident when an infected COM file is executed and will intercept interrupts 08h, 13h, 21h and 60h, installing itself as a system TSR. The TSR is 2128 bytes in length. At the time at which the virus becomes resident it will attempt to infect the master and DOS boot sectors. Other diskettes accessed when the virus is active in memory will also be infected. When the system is booted from a disk containing the virus in the master or DOS boot sectors, the virus becomes resident in high system memory, reducing the available memory by 77 840 bytes. The virus will then attempt to infect any COM programs executed.

4.13.3.4 Multi-architecture Viruses

It is also worth noting that the trend to permit other hardware architectures (such as the Atari ST) to read DOS formatted disks has led to the risk of multi-architecture viruses. Since both the Atari ST and IBM PC will read a boot sector from a DOS formatted disk and attempt to execute the incorporated code, it becomes possible to produce a boot sector virus which will spread on both systems. The significant difference between architectures is of course the use of the Intel 80X86 processor on the IBM PC, and the Motorola 68000 processor on the Atari. Tailoring of the initial jump instruction in the boot sector can produce an instruction sequence which will read:

Hex	Motorola 68000	Intel 80386
60	BRA.S	PUSH A
90	offset	NOP
EB	-	JMP
XX	-	offset
XX	-	offset

This instruction sequence allows two separate jumps to be incorporated within the available 11 bytes, thus splitting flow of control in two ways, depending on the executing processor.

4.13.3.5 Architecture Dependent Viruses

The opposite to a multi-architecture virus must be the extreme examples of the IBM PC-DOS viruses which will not execute on different processor chips (8086, 80286, 80386 and 80486). This non-operability may be caused by the use of extensions in the processor instruction set or in the case of the "Yale" virus by its use of an instruction marked as "undefined" in the 8086 set.

The 8086 processor (despite Intel specification that the instruction code was not used) interpreted instruction code 0F as being POP CS. This caused the virus (which relied on the instruction) to fail on 80386 processors. The latter processor had used the code as an escape to a two byte enhanced instruction set.

The original Yale virus thus caused an invalid opcode exception when run on a 80386 processor. The virus had thus become obsolete through the introduction of new (and not strictly backward compatible) hardware.

A similar example is the use of the "MOV CS,AX" instruction by the Italian virus which was permitted on the 8086, but trapped as illegal by the 80286/386 processors.

Other examples are viruses which exploit less obvious features of the processor architecture such as the instruction pre-fetch queue or pipeline. The virus modifies an instruction which is immediately in front of the instruction being executed. This will cause the virus to execute the unmodified instruction (since this has already been fetched by the processor and is awaiting execution). Disruption of the flow of control (such as might be caused by single step debugging) will flush the pipeline, and cause the virus to execute the modified instruction. The length of this pipeline varies between processors. Examples are 4 bytes for the 8088, and 6 bytes for the 8086.

Chapter 5

Management of PC Viruses

5.1 Perspective on Security

In Chapter 4 we painted a bleak picture of the wide range of camouflage techniques and replication strategies adopted by PC viruses. In this chapter, methods to prevent, contain and recover from computer virus infection will be discussed. Together, these methods provide comprehensive protection from significant damage to vital programs and data from virus (and trojan horse) activity.

The first important point to note is:

A trade-off between security and convenience always exists

A possible means of preventing computer virus infection would be a PC with a pre-formatted and installed hard disk, no floppy drives and anti-tamper alarm systems. This has significant disadvantages, namely:

Inability to install or transfer data and programs

In some environments such an inconvenience may be acceptable; in others it is crippling. The extent of the anti-viral precautions adopted by an organisation is a management decision. Such a decision must be based on:

- An estimate of the risk of data and program corruption by viruses
- The financial cost of such damage to the organisation
- The recurrent financial cost of regular anti-virus measures

In most circumstances, organisations may accept an element of risk to minimise security overheads and employee inconvenience. At the moment, when considering each proposed policy, ask:

Do the advantages of this policy justify its implementation costs?

5.2 Components of a Virus Control Scheme

The components of an organisation's reaction to computer viruses can be divided into:

- Prevention
- Detection
- Containment
- Disinfection
- Recovery

Prevention of a virus refers to precautions such as controls on software run on test systems, physical and electronic security controls on external software installation, policy constraints on shareware and public domain software, and user education in software use and clean machine practices.

Detection of a virus refers to the careful monitoring and logging of anomalous system activity, together with the use of a range of anti-viral and software integrity verification schemes.

Containment refers to the establishment of clear procedures for reporting of viral infection, controls instigated when a virus is detected in an organisation and the establishment of skilled anti-virus groups within the organisation.

Disinfection refers to the removal of all viral material from the organisation's computer systems through the reformatting of disks, removal and re-installation of software or the use of specialist viral disinfection tools.

Recovery refers to the ability of an organisation to restart vital work disrupted by the virus, including the ability to restore potentially damaged data from archive materials. Techniques such as redundant copies of data files, standby systems and careful contingency planning are all part of an organisation's recovery plan.

Management plans must also address issues such as the maintenance of public confidence in an organisation after a viral attack.

5.3 Prevention of Virus Attack

Viral infection can be prevented by controlling the ingress of viral material into the controlled environment which represents the company computers. Such environments can be broad, encompassing the entire company (including PCs removed by the user for home working), or restricted, covering a minimal range of PCs in a controlled access and closely supervised area.

In general such environments are structured in a hierarchy of risk:

- Universal – all computer systems with unrestricted software use and traffic
- Home use – computer systems taken off the corporate site or outside corporate control, i.e. home use of company PCs
- Corporate use – computer systems physically restricted to the corporate site but with no forms of access control
- Restricted use – computer systems restricted to the corporate site and employing a range of access controls and subject to supervision and auditing

As the value of the data stored on systems increases, or the imperativeness of retaining uninterrupted operation increases, so increasingly restricted environments must be established. Software flow either physically (via media transportation) or electronically (via networks) must be restricted to preserve the integrity of the environment.

To prevent a virus attack, we can constrain the propagation of viral code using a wide variety of methods. These may be divided into three categories:

- Physical constraints on the movement of viral code via media (or personnel) between environments
- Electronic constraints on the communication of viral code via networks
- Ideological constraints on the desire of the user to initiate either of the above

5.3.1 Physical Access Constraints

The most effective way to prevent viral code spreading is to isolate systems physically and electronically, then to control the movement of viral code either via media (floppy disk, tape, removable hard disk, CD-ROM etc) or personnel (through entry by keyboard or OCR). This can be achieved by:

1. Physically segregating PCs – restricting access to the PC by lock or guarded access control point. Depending on the installation, this can include drastic measures such as "mantrap" access gateways under human supervision with electronic card locks and personal code entry. In general, such measures are only appropriate when:
(i) Data integrity is vital (e.g. finance or banking)
(ii) Prevention of denial of service is vital (e.g. air traffic control)
(iii) Data confidentiality is vital (e.g. military)
Less stringent physical segregation may just consist of preventing PCs being removed from the corporate office by suitable alarm mechanisms, thus restricting the opportunities for installation of alien software.

2. Media transportation controls – such as physically searching employees entering or leaving the secured environment, or through the use of detectors capable of signalling the passage of a metallic media (such as the ferric and chrome dioxide coating on magnetic disks, or the metallic backing plate on quarter-inch cartridge tapes).

3. Minimisation and centralisation of replaceable media – this technique involves restriction of the number and location of machines with removable media. This subset of machines is placed under careful supervision and control. From these machines software is transferred by network to the hard disks on other machines for day-to-day use. (Naturally this has the disadvantage of rapidly spreading infection should an infected program bypass the careful checks.)

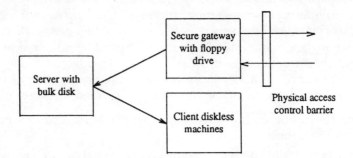

4. System operation constraints, such as the inclusion of physical locks which prevent the machine being operated by unauthorised personnel (preferably not easily bypassed by shorting two wires when the IBM PC case is open, possibly enforced by tamper resistant casings and alarm mechanisms). Access to the media may also be restricted by locks preventing access to floppy or tape drives.

5. Network security constraints – restricting access to, and tampering with, networks through the use of such methods as:

(i) Pressurised ducting, with pressure drop detectors and alarms

(ii) Line characteristic monitors, capable of detecting breaks (such as unplugging of an Ethernet connector to insert a tap) or changes in line capacitance or inductance caused by such a tap

(iii) Minimising cable in vulnerable or accessible locations

5.3.2 Electronic Measures

A wide variety of electronic access restriction and user authentication techniques exist, many of which can easily be adapted to the personal computer environment. They form a less onerous, although less foolproof, alternative to physical constraints.

In many cases an expert can circumvent electronic access control mechanisms by exploiting known bugs or loopholes in the mechanism.

Electronic access control is based on three characteristics of the user:

1. What the user is – physical feature verification.
2. What the user knows – knowledge verification.
3. What the user has – possession verification.

The most common techniques are adopted from groups 2 and 3, since such knowledge or possession can easily be confirmed electronically. Unfortunately such knowledge or possessions can easily be transferred, making these checks easy to circumvent.

Group 1 mechanisms are most difficult to forge (consider the difficulty in forging a fingerprint to gain such access) but are still in the development phase. They are often unreliable and error prone, causing the following types of errors at a rate which is unacceptable:

- Accidental permission of access to an unauthorised person
- Accidental denial of access to an authorised person

The mechanisms may also involve considerable personal inconvenience or prove ideologically unacceptable (i.e. all employees must be fingerprinted for recognition).

5.3.2.1 Physical Feature Verification

Examples in this group include (in order of inconvenience):

- Retinal pattern recognition – recognition of the pattern formed on the retina of the human eye by blood vessels, normally involving personal inconvenience although difficult to forge
- Fingerprint recognition – often ideologically unacceptable
- Voice recognition – unreliable and easily distorted by stress or illness
- Reaction time recognition – insufficiently discriminating in isolation; normally coupled with password entry using typing rate analysis
- Facial recognition – unreliable and easily distorted by facial hair, tanning or make-up

5.3.2.2 Knowledge Verification

Into this category fall the bulk of all computer user authentication schemes. The verification of knowledge can take the form of:

- Passwords
- Pass phrases
- Background history enquiry

These include the installation of password checkers on IBM systems. Obviously, an authentication mechanism must be in place as soon as possible in the boot sequence, and should be tamperproof. In this respect the authentication system should be in ROM, or incorporated into the master boot record on the hard disk or network server. It must be secure against being bypassed by:

1. Insertion of bootable floppy media (which will be selected prior to execution of hard disk initialisation code).
2. Abort sequences such as Ctrl-Alt-Del and Ctrl-C from the keyboard.

3. Execution of a command sequence from a trojan horse program run under the control of an authorised user, such as the installation of a "trapdoor" which can be utilised by an unauthorised user.

A number of IBM PC authorisation mechanisms have flaws which may allow them to be bypassed. This is one case of a general problem related to tampering with system software. It is preferable from an integrity viewpoint to incorporate as much as possible of the system boot and initialisation code into ROM. The incorporation of the BIOS, DOS and COMMAND.COM into ROM would ensure a clean system environment at boot time (up to the point at which the user invoked a non-built-in command from the command interpreter). Even in such ROM based systems (such as the Atari ST and newer Mac OS releases) facilities normally exist to override components of the ROM code to allow the installation of system patches and upgrades. The additional incorporation of the authentication mechanism into ROM would ensure that only initial authorised use would be permitted. Once an authorised user was active he or she might inadvertently introduce a trojan horse or virus infected utility into the clean environment. The issue of ensuring software integrity is addressed in the Biba extension to the Bell-LaPadula security model dealt with in Chapter 7.

5.3.2.2.1 Passwords

The password is the principal method of authenticating a user in most systems. A wide range of guidelines exist (such as the DOD password management guideline) on the choice of passwords. A well designed password control system would include:

● Restriction of acceptable passwords:

(i) to be in excess of a minimum length

(ii) to be chosen from a rich character set (multicase and alphanumeric)

(iii) not to be related to the user's login name or real name

(iv) not to appear in the standard English dictionary

(v) not to be a pronounceable word through restriction on the trigrams (groups of three letter combinations) appearing in the word to those which do not occur in the English language

● Reduction of system information which might allow passwords or logins to be guessed:

(i) avoidance of system login banners and welcome messages, which might permit identification of the type of operating system and thus derivation of the characteristics of typical passwords

(ii) non-repudiation of invalid logins until a password has been entered, prohibiting a rapid search for possible logins

(iii) insertion of a time delay into the password verification routine, thus delaying a response until a number of seconds after password entry which reduces the rate at which login/password doublets can be tried

Passwords can be extended to include complete phrases or sentences, thus allowing further complexity and increasing the search space for password guessing. Such pass phrases may still be comparatively simple for the user to memorise. Finally, the password mechanism can include an analysis of typing rate and inter-character delays (offering limited physical feature verification).

5.3.2.2.2 Background Verification

The user may be queried during the login session to determine his identity. Such queries can be generated from a system database of personal information, e.g. the infamous example used by some credit card firms: What is your mother's maiden name? This method has fundamental drawbacks:

- Personal resistance to compilation of such a dossier and its storage on computer (including the implications of the Data Protection Act)
- Limited background research by unauthorised users (who may be a friend or relation of the legitimate user) can allow the correct answers to be discovered

5.3.2.2.3 Other Techniques

A twist in the knowledge verification technique is to require the user to memorise a simple algorithm. A challenge issued by the system is transformed by the user (using a stand-alone system or calculator) under the known algorithm. The response is then entered at the keyboard and is verified by the system.

5.3.2.3 Possession Verification

The final category involves such systems as magnetic card or badge readers attached to the computer system. These are, however, easily duplicated, stolen or borrowed by other users. The use of complex patterns of magnetic flux intensity can complicate the duplication process. Possession verification includes the issue of "boot disks" without which the system is unusable (although this is a potential channel for the introduction of viral code in the form of the boot sector virus), and of software protection "dongles". The dongle is a hardware module attached to an external system interface (possibly in the form of a compact "smart" card) which in its simplest form comprises a PROM readable by the host. More complex varieties include stand-alone cryptographic modules which can be "challenged" by the host and will return an encrypted version of the host's challenge for verification.

5.3.3 Media Access Controls

The previous methods have concentrated on the restriction of personal use of the computer system. Virus code can also be restricted by limiting the loading of code from physical transportable media. Examples include:

- Restricting automatic loading of code on media insertion
- Checksumming or scanning for viral code on all inserted media
- Prevention of unauthorised software installation

A major problem on the Macintosh series has been the WDEF virus. This virus appears in a configuration file on each disk known as the "Desktop". This file controls the placement of icons and windows on the screen and permits the location of application programs via a four-byte signature. This file is automatically included in the code search path when the disk is inserted into the system, thus causing the implicit loading of the viral code in the WDEF virus infected Desktop. In the IBM PC, and other related systems, which are incapable of detecting media changes (i.e. removal or insertion of a floppy disk) such implicit loading is fortunately not a problem.

The integrity of the inserted disk can be automatically verified if the medium carried a unique value identifier. The identifier may comprise either a serial number (e.g. the Atari ST disk BPB) or a value identifier (in the Mac volume information block or IBM PC root directory). Unfortunately IBM PC systems have not adopted a standard convention regarding volume labels, and these are often duplicated across disks or missing entirely.

If a disk change can be identified (which may not imply automatic loading of code on media change) the system can:

- automatically calculate a checksum over the boot sector, directory information and disk areas then verify this against a checksum stored on the disk, or in a master directory in the hard disk
- automatically scan for known virus signatures or code within the executable files on disk

An example of such an automated scanner is the desk accessory "Virus Detective" on the Macintosh. This is capable of detecting disk insertion, which causes a scan for a series of search strings (defined using a simple but flexible definition language).

5.3.4 Network Access Controls

The preceding sections have dealt with physical and electronic user authentication and media authentication. In the modern corporate environment many systems are interconnected via local and wide area networks such as Ethernet and X25. It is common practice to provide a wide range of services from remote sites, including login and remote execution of code or utilities.

Networking increases the potential for unauthorised access, and permits the rapid spread of viral code. The particular problems posed by networks are:

- Identification of access channels

- Distributed trust
- Centralised network file servers
- Network transport by public carriers

5.3.4.1 Identification of Access Controls

A number of alternative routes normally exist by which code can be transmitted across the network either for local storage (with delayed execution via a trojan horse mechanism) or immediate execution under remote control. The identification of all possible channels, together with their audit and control is vital. Typical channels include:

- Remote logins or command shells
- Remote file transfer or access facilities
- Remote code execution or procedure call
- Electronic mail facilities

Other network services providing restricted services may be open to subversion bugs and loopholes in the (often highly privileged) utility providing the service.

A gateway or gateways should be established which represent the interface between the outside world, external corporate sites and local networks, e.g.:

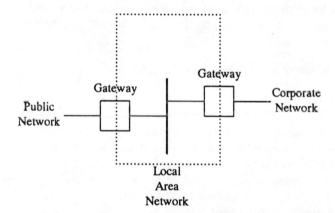

Such systems tend to implement enhanced security and integrity controls, including extensive auditing and monitoring of network traffic. Such monitoring often includes expert systems to identify anomalous activity which may be characteristic of a security breach.

5.3.4.1.1 Centralised Network File Servers

Similarly, central file servers may be established on LANs to allow attachment of diskless machine nodes, or sharing of specialist software. Such servers offer a haven for viruses, which may replicate rapidly on the server machine. The infected server may then spread the infection to the client machines which it serves (the infected binary being transferred from the server for local execution on the client machine). Having spread to the client, the virus may spread normally amongst the local media of the client.

Servers must therefore exercise a high level of security controls, including extensive anti-viral and checksumming software, security measures in the form of discretionary or mandatory access controls, physical access controls to the server, and careful monitoring of the server.

With careful control, the server can provide an assurance that the system and application software remains uninfected (including that run on diskless client machines). Obvious measures are:

- Use of an alternative operating system on the server to prevent infection of the server through execution of viral code introduced from a client system
- Write-protection of all executable files, with limited client rights to modify or remove the write-protection attribute

5.3.4.1.2 Distributed Trust

Network systems often make use of less stringent access controls between nodes on local networks, and between trusted nodes such as related or customer firms. This can lead to the establishment of a hierarchy of trust in which:

Node A trusts Node B, Node B trusts Node C, etc.

A viral infection of node C can therefore spread rapidly through the remote execution of code on node B under the control of a user on node B, and thence to node A. In a similar manner a virus executing on node C can copy its code to the file system on node B, from whence it may execute and copy its code to node A. This bi-directional propagation of trust is a typical feature of traditional discretionary access models. Thus, complex multi-link infection paths can exist, often leading to infection of distant machines which are not trusted by the source machine (except indirectly).

5.3.4.1.3 Network Transport by Public Carrier or Accessible Media

Finally, consideration must be given in high security environments to the accessibility of all communication channels linking secure systems. On broadcast network systems (such as Ethernet CSMA/CD) any node is capable of intercepting packets destined for another node (a confidentiality risk), or of injecting packets appearing to originate on another node (an integrity risk).

Thus an untrusted node can intercept a request to load a remote file, and can transfer a virus infected file in its place.

Where a network is routed via a public space, or indeed over intermediate public carriers (PTTs), it becomes possible to intercept a file transfer request destined for a remote system. Such a request can then be answered by the untrusted intercepting system.

A number of digital authentication schemes can be adopted based on public key cryptosystems such as RSA prime factoring algorithms. The interested reader is referred to Appendix 16 for details of suitable further reading.

5.3.5 Ideological Controls

Anti-viral techniques require the co-operation of the user community in observing:

- "Good" software policies
- Use of technical anti-virus utilities
- Monitoring of anomalous system behaviour
- Reporting of possible viral infection

This co-operation is vital and can only be achieved through careful management of personnel – a mixture of education, involvement and supervision. It is not sufficient to educate users in the technical aspects of anti-viral software utilities without addressing the rationale for such inconveniences. It is vital that the potential for viral damage is described (possibly using illustrative case histories), and that measures are taken to ensure that employees realise that they have a responsibility for viral protection and can take an active role in detecting and destroying this menace.

The principal ways of establishing user acceptance of good anti-viral policies are:

- Education
- Motivation
- Supervision
- Discipline

5.3.5.1 User Education

A wide range of training materials are now available from commercial security firms such as Sophos, S & S International Ltd., ISIS or the Federation Against Software Theft (FAST), including provision of instructional seminars, demonstrations of computer viruses, information packs, software documentation and news bulletins. Contact addresses for these organisations are given in Appendix 14.

Training tends to split into three phases:

1. A basic introductory course – for end users.
2. Detailed technical courses – for systems programmers and administrators.
3. Management overviews – for senior management and executive levels.

A typical two-day introductory course might comprise:

- What is a virus? Terminology, descriptions of trojan horses, logic bombs, viruses and worms
- How does it operate? Brief overview of how a virus spreads in the PC environment, examining a few selected viruses, possibly with a demonstration of viral spread (preferably simulated)
- What damage can it do? Look briefly at the damage caused on activation. Show how data and program code may be destroyed and indicate the cost of such damage
- How do we prevent it? Describe good software practices. Describe technical preventive measures and demonstrate use of selected in-house anti-virus software. Backup and integrity policies
- What to do when a virus is detected? Corporate reporting procedures. Recovery procedures: re-installation and disinfection. Public relations and legal aspects

During the entire course the corporate data security policy (described below) must be stressed. As much visual material as possible should be used, including demonstrations of viral activation, hands-on use of anti-viral software, etc.

Unfortunately, there is a need for accurate simulations of the behaviour of anti-viral products on detection of a virus. In this respect, harmless simulators can be constructed which:

- Demonstrate the virus' obvious symptoms, such as characteristic screen displays, musical effects, etc. Such simulators can also simulate the growth of files on infection and change in file characteristics
- Cause activation of the "Alert" messages on anti-viral products (by simulating an attempt to write to an executable file, for instance)

In some cases a need may exist for the use of live (unattenuated) viruses, although this should be carefully considered and minimised to reduce the risk of accidental spread to live corporate systems (or indeed copying by participants on the training course). In the event that such a potentially risky demonstration is undertaken, always:

- Backup all data on hard drives
- Select a number of scratch floppy disks for demonstration use, and clearly label them as "infected"
- Segregate the demonstration system both physically and electronically

- Supervise the infected machines at all times; do not permit anyone to insert or remove media while the machine is infected
- After the demonstration switch the machine off and leave for at least 30 seconds. Switch on and boot from a "clean" write-protected copy of the system master boot disk
- Reformat all hard drives (using a clean copy of the formatter program), preferably at low level. Alternatively, always rewrite the master boot record for each physical drive
- Erase (using magnetic flux coils) or destroy all removable infected media
- Maintain a careful watch on all systems for a period of time after the demonstration

Normally such demonstrations are of limited use (other than the glamour of handling live viral material), and are best left to specialists.

Technical courses are appropriate only for personnel who need to know the details of viral replication and of the detailed operation of anti-viral measures. An example might be the virus control or personal computer security group within a firm.

The technical course might also be held over two days (preferably on completion of the end user course), and might include:

- Detailed examination of how viral code can be executed, i.e. the boot sequence
- How a virus replicates, i.e. patching of binary files by link viruses
- How a virus remains active: terminate and stay resident methodologies
- Detailed examples and descriptions of the operation of common viruses, such as Israeli, Cascade, Brain, Italian, WDEF and nVIR
- An examination of the operation of anti-viral software products: checksumming, vector interception and signature recognition (including shortcomings)
- Re-installation and disinfection of infected systems
- A hands-on walk-through of the detection, analysis and disinfection of an infected system
- Possible panel or discussion session on future trends and developments in virus technology – always interesting, often worrying

The final form of course is aimed at senior management and thus has a risk assessment, public relations and legal aspects bias. Such a course might run over one day and cover:

- General introduction to computer viruses – introduce the concept and give examples of damage caused to affected organisations, including illustrative media coverage
- Risk assessment – if possible, give illustrative statistics on the risk from computer viruses, and review the potential seriousness of damage to corporate data, denial of service or data compromise

- Corporate policy – outline the corporate data security policy and detail the management and procedural structures in place to handle virus infection
- User education – detail the education programs available within the company, and the emphasis during induction courses
- Public relations – detail the handling of reporting to the press, relations with clients, reporting to official organisations and dissemination of information within the organisation
- Contingency planning – detail the corporate data recovery policy and the contingency plans available to permit data recovery and uninterrupted operation
- Discipline and legal issues – discuss the contractual recourse against guilty employees, and the corporate policy on initiation of legal proceedings against employees or outsiders guilty of virus or trojan horse introduction

The flavour of each course is very different, and in each case the material and style of presentation are highly biased towards the audience requirements. Brainstorming and active participation is vital.

User education does not finish with the introductory course – it is an ongoing activity seeking to continue the high profile of software security measures as well as informing users of new trends in viral threats.

A large number of specialist magazines are available for technical staff, such as *Virus Bulletin*, *Virus News International*, *Computers and Security* and *Computer Fraud and Security Bulletin*, together with detailed reference listings and catalogues of known or reported viruses, such as the University of Hamburg virus catalogue, Homebase Bulletin Board catalogue, *Virus Bulletin* catalogue, and the Dirty Dozen trojan horse listing.

A similar range of electronic discussion forums deals with reporting of new viruses and discussion of the general field of anti-viral measures. The principal forum, Virus-l, is co-ordinated by Ken Van Wyk of CERT.

These detailed discussion forums are often inappropriate for end users and management, who may benefit from a precise or abstract service. This service might take the form of a monthly electronic mail bulletin, occasional warning circulars or a column in the company magazine. Such bulletins may contain:

- Warnings of new viruses or errant software
- Notices of upgrades to selected anti-virus software
- Changes in, or reminders of, corporate data security policies and standard anti-virus procedures
- Contact numbers of people in the reporting chain for virus discoveries or who can provide technical advice
- Dates of anti-virus courses and descriptions of educational resources

Management may benefit from a similar condensation including revised risk assessments and changes in current legislation.

5.3.6 Management Policies

This section is concerned with the detailed measures available to reduce the threat of computer viruses (and trojan horses). From it can be extracted a management policy framework. Such policies must be tailored to the individual needs of the company (including an assessment of the value of the company's data and computing resources). Aspects of a policy include:

- A general statement of the company's desire to ensure the security and integrity of its computing systems, normally signed by the managing director or company chairman
- Policy on training and education of employees
- Policy on anti-viral measures, including:
  (i) Use of external software
  (ii) Use of technical anti-viral measures and software
  (iii) Reporting of viral infection
  (iv) Establishment of a group with special responsibility for viral advice and disinfection
- Public relations policy
- Disciplinary and legislative policy
- Policy on contingency planning for data recovery

Such an anti-virus policy will normally form an integral part of the broader general corporate security or corporate IT security policy.

5.3.6.1 Training of Employees

An education policy should provide for initial training of new employees (possibly via compulsory attendance at the end user course as part of the corporate induction program). It should also provide access to advanced courses where appropriate (i.e. to system programmers and members of the anti-virus unit in the case of the technical course, and to senior management in the case of the management course).

Educational policy should also require that updates to new viral developmets be tracked, and that employees be informed. This can either be achieved in-house by the anti-virus group or externally by consultancy services from specialist security firms.

5.3.6.2 Use of Anti-viral Measures

This is a major component of the management policy statement. It sets the company attitudes and practices for viral prevention. Firstly, it must address the installation procedures for new software, and may include:

1. Restrictions on software not from trusted vendors (including items from public domain bulletin boards, "cowboy" firms and other unknown sources). While this may restrict viral infection, it is worth noting that the so-called "shrink-wrapped" software does not provide absolute protection. Even reputable companies have distributed virus infected software by accident. Examples are given in Chapter 2 and Appendix 9. Certain major bulletin boards now apply extensive anti-viral scans on new products. They may, however, be an attractive target for the upload of software infected by newer viral strains. Thus, there is a reasonable guarantee of software free from known existing strains. These boards include major archives such as Simtel-20, Lancaster PDSOFT and Usenet (a UNIX conference system), providing many news groups which distribute software in binary form. Most are now applying quite advanced checksums to software posted. Unfortunately since such news messages can easily be altered in transit (or indeed forged) this provides limited protection. It is likely that boards will move to digital signature algorithms based on "public key" cyphers in the near future. Key distribution could then be via an alternate channel (indeed including a single master public key distributed with the news software which authenticates public keys for known authors, which are then used to authenticate software sent by these authors). Software policies must be enforced. This can be achieved either by casual observation or by direct auditing of installed software. Organisations such as FAST can provide guidance in this area.

2. Recording of software configurations: in conjunction with restrictions on software installation, there is a need to accurately record the software configuration on each system. This allows monitoring of file characteristics changed by viruses, provides an aid to diagnosis of abnormal behaviour and finally permits rapid re-installation and recovery after infection. Such a log may be kept manually in logbook format, or electronically (possibly automated). The latter must be carefully backed up (possibly separately from the normal backup procedures, via alternate media or hard copy printout).

3. Use of technical anti-viral measures: this policy must describe the "prescribed" anti-viral measures which must be taken by the organisation. There are many anti-viral software utilities available, often purporting to be best in the field. In general they divide into: (i) utilities which are resident on the PC and will detect and attempt to prevent a virus spreading; (ii) utilities which may be run on an irregular basis to find characteristics of files indicative of a viral infection; and (iii) utilities which can identify a change from a standard configuration (which may be due to viral infection).

A software policy should describe which products (possibly in each category) are to be run on computer systems. The need to ensure the "cleanliness" of systems may of course vary. The most important are generally:

- Production and operational systems, whose disruption may be immediately visible to clients and may delay critical projects

- Administrative systems, where a significant rate of change in data occurs with consequent rapid disruption of the organisation if impeded
- Development systems: with correct backups little delay or loss should occur
- Other systems, including public machines, managerial systems, etc.

While the criteria above are dictated purely by the direct impact on corporate operation, other indirect criteria (such as the risk of infecting a valuable client) may alter priorities.

Many of these products change rapidly while attempting to track new viral developments. In this regard the policy must address:

- Responsibilities for monitoring of software updates
- Frequency and procedures for issuing and installing updates within the organisation
- Measures to audit or monitor the versions in active use

5.3.6.3 Compartmentalisation

A technical area which should be covered by the management policy is that of compartmentalisation. This is taken to be the division of an organisation's computer installations into one or more groups, between which software interchange (and therefore networking) is forbidden or restricted. Each group may also include requirements for different anti-viral measures, audit procedures and backup procedures.

A typical segregation is to group all operational and production systems into one (or more) compartments which are isolated from the remainder of the organisation. Thus if a function of an organisation is the bulk copying of software for distribution, then it is vital that the copying machine and the repository of production master copies are free from infection.

The production compartment may impose severe restrictions on the introduction of untrusted software, use extensive anti-viral checking and use secure operating systems and hardware support.

Compartmentalisation may also be required by standard financial security practices (such as the segregation of operational systems using live data from development systems modifying program code).

5.3.6.4 Centralisation

While apparently contradictory to good viral practice (since it encourages software sharing) some form of software centralisation is beneficial as it may permit greater control to be exercised over software update, issue and modification.

A common example is the establishment of a group master software repository in which all "master" copies of software are maintained. When a user initially wishes to use a package, a copy is obtained from this master archive and transferred (either electronically or manually) to his/her work machine. The repository is subject to continuous monitoring, careful anti-virus checking and possibly physical access control. No writes are permitted via network facilities to its storage. This allows:

- Control over all "master" copies of software
- Backup of master copies
- Use of stringent anti-viral measures

The repository machine would normally be under the control of the anti-viral group within the organisation, although preferably segregated from any analysis or testing machines.

Compartmentalisation and centralisation basically permit identification of a critical component within the organisation, and the cost-effective improvement of security and integrity measures within this critical component.

5.3.6.5 Personnel Policies

Finally, viruses can be prevented or reduced in probability by personnel measures such as:

- Incorporation of "damage" clauses and disciplinary clauses into contracts of employment
- Encouragement of professional ethics within the group
- Disciplinary action against viral perpetrators
- Vetting of personnel

In the first case the organisation may wish to ensure that an employee can be held liable in a civil action for any damage which may be caused to the employer's system by the introduction of a virus or trojan horse.

In the final case we seek to apply psychological testing (and possibly background investigation) to determine if an employee has a history of hacking, software copying or abuse, or the creation of viruses, or has a profile which would suggest unethical or cavalier behaviour. This technique is of course very rough but may enable an organisation to avoid obvious risks. This may also reduce premiums on software related damage insurance policies.

5.3.7 Vaccination and Inoculation

The analogy between biological and computer viruses can be extended to include the concept of a vaccine which when administered will prevent viral replication. Such viruses operate by attaching a virus signature or signatures to the boot sectors and files within the system environment to prevent infection by common viruses. Thus the Vienna timestamp flag (setting the seconds field in the date/time stamp to 31 = 62 seconds) could be added to all executable files within the system, thus preventing the virus (and most of its derivatives) from infecting the system. This technique is particularly useful in the case of boot sector viruses. On non-system disks it is often possible to add a wide range of signatures including those of most common boot sector viruses. Since the boot sector is effectively unused in a non-system disk, these signatures may safely be added without cost to the user. They guard against possible accidental infection of a non-system disk by a boot sector virus (and subsequent transfer of the infection if an attempt is made to boot from the non-system disk).

Examples of multiple inoculations of a boot sector include:

Virus	Offset in boot sector	Signature
Italian	1FC hex	57 13
Brain	004 hex	34 12
Disk Killer	03E hex	CB 3C
New Zealand	0 hex	EA 05 00 C0

An extension of the vaccination principal is the self-propagating vaccine. In this case the vaccination code and signatures are coupled with a replication component which will automatically write the vaccine and associated replication code onto all available drives. The vaccine thus spreads throughout the community, being transported when disk media are moved between systems. As with the concept of anti-virus viruses (discussed later in this chapter) which seek to disinfect and destroy other viruses, self-replicating vaccines raise a number of problems. It is questionable whether many users would wish any form of self-replicating code to be active within their system environment, whether virus or anti-virus.

5.4 Detection of Viral Code

5.4.1 Monitoring and Logging

The first (and simplest) way in which a virus may be detected is through the symptoms it causes within a computer system. Each system (or group of systems) should have a log of abnormal activity (which will also prove of use to engineers when debugging hardware faults). Examples of unusual activity caused by viruses are:

- Graphical displays – bouncing balls, falling letters, cryptic messages, colourful graphics, etc.

- Musical displays – selection of tunes, abnormal beeps or clicks
- Keyboard and text manipulation – substitution of characters in text files, toggling of keyboard Caps Lock or Num Lock, insertion of new characters into the keyboard buffer
- Memory – reduction in available memory or corruption of user memory blocks
- Disks – unexpected disk activity, loss of available disk space, growth of files, changes in attributes or alteration dates, cross-linking of disk sectors, inability to read a disk partition, missing or lost files
- Programs – longer startup or execution times, unexpected failures
- Machine – changes in standard reboot sequence, hangup or spontaneous reboot of machine, general slowdown

Once active, a virus can generate a wide range of such activity by manipulating any facet of the IBM PC's operational characteristics.

Automated tools are available to aid in the monitoring of system configuration. These include the checking of the directory layouts, file lengths, alteration times and attributes, and, finally, checksumming of file contents.

The former are comparatively simple utilities which generate a saved state in a file, which can later be compared against the current system state. This will allow the detection of deletions or creations of new executables, and change in characteristics of an executable.

A more powerful technique is checksumming. Since most modern viruses actively conceal their presence (by restoring changed file attributes, alteration times, etc.), this is vital. The checksum of a file is a complex function of all bytes within the file. An important characteristic of the function is that it should reflect any change to the file. Many examples exist in other fields of computing, such as:

- Cyclic redundancy checks, commonly used in communications such as CCCITT CRC 64 algorithm
- Hash keys, used in standard hash indexing techniques
- Digital signatures generated using variants of the data encryption standard (DES), or based on public key algorithms such as RSA

Possible choices include the MD4 message digest algorithm proposed by Rivest, or the SNEFRU One Way Hash function adopted by Xerox. Implementations of both algorithms are available in the public domain.

The checksum utility is run to generate checksums over all files (or, less stringently, over all executable files). The resultant checksum may either be stored locally or backed up on an alternate system or archive. Checksum utilities typically take a considerable amount of time to generate checksums on all files (an important characteristic being the "unforgeability" of the checksum – often ensured via complexity of the checksum function).

The checksum generator must be re-run on a regular (daily or weekly) basis to compare the current system against that saved earlier. Any change in checksum represents a change in executable file content, and thus a possible viral infection. Naturally, when active code development work is being carried out false alarms may be generated.

On Macintosh systems, the CODE resources together with any additional resources containing executable code (see Chapter 6) in the resource fork of all files must be checksummed. Note that data files may contain resource forks. Such forks will be inserted in the search path for executable code when the data file is opened by the application.

On IBM PC systems it is normally appropriate to checksum the entire executable file (normally those with COM, EXE, BIN, OVL or SYS suffixes). To ensure full protection it is worth remembering that data files may be interpreted or compiled by applications such as macros, batch files (BAT), hypertext or program source. Such files must also be checksummed to give full protection.

The checksumming can be extended to other static code areas in the system, such as:

- Checksumming of DOS boot sectors
- Checksumming of master boot records

A regular checksum verification does however permit a limited window in which a virus can infect before detection on the next verification run. The assessment of this risk must determine the frequency of such verifications, and the need for other, more specific, detection techniques.

There is also the risk that if a checksum package is well known (e.g. "Checkup"), the virus will specifically target its algorithm by:

- Modifying each infected executable by adding padding bytes to ensure that the eventual checksum is identical to that of the original application. This is complicated if the checksum algorithm is difficult to "invert", so that the requisite padding bytes cannot be determined. Multiple checksum algorithms can also be utilised by the same product. A further technique is to dynamically (on a per host basis) vary the size of the block in the executable over which the checksum is generated.
- Locating and modifying the saved checksum file – avoided by backup of the file, or encryption of the saved checksums.
- Locating and modifying the actual checksum program to ignore the modifications to specific files – difficult unless the program is well known, but easily prevented by running a clean copy from a software master disk.

General attacks which might be applied to defeat checksumming (and signature recognition) operate by concealing the alteration to the code of the original executable. This is the technique adopted by Stealth viruses such as the 4096.

Checksums can also be verified on program load (allowing rapid detection of executable alteration), by:

1. A small TSR which intercepts the DOS load and execute interrupt, recalculates the checksum and compares it against a stored value.
2. Self-checking code incorporated into the program itself (normally recommended for anti-virus software which must ensure its own integrity).
3. Hardware support to checksum executable code segments and compare against a saved checksum stored in the executable file. This may require support for public key algorithms to inhibit forgery of the signature value when the algorithm is known.

In the IBM PC environment, approach 1 is easily implemented. On more complex architectures (where the hardware has a segmented memory architecture and virtual memory support) it is possible to checksum each executable code segment associated with a utility at load time and to compare the resultant checksum(s) against a vector stored in a well-known location in the kernel or supervisor space.

5.4.2 Signature Recognition

While a checksum seeks to detect change, the techniques described in this section seek to detect a characteristic of a known trojan horse or virus. Viruses may be recognised by the presence of a code pattern in the infected executable; by the actual signature marker used by the virus itself; or by generic "expert" systems capable of recognising suspect code sequences.

Virus specific recognition sequences require that the signature recognition utility detects a specific sequence of bytes (normally 8–16 bytes) within the code file. Such systems require a database of built-in recognition strings which must be constantly updated as new viral strains appear. Tables of such recognition strings regularly appear in *Virus Bulletin*.

The choice of a virus recognition string is a non-trivial task. It must be:

1. Unlikely to give rise to false alarms when scanning uninfected files. Thus strings in the locale of common DOS call sequences are inappropriate, as are strings appearing in libraries used by common compiler systems, and typical code sequences such as register save/restores. In general, testing against a wide range of commercial utilities is vital.
2. Common to all files infected by the virus, i.e. not dependent on a particular characteristic of the host being infected or part of the variable area of the virus.
3. A vital part of the "core" of the virus, such as its replication code.

Item 3 is aimed at allowing the recognition of the common form of viral code produced by simple modification of an established virus, the so called "clones". Choice of multiple search strings, one of which is a common characteristic of the virus family (e.g. Jerusalem strains) and a second which is characteristic of a particular member, may be advisable. This technique allows the flexibility of family identification, coupled with exact id of the actual virus.

When a virus is roughly identified it is possible to confirm the initial identification of the virus by comparing a checksum of the static portion of the virus with that of the reference sample. This allows a detailed analysis such as:

Virus is Jerusalem family, particular strain Anarkia

or

Virus is Jerusalem family, Anarkia signature but sample has been modified

In the Macintosh case the patterns of resource ids, names, sizes and types can also be used as an input into the virus signature recognition process. A large number of nVIR B clones avoided detection by the simple expedient of changing the type of the auxiliary resources used to store viral code. The type was changed from "nVIR" to "Hpat", "AIDS", "MEV#", "Jude", etc. It is vital that a chosen signature or characteristic must be robust and resistant to simple modification (e.g. binary editing) of a viral string.

It is of course possible to look for the same recognition string, directory entry or resident call characteristic as the virus itself uses as a signature. This is discouraged because this string is frequently changed when a virus is modified (or even upgraded by the author) to produce a new strain.

Whatever the chosen recognition string it is vital that it is encrypted in the scanner. Unencrypted recognition strings are often detected by other scanners as virus fragments (thus causing the common problem of virus scanners detecting each other as being multiply infected). A further advantage is that it may prevent the virus author from discovering the minimal modification necessary to his virus to avoid detection.

Checksum and scan utilities can be converted into incremental scanning utilities which are permanently resident in memory, carrying a slow incremental scan or checksum verification of the directory hierarchy (in much the same way as a direct action virus does).

Utilities can also be automatically executed at system startup or termination, or on insertion of a new disk media (possible in the Mac case, uncertain on IBM PC systems because of the lack of a hardware media change indication).

5.4.3 Generic Code Recognition

The final form is potentially unreliable, but has the potential to detect new emergent strains without being upgraded. It also provides a method of detecting trojan horse code (without running the potentially damaging code).

A generic recogniser consists of an expert system which attempts to recognise sequences of code that are suspect, hostile, or represent virus camouflage, replication or manipulation code. Examples include:

- Manipulation code: calls to formatting DOS calls, direct BIOS calls, calls to absolute DOS sector I/O, calls to modify the DOS/BIOS vector table, interrupt call simulation code (by pushing the flag register prior to a subroutine call), suspicious text strings (including expletives)
- Replication code: calls to DOS TSR functions, sequences of byte moves which originate within the executable code or are targeted to the executable code (self- modifying)
- Camouflage code: writes to track 40/80 or beyond, manipulation of system file table or file control blocks, modification of memory control blocks, known camouflage modules (such as the 80386 pipeline mode test code), etc.

Recognition is complex, and, as explained in Chapter 3, can never be 100 per cent effective. A code sequence can normally be rewritten to perform the same task, but with a completely different set of instructions, e.g.

$$Y = X + 4$$
$$Y = (X-3) + 7$$
$$Z = X + 2; Y = Z + 2;$$
$$PUSH\ X; POP\ Y; Y = Y + 4;\ etc.$$

This is a developing area which, despite its many false alarms, may tag public domain software which requires further inspection or investigation.

Signature recognition utilities suffer from three major drawbacks:

- In a similar manner to checksum utilities, they must be run regularly (taking a considerable time to scan all executables on disk) and must therefore leave a window of time between which infection and replication may occur
- They (excluding generic techniques) require regular update as new viruses appear
- Second generation self-encrypting viruses minimise the recognisable code string within the virus

The signature recognition can be carried out at object load time (in a similar manner to the dynamic checksumming process described earlier).

5.4.4 Sacrificial Lamb

A final common technique used to detect viral infection (and indeed trojan horses) is the sacrificial lamb. All new software is installed on the system, all games and public domain software likely to be used is collected and installed. This is done to ensure that the system will become infected if a virus is circulating. The system clock is normally run at least a fortnight in advance in the hope of detecting activation of unknown viruses or time bombs. The time advance must be calculated to match the estimated time to analyse a new virus and disseminate effective warnings within the company.

The sacrificial lamb system is then carefully monitored, and has a range of anti-viral software run upon it. If an infection is detected it is traced to its originating package and a warning sent to the remainder of the organisation.

Software releases can be delayed for a few weeks while samples are under test. Such testing, if extensive, may also detect general bugs or software inter-operability problems.

5.4.5 Auditing

A further approach to the detection of viral code is to apply auditing using manual or electronic mechanisms to significant components of the system's behaviour. Such auditing is incorporated in many implementations of secure systems (including the DOD TCSEC at level C2). The auditing normally tracks all security related events (i.e. those which arise from the user authentication process and the transfers of information subsequently initiated by that user).

A typical audit trail (based on the Sun C2 security option) is considered below. In this scheme audit trail entries comprise records written to a secure directory (owned by a special audit user id) for each of eight classes of system event, namely:

short name	long name	short description
dr	data_read	Read of an object
dw	data_write	Write or modification of an object
dc	data_create	Creation or deletion of an object
da	data_access_change	Change in object access controls
lo	login_logout	Login, logout or batch job commence
ad	administrative	Various operator administrative functions
p1	minor_privilege	Privileged operation
p2	major_privilege	Privileged operation

The records written to the audit trail contain sufficient information to identify the time, date, initiating user and terminal, and the object being acted upon or operation being invoked. A typical sample record is for the "execve" process creation operation. This writes a record in the following format:

- Current root directory being used by the parent
- Current working directory being used by the parent
- Pathname of program to be invoked

Added to this specific record is a general header including the event time, real and effective user and group ids of the program causing the event, process id of the invoking process and the result code returned by the operation.

Such audit trails can be generated on most systems by interception of low level system calls at the BIOS/DOS interface, Mac OS or at the level of UNIX system calls. Important features of the audit trail generation mechanism are:

1. That the audit generation mechanism must be tamper resistant.
2. That the generated audit trail must be tamperproof.

The former requirement implies that the audit mechanism (if using system call interception via the interrupt vector table) must prevent any alteration of the system interrupt vector table which might allow disconnection of the audit facility. Equally, it must also prevent undermining of the audit mechanism by use of low level facilities, direct subroutine jumps to memory resident OS components or direct use of the system hardware.

At the very least, it should detect such attempts even if the system security environment is incapable of inhibiting such tampering. In an environment without memory management protection facilities this is probably impossible. Thus, certified audit subsystems are unlikely on PC or Mac platforms (except as part of a re-engineered kernel/OS which make use of the memory protection facilities provided by the 80386/68030 chip and associated memory management hardware). Thus, many personal computer audit trails are advisory rather than definitive (i.e. they may detect hostile behaviour, but this is not guaranteed).

The latter requirement can often be satisfied via "WORM" (Write Once, Read Many) devices. Such devices are tamper resistant in that the audit trail once written cannot be modified.

To detect viral code propagation, auditing must detect all creations or modifications of objects (to detect corresponding file techniques) which might be potentially executable. Such objects may be comparatively low level, such as an operating system boot block, or as abstract as the C source for a program or utility.

In general it is also useful to monitor behaviour which might be characteristic of a virus attempting to bypass the audit mechanism (such as utilising OS calls to modify interrupt vectors or operating system memory, or unexpected state changes in external hardware characteristic of direct manipulation by a virus).

For information on auditing requirements the user is referred to the NCSC manual, *A Guide to Understanding Audit in Trusted Systems*.

5.4.6 Use of Expert Systems to Analyse Viral Behaviour

Unfortunately, indiscriminate auditing can generate vast quantities of information. This results in the typical "needle in a haystack" problem. The audit trails are thus often relegated to a means of tracing the source of erroneous system behaviour after the event. To be of use in immediate detection of problems the audit trail must either be condensed (losing vital information) or the human administrator must be aided when interpreting the trail.

To achieve the latter, it is possible to design an expert system to perform occasional (or, in larger systems, on-line) audit trail analysis. Such an expert system includes a number of heuristics and metrics relating to the form of user behaviour which is indicative of hostile action. In a similar manner, activity profiles can be constructed for users. When a user shows a significant departure from his/her activity profile (such as a secretary who uses the system only for editing and printing beginning to compile and run programs; or a user suddenly shifting from his favourite language, compiler, editor and utility set) a warning can be flagged. A possible example is the runtime intrusion detection system developed at Stanford.

To detect the presence of a virus it is normally sufficient to flag any generation of executable code by unexpected (i.e. non-compiler) utilities, to detect the modification of source code or batch files by unexpected utilities (i.e. non-editors). The audit trail may also detect the violation of system software policies (i.e. copying of utilities or importation of bulletin board software).

The auditing trails and expert system can thus provide a limited degree of relief from failures in the security environment provided by the operating system.

5.4.7 Fighting Fire with Fire

A common method of viral code detection on the Commodore Amiga platform is the idea of an anti-virus virus. The virus detection software is written as a boot sector virus which when booted will become memory resident automatically. The anti-virus then checks all disks inserted (including hard disk partitions) for known viruses. If a virus is detected it is overwritten by the anti-virus. In most cases the anti-virus also replicates on all available disks and partitions.

It is questionable whether the concept of a anti-virus spreading unchecked is preferable to a genuine virus infection. Both anti-virus and virus use valuable system memory and slightly degrade performance. It is also likely that anti-viruses which exploit undocumented system functions may become potentially damaging on future operating system releases.

The picture that can be painted in the Amiga world is one of anti-virus chasing virus, and indeed anti-virus chasing anti-virus since most upgrades automatically detect and remove previous versions of themselves. Admittedly, the removal of the anti-virus or virus is normally done with the user's consent and knowledge.

The table below gives details of the known anti-viruses on the Commodore Amiga platform as of July 1990:

Detects	Anti-virus virus product				
	ASS 1.0	North Star I	North Star II	Pentagon Circle	System Z 3.0
Byte bandit	X	X	X	X	X
SCA	X	X	X	X	X
North Star I			X	X	
North Star II				X	
System Z 3.0			X	X	
System Z 4.0				X	
Paramount				X	
Lamer exterminator 1.0					
Lamer exterminator 2.0					
Byte warrior					

Detects	Anti-virus virus product			
	System Z 4.0	System Z 5.0	System Z 5.3	VKILL 1.0
Byte bandit	X	X	X	X
SCA	X	X	X	X
North Star I				
North Star II	X	X	X	
System Z 3.0	X	X	X	
System Z 4.0		X	X	
Paramount				
Lamer exterminator 1.0		X	X	
Lamer exterminator 2.0			X	
Byte warrior	X	X	X	

Of the viruses in the above table only "SCA", "Byte Bandit", "Byte Warrior", "Paramount" and "Lamer Exterminator" are actually viruses; all others are anti-virus products which are earlier or rival systems.

On the IBM PC platform there have been a few cases of anti-virus viruses, one example being the Denzuk virus which contained (buggy) code to recognise and remove Brain virus variants.

In the Macintosh world the existence of the commoner nVIR strain is directly attributable to the recognition of an early destructive nVIR strain (occasionally referred to as nVIR C), which randomly removed files from the system folder. The person who detected the strain then modified the destructive nVIR strain to produce the (now ubiquitous) benign nVIR strain. The newer strains (including nVIR A which uses MacTalk to speak the words "Don't Panic!") beep when an infected system is rebooted or an infected application is launched (for nVIR A 1/16 and 15/128 probability of each, for nVIR B 1/8 and 7/32 probability of each).

5.5 Containment of Viral Code

Containment can be achieved via a variety of techniques mainly dependent on hardware support for correct operation. It is into this category that the mainframe security kernels belong, as do the cruder PC interrupt monitoring utilities.

5.5.1 Hardware Compartmentalisation

The most effective protection is provided by dedicated hardware techniques backed by formally verified secure kernels. This is an extremely costly technique. A limited hardware support environment is, however, available even in readily obtainable 80386 processors.

5.5.1.1 *Virtual Machine*

The virtual machine concept supported by the Intel 80386 (and 80486) chips is based on a simple idea: that of providing each user (human or program) of the machine with a segregated environment in which the user is unaware that he/she/it is sharing with other users. The user can access a subset of system memory, filestore and hardware peripherals which present a "virtual" machine to the user. The user cannot access any of the physical machines facilities which have been allocated to other user's "virtual" machines without the intervention of the operating system.

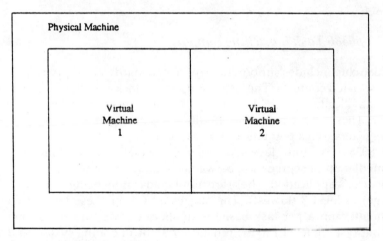

Each virtual machine comprises:

1. A virtual memory space which appears to the user as contiguous physical memory. Such virtual memory is a subset of the physical memory of the actual machine (in advanced versions data in part of the virtual memory space may be paged or swapped out onto secondary storage media; the operating system will manage reloading of data when the user accesses the section of memory which was paged out).

2. A virtual processor which appears to run only the user's program (this may include even concealing variations in loading caused by other virtual processors running on the same physical processor).

3. A set of virtual peripherals which permits use of a subset of disk space, and limited access to printers and communication facilities. Part of the physical disk appears to each user as his own (exclusive use) disk. Printout sent to printer devices is automatically spooled to prevent interference with other users of the printer (which is basically an exclusive access device).

This idealised virtual environment effectively isolates every user of the system. While totally preventing viral propagation across boundaries (except via external communication links), this does also inhibit useful exchange of data. Thus a limited number of closely controlled channels are provided which can cross virtual machine boundaries. Each channel is carefully monitored by operating system components which themselves execute in a privileged virtual machine.

The 80386 processor provides extensive hardware support for this concept including:

- Segment and paging support for virtual memory
- Task switching with automatic context switching
- Hierarchy of protection levels
- Privileged instruction

5.5.1.1.1 80386 Task Switching Support

The 80386 chip includes support for a number of hardware supported tasks and their associated contexts. The latter comprise a block of system registers which are automatically switched when processing transfers from one task to another. These registers include traditional data registers, memory management registers, stack pointers and privilege flags.

The 80386 has four levels of privilege which are fundamental to the implementation of segregation between components of the operating system and the user's application. These are numbered commencing at level 0 (highest privilege) to level 3 (lowest). The suggested use of these levels (which are implemented on a per task basis) is to allocate level 0 to the kernel of the operating system, level 1 to the remainder of the operating system and level 3 to applications, level 2 being retained for supervisory applications such as printer spooling, mail daemons or user level batch schedulers.

5.5.1.1.2 80386 Paged Segmented Memory

The 80386 chip when operating in protected mode (i.e. not 8086 emulation in real mode) provides the facility to establish complex mappings between the process virtual memory space and physical memory. These mappings are achieved via two levels.

Segmentation introduces the concept of a segment of memory which is a variable sized block of memory identified by a handle – the segment id. All memory references are expressed as a 48 bit address containing a 16 bit segment selector, and a 32 bit offset within the addressed segment. The segment may either be implicitly specified using the active segment value in the segment register appropriate to the transfer taking place (e.g. DS, the data segment register, or CS, the code segment register) or through an explicitly specified segment override.

15..0	31..0
Selector	Offset within segment

Each memory reference is mapped by the 80386 via one of two tables: a global descriptor table (GDT), and a local descriptor table (LDT). Each of these tables holds 2^{13} segment descriptors. When a memory access request is made the segment register associated with the address (e.g. ES) is used to index one of the two segment descriptor tables. The table accessed depends on the state of bit 2 in the segment register. If this bit is 0 then the GDT is accessed, otherwise the LDT.

The LDTs are context switched each time a change in executing task occurs, and thus permit task specific memory to be referenced. The GDT is global to all tasks within the system permitting access (under strictly controlled conditions) to data and memory in the virtual memory space of other tasks or the operating system.

Normal references to data or executable code are mapped by the 80386 by locating the segment referenced by the segment register associated with the address register being used to access the data or code. This is achieved by indexing the segment descriptor table entry specified by the selector, then accessing the location given by the base field of the segment descriptor plus the offset specified in program address register/program counter or stack pointer.

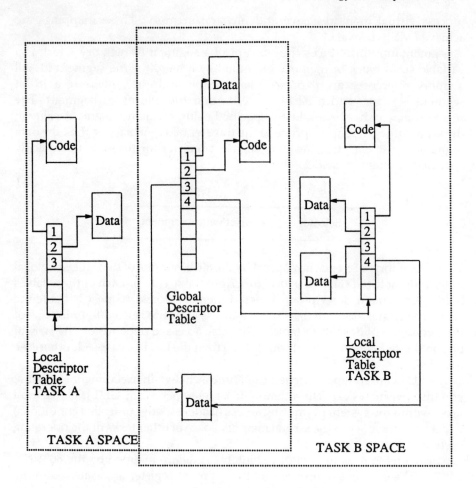

Illustration Of 80386 Descriptor Table Addressing

The format of the segment descriptor (for standard memory segments) is:

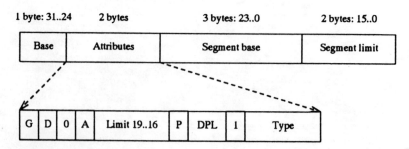

The fields which are important from a security viewpoint are:

Base	32 bit	Pointer to base of segment in linear memory
Limit	20 bit	Size of segment in bytes or pages
Granularity (G)	1 bit	Whether size is specified in bytes or pages (4K)
DPL	3 bit	Descriptor privilege level
Type	4 bit	Protection information for segment

Other fields are connected with memory management and the implementation of the illusion of virtual memory (which may require data to be transferred to and from backing store) in software.

First, during address translation the offset is verified against the segment limit value (causing an exception if in excess). This prevents addressing outside the memory segment boundary, such as overwriting the base of the stack.

Second (for executable code), the protection bits serve to control access to the associated segment. The current privilege level (CPL) of the task attempting the access to memory is checked against the descriptor privilege level (DPL). If the task has a privilege equal to the privilege of the descriptor then the access is allowed. Otherwise a protection violation is generated. Code segments can be marked as "conforming" in which case they will permit calls to be made when the CPL is greater than (remember 0 is the highest privilege) the DPL. This is the case when library routines (such as the maths library) are exported (from say ring 2) to an application (in ring 3).

Thus, memory can be effectively divided into segments at each level of privilege, i.e.:

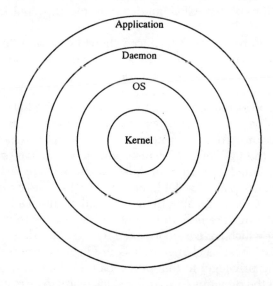

Furthermore, since each task has its own LDT, it can be further limited in the segments it can address. Thus each ring can be divided into further compartments restricted to the segments (at that privilege level) which can be accessed by the task.

Modification of descriptor tables is also a privileged operation. In fact the GDT contains segment descriptors which point to each LDT and determine the access allowable to the LDT.

5.5.1.1.3 Accessing OS Code

In the strict model above it is impossible to execute a code module which has a higher privilege level than the active application. In older processors with hardware protection levels this was implemented by generating an interrupt when the access was attempted. The interrupt would be processed by the processor in "supervisor" mode. In this mode the processor could determine by analysis of the saved registers on the stack whether this action is allowable. The processor could then service the interrupt request and return control (with consequent resetting of supervisor status on return) to the invoking "user" mode application. This was the technique used by the 68000 processor. This chip had two modes of operation (supervisor and user). The mode was signalled to the external memory management unit (MMU) using the chip function code lines. Thus, the MMU could flag a protection violation when the user attempted to access a location in the supervisor space. By reloading the MMU registers and CPU registers (in supervisor state) the operating system could affect a task switch. Certain basic instructions were inhibited in user mode (namely modification of the CPU mode and interrupt masks, stop and reset processor).

The 80386 processor introduced the concept of a "gate". The gate is a mechanism which permits the controlled execution of privileged subroutines or code by a user application. The gate is a special form of segment descriptor which contains an indirect pointer to a further code segment. When the user references a gate segment via the LDT or GDT, the user's CPL must be more or equally privileged to the gate descriptor's DPL. The gate descriptor contains a new segment selector which is used to again reference the LDT or GDT. This points to the actual code segment which will be executed. A further permission check is applied to ensure that the task's CPL is equal to the DPL, or vitally in the case of conforming code that the task's CPL is greater than or equal to the DPL (note calls to less privileged rings are not supported – only returns from procedures in the inner ring which have been invoked by the outer ring).

In the latter case a change in task privilege occurs as the CPL is lowered (increasing privilege) to that of the DPL of the called code. This includes storage of the previous CPL on the stack ready to be restored when a return is made. In summary, the sequence of access to a privileged system routine via the 80386 gate mechanism is:

1. Application segment register or segment override references a descriptor in the LDT or GDT which is flagged as a gate.
2. Check that the application's CPL is less than or equal to the gate's DPL, otherwise protection violation.
3. Use the new segment selector in the gate descriptor to access the LDT or GDT.
4. Check that the application's CPL is greater than or equal to the referenced descriptor's DPL.
5. If the application's CPL is greater than the descriptor's DPL then create a new stack saving the old CPL value, upgrade the CPL to the descriptor's DPL value.
6. Execute the code specified by the segment base in the referenced descriptor offset by the offset value specified in the gate descriptor.
7. On return restore the stack and the task's old CPL.

Thus, the gate concept allows the temporary raising of process privilege while executing an operating system function. The latter are carefully delimited through the creation (by the operating system when establishing a new task) of gate descriptors in the GDT or the per task LDT.

5.5.1.1.4 Segment Permissions

Finally, in addition to the privilege level ring mechanism and LDT compartment mechanisms, each descriptor carries a series of read/write/execute attributes. These are stored in the "type" field of the segment descriptor. The values available are:

Data segments		Code segments	
0	Read only	8	Execute only
1	Read only, accessed	9	Execute only, accessed
2	Read/write	A	Execute/read
3	Read/write, accessed	B	Execute/read, accessed
4	Read only, grow down	C	Execute only, conforming
5	Read only, grow down, accessed	D	Execute only, conforming, accessed
6	Read/write, grow down	E	Execute/read, conforming
7	Read/write, grow down, accessed	F	Execute/read, conforming, accessed

The attribute "accessed" records the fact that the segment has been written, read or executed. "Conforming" was described previously. The read, write and execute attributes provide fine control over the segments referenced by the descriptor. Note that descriptor table entries can only be changed by tasks with write permission to the LDT (referenced by the GDT), or in the case of the GDT programs at privilege level 0.

5.5.1.1.5 Paged Memory Operation

Below the segmented memory subsystem is the paging subsystem. Each segment may be further divided into 4 K pages of memory. A mapping can be established via the use of page tables held in RAM between each logical page within a segment and its actual physical address in memory.

This permits the operating system to page out blocks of user processes onto secondary storage. The entry in the page table is carefully marked with the address at which the 4 K block has been stored on backing store. Any access to this "paged out" block is trapped by the 80386 chip and causes an exception to be raised. This exception is trapped by the operating system, which then reloads the block and marks it as present in memory, permitting the 80386 to complete its memory access.

This powerful system permits the "virtual" memory to exceed that available on the system, by using disk as an extension of the memory space. It also permits a finer granularity of protection through the use of page level protection bits. Each page table entry (PTE) has two protection bits associated with it, namely the R/W (read/write bit) and the U/S (user/supervisor bit). These bits only restrict access at the lowest privilege level (level 3) and are bypassed by more privileged tasks. The U/S bit if set permits the page to be accessed by applications at level 3, otherwise only level 0–2 tasks can access the page. The R/W bit is set to indicate that a page can be read, written or executed. If reset it restricts access to reading or execution.

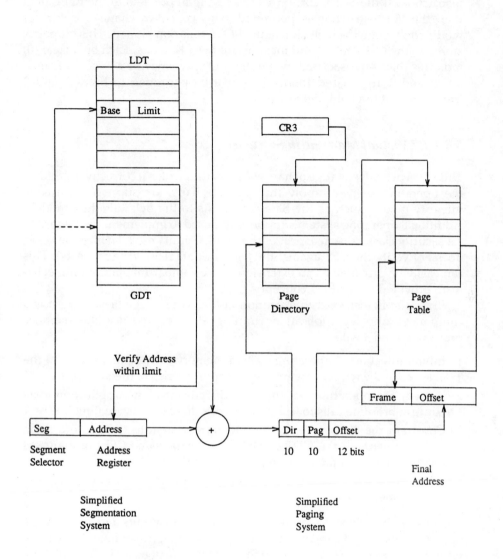

LDT

Base | Limit

CR3

GDT

Page
Directory

Page
Table

Verify Address
within limit

Frame | Offset

Seg | Address

+

Dir | Pag | Offset

Segment   Address
Selector   Register

10   10   12 bits

Final
Address

Simplified
Segmentation
System

Simplified
Paging
System

80386 Paged Segmented Memory Address Translation

5.5.1.1.6 Input/Output Operations

The 80386 next addresses the protection of I/O operations using the IN, INS, OUT and OUTS instructions. Each task when created has an IOPL (input/ output privilege level) stored in the EFLAGS register in the task context. This register determines the minimum privilege required to execute an I/O instruction. If the task's current CPL is less than or equal to the IOPL field then the I/O instruction is permitted. This coarse mechanism is further modified through the inclusion of the I/O permission bitmap. This bitmap is stored in the task context and includes up to 64 K of bits. Each bit if clear (0) indicates that the associated byte in the I/O space may be accessed. Thus if bits 2 and 3 are cleared then access will be permitted to bytes 2 and 3 irrespective of the IOPL field value.

5.5.1.1.7 Virtual Machine in Software

The 80386 provides a range of hardware facilities which if correctly utilised by the operating system supply the requisite hardware support for a code integrity model (such as the Biba extensions to the Bell-LaPadula model). Additional operating system support is required to implement the hierarchical security classification aspect of the Bell-LaPadula model (since the 80386 does not verify the CPL against the DPL for data read/write requests). This can easily be provided as an extension of the compartmentalisation mechanism provided by the LDT concept.

Viral code is restricted to execution at lowest privilege (assuming it is a component of user application running at level 3) since the memory protection model will:

1. Inhibit infection of operating system memory or code areas (due to the absence of the requisite segment descriptor entries in the task LDT).
2. Prevent the operating system from directly invoking application code (since subroutine calls to less privileged code segments are inhibited).
3. Constrain the virus' calls to the operating system to those conforming code segments in the GDT or task LDT (at the same CPL) or via gates defined by the operating system to higher privilege levels.
4. Inhibit access to external peripherals via the IOPL and I/O permission bitmask mechanisms.

Gates can be subject to careful access control constraints and audit by the operating system. This may, however, allow limited trojan horse activity by viruses invoking "risky" operating system functions via the call gate mechanism.

The memory management model outlined above also provides scope for the automatic verification of executable code checksums at task load time. The operating system maintains a public key encrypted vector of checksums for each executable segment in the task object file as a special segment. This special segment may either be generated by a trusted compiler (possibly after requesting a password from the user). The password is the private key used to encrypt the checksum vector for all executable code segments. When the kernel loads the task the public key part is used to decrypt the checksum vector, and each checksum is verified against the corresponding object code segment. As with any checksumming approach this implies existence of a trusted component in the system which handles the private key. It does however reduce the problem to verification of compiler integrity.

5.5.1.2 Automatic Flow Verification

A further approach to the automatic verification of program integrity is the use of signed flow graphs for each process. It has been proposed that a second co-processor be utilised to verify the operation of the main CPU. The primary function of the co-processor would be the verification that the CPU has not departed from the execution behaviour expected of the currently executing program. To detect such deviations the creation of a program flow monitor (PFM) was proposed. The PFM detects unexpected branches from the normal sequence of program execution (such as might be generated by a virus). To detect such branches each compiled program has a control flow graph (CFG) associated with it. The CFG is a signature which represents the flow of control within the associated program. Deviations can thus be detected by the co-processor.

A possible technique for CFG generation is to produce a graph which has as its leaves a checksum generated for each sequential (i.e. non-branching) sequence of instructions in the user program. The graph of checksums is then loaded at execution time onto the co-processor system. The support hardware then regenerates the checksum as the CPU executes the sequence of instructions. Whenever a branch is encountered the co-processor takes the current checksum and compares it with the stored checksum in the CFG. If the values differ then it can infer that a change in flow pattern has occurred. If the values remain identical then the co-processor can permit the main CPU to branch to the next sequential code block. The co-processor then fetches the next checksum value for this block and begins to recalculate the checksum as the CPU continues execution.

If the values differ the co-processor will abort the main CPU and record the location of the deviation for further analysis. The program may be restarted to determine if this is a transient variation (possibly caused by a memory parity error) or a permanent variation representing a change in executable code. The co-processor may be relieved of the work of checksum generation by using a hardware linear feedback shift register (LFSR) to generate a CRC polynomial.

It has been further suggested that one of a variety of checksums be selected at compile time, and that the LFSR generator be programmed with the checksum characteristic. The CFG and perturbation characteristic are encrypted for further protection. This verification scheme (as with the cryptographic schemes) does not rely solely on write-protection of code files to ensure system integrity maintenance.

In CFG schemes which do not employ encryption using user supplied keys, a possible attack scheme has been proposed. This scheme, known as "back track", relies on the fact that the assembler is considered trusted (i.e. has access to the CFG encryption keys). Thus a possible way in which the virus can forge the CFG is to:

1. Disassemble the executable (or indeed decompile).
2. Add the virus to the disassembled assembly code.
3. Assemble and re-link (this process generates a new valid signed CFG).
4. Replace the old version with the forged infected version.

In general, if a route can be found to the source code (either by decompilation or by direct access to the appropriate file) then it can be tampered with and then recompiled.

5.5.1.3 Software Distribution: Ensuring Trust

The encryption and CFG approaches can both be used with public key systems to verify the integrity of distributed software. This operates by encrypting software using the vendor's private key (or possibly just the checksum or CFG value). This software is then loaded and verified at loadtime (using the checksums decrypted by the vendor's public key) or at runtime (using the CFG). A hierarchy of trust backed by the assurance of tamper free distribution can thus be established.

5.5.2 Software Compartmentalisation

The previous methods have effectively relied on hardware to support a basic protection model or to support flow verification. This section addresses the extensions to the existing software environments which are necessary to contain viral code.

The first cases considered are those methods appropriate as a stopgap in operating systems which are not designed for security (em, PC-DOS!). Consideration is then given to how such systems can be redesigned to conform to a formal security model.

5.5.2.1 Interrupt Trapping Code

The first technique (commonly used by PC anti-viral utilities) is to attempt to intercept all system activity through the use of interrupt vector trapping utilities. As previously mentioned, all DOS system (and Mac OS/toolbox) calls are routed via an interrupt vector table. By revectoring all significant interrupts it is possible to intercept all system activity.

The interrupt vector monitor thus re-vectors all interrupts to point to its own code. Thus a virus invoking Int 21h (the DOS service interrupt) will cause a branch to the monitor routine in RAM. The monitor can then screen potentially unacceptable behaviour such as writing to executable files.

On detecting "suspect" or "risky" behaviour the monitor will generate a warning message on the user's screen, and request whether the user wishes to permit such activity to continue. This infers that a trusted channel exists for the messages produced by the monitor, and the user's responses to such messages. If this is not the case then the monitor's messages may be intercepted by the active viral code, and suitable responses inserted directly into the keyboard buffer on the target system. (The general issue of ensuring that a trusted path exists between the security kernel and the user is addressed by the B-2 TCSEC criteria. These criteria include a further requirement that such a trusted channel is uniquely identifiable and distinct from all other communication channels.)

In general, interrupt monitors provide a useful tool in non-development environments. In environments where active development is under way, a significant number of false alarms can be generated, which may screen illegitimate virus activity. For instance in the typical "edit-compile-run" development environment, a significant number of writes (admittedly by trusted compilers) are generated to code files.

5.5.2.1.1 Configurable Monitors

To be useful in such a development environment, the interrupt monitor must be configured to permit trusted utilities to execute certain functions without user intervention. An example is the "gatekeeper" public domain software package on the Apple Macintosh. This package traps all attempts to modify or amend:

File attributes:	Self	System	Other
Resource information:	Self	System	Other

In this case events are divided into two categories: file attribute modification and amendment of resource contents. Each program is permitted to modify either file attributes or resources for itself, system files or all other files. When a program attempts a monitored operation (such as adding a new CODE segment to a resource fork) the gatekeeper will trap the request and verify the program's name against the access control list configured with the utility. If access is denied (i.e. the user has not configured the utility to permit the program to carry out that category of operation) an alert will be presented and the user prompted for a decision.

Careful configuration of such a utility is required, but once in place it can prove extremely successful. Examples of functions permitted to programs may include:

• Permit trusted programs such as binary editors, compilers and linkers to write executable code resources

- Permit resource editors general rights to modify resources
- Permit certain self-modifying utilities rights to modify their own code (a common practice when programs carry internal configuration information in their executable files, an example being paths to various files)

A typical list of trusted program utilities might include:

- Binary editors: can alter executable code
- File manipulation utilities: can alter file attributes
- Disk backup software: can write to executable files and manipulate file attributes
- Compilers, linkers: can write to executable files
- Archive maintenance utilities: can write to executable files and manipulate file attributes
- Executable manipulation utilities (e.g. stripping symbol table): can alter executable files
- Patching utilities: can write to executable code

Such configurable utilities normally come with lists of privileges required by standard programs, together with a simple facility to add such privileges. It should be noted that when powerful binary editing or manipulation services are available these may be used by a virus to bypass the restrictions, i.e. virus runs trusted program (e.g. DEBUG) which can write executable files.

The concepts of trusted channels and the grouping of objects in the file system by type have been fundamental to integrity schemes such as the F6 Information Technology Security Evaluation Criteria (ITSEC) high integrity scheme (described in Chapter 7) and the Burroughs file system architecture. In the latter case every file has a file type which reflects the program which created the file. Certain file types (mainly executable) could only be created by trusted system compilers. The compilers thus provided a barrier to direct manipulation of executable code.

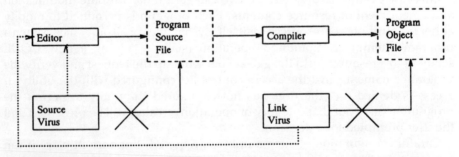

Only trusted components may modify specific file types. Dotted lines indicate reverse engineering of object, which may permit a virus to insert itself by source modification. To complete trust, the editor must be invoked by the user via a trusted channel mechanism.

5.5.2.1.2 *Operation of a Monitor*

A monitor utility redirects one or more system interrupts (or traps) when it begins operation. These interrupts are changed to invoke the monitor utility's code. The monitor screens the interrupt request and then passes control (if the request is permitted) to the operating system.

In the IBM PC, for instance, a monitor would intercept the BIOS and DOS service interrupts (including such auxiliary DOS interrupts as the absolute disk read and write interrupts).

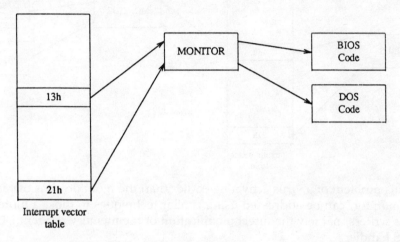

The point at which such a monitor becomes active is crucial in that a virus must become active after the monitor for the latter to be effective. For instance, if the virus is resident before the monitor (and has intercepted the DOS/BIOS interrupts) and then the monitor becomes active, we have:

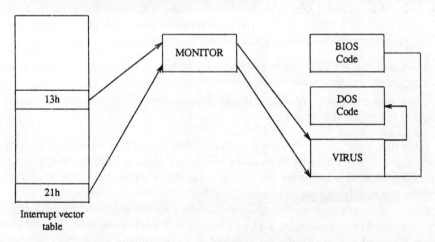

The virus may thus use the unaltered DOS and BIOS interrupt calls. If the virus becomes active after the monitor is resident in memory, then the monitor will be effective. The virus redirects the DOS/BIOS interrupts to point to its own code, and executes its infection/manipulation task. During this task any services it requests of DOS/BIOS will be made via the interrupt address – which points to the monitor. Thus the monitor is effective. The monitor cannot, however, prevent viral code from being invoked: it can only prevent the virus utilising DOS/BIOS services via the conventional route.

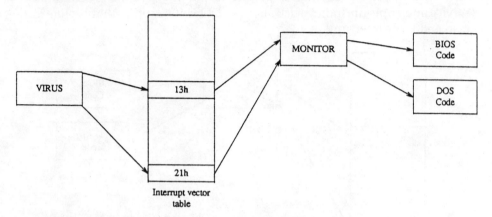

Interrupt vector
table

This problem of a virus activating earlier than the monitor, thus bypassing the monitor, can be addressed using similar techniques to those adopted by virus writers, namely the direct modification of the memory resident DOS or BIOS handler.

The monitor patches the DOS handler to contain a jump to the monitor routine, storing the original bytes (which were modified) in a storage location. Thus, irrespective of the time at which the virus becomes resident, it will cause a jump to be made to the monitor. The monitor executes its code, and then executes the stored DOS handler instructions followed by a jump to the remainder of the DOS handler. This technique requires a degree of knowledge of the structure of a particular DOS release to permit:

1. Location of the DOS handler in memory, without relying on the potentially compromised interrupt table pointer.
2. Determination of a suitable strategy for ensuring that the original handler code is executed correctly.

With the presence of viruses which also alter the DOS handler it becomes once more a race between virus and anti-virus program. Specifically, if a virus alters the DOS handler after the monitor has modified the handler, it will gain control but will be subject to monitoring by the monitor.

A hack is to arrange for the monitor to use a number of interrupts, some of which would not be used by a virus (i.e. clock, mouse or video). The monitor when invoked can verify the integrity of its "tap" on the main DOS and BIOS interrupt vectors and if these have been disconnected reconnect them. This technique was used by a multi-tasking virus on the Commodore Amiga which consisted of two tasks. One was the actual virus, the second a simple utility which verified that the virus was still in control and connected to the interrupt vectors. If this was not the case the virus was reconnected.

5.5.2.1.3 Extensions to Real Time Monitoring

While not strictly part of viral containment, it should be noted that the resident monitor can be extended to carry out incremental scanning of memory for viral code, checksumming of critical system areas and validation of the interrupt vector table. Such a utility would provide a degree of "defence in depth" by acting as a monitoring utility, virus scanner and checksum verification utility.

5.5.2.2 OS Support

It is greatly preferable for an operating system to provide (with hardware support) an extensive security environment which permits the establishment of user specified compartments within the system. Such compartments may reflect natural divisions in function or data, or be driven by confidentiality or integrity requirements. Often such software compartments may serve as a cost effective substitute for organisational compartmentalisation or segregation.

A number of formal security models which are appropriate to a mainframe or mini computer system with hardware support (e.g. an 80386 processor) are addressed in Chapter 7. These models reflect the commercial or military requirements for data confidentiality and integrity.

5.5.3 Network Compartmentalisation

With the advent of networks many of the physical compartments which had existed either strictly through machine segregation or effectively (due to constraints on physical movement of media between systems) were removed. Networks permit interconnectivity and are thus opposed to compartmentalisation. A natural trade-off between the obvious benefits of information exchange and the risks of information compromise or alteration exists.

Network software normally permits the establishment of barriers between systems which restrict information flow. Normally such barriers are estab lished at "gateway" hosts which link smaller LANs. Such gateways may run an extremely restricted range of carefully verified software, providing a minimal (and management approved) range of services. In general, a careful management decision needs to be made about the benefits of close or loosely coupled networks, based partly on an assessment of the value of the service and partly on the integrity of the networks being interconnected.

The principal network protocols are considered in Chapter 8, which gives a detailed introduction to the problem of virus propagation via networks. At this time it is sufficient to note that a significant risk attaches to uncontrolled file server systems.

In such open file servers a virus infected file may be uploaded or written. This file is then instantly available to all other client systems. If the file server is transparent then a virus on a client system may infect any of the files from the server.It is vital that the software environment on the server is configured to restrict access by clients to read-only. The need for careful configuration again adds weight to the case for the server being under the direct supervision and administration of the systems group (possibly even the computer security group) within an organisation.

Without a file server it requires the explicit action of a user to transfer a virus: with a transparent file server the virus can spread organisation-wide in a matter of seconds.

Used carefully, a file server can provide an extremely secure repository of software. If anti-virus software is operational on the server it can provide a high level of assurance that software used by the organisation is clean, and permit an infected system to be booted easily to a clean state from which disinfection of local disks can begin. The security environment on the server can often permit detection of viruses active on client systems (by detecting suspicious write requests to executables on the server originating from an infected client).

The ultimate solution is of course to completely centralise file storage on a single (or group of) server which is closely controlled. All other nodes are diskless or at the least have a security environment at startup (booted by network from the server) which inhibits the introduction of executable code.

5.5.4 Investigation and Response

Finally, it must be accepted that a virus infection may occur. If this happens the structure to react to the incident rapidly and effectively must be in place. Such a structure must permit rapid analysis of the threat, rapid dissemination of advice and counter measures, supervision of disinfection or removal of the virus infection (or trojan horse) and, finally, recovery of damaged programs or data. Such a response must also address the difficult area of maintaining confidence (client, employee or public) in the company. The public relations issues are addressed later in the section on recovery from viral infection. At the moment we will concentrate on investigation, determination of the extent of spread, and dissemination of information on the virus infection.

5.5.4.1 What is the Infection?

The first question must be to determine the type of the infection. This can be achieved in most cases through the use of virus specific scanning software. These utilities will recognise an infection by its signature or by checksum comparison with known virus samples. This will permit reference to be made to one of the many catalogues of known viruses, and an assessment of the potential damage which the strain may cause.

In a few cases, however, it will be necessary to analyse the sample either using on-site expertise or with the co-operation of one of the many specialist firms consulting in anti-virus measures. The latter is often preferable because virus disassembly is highly specialised. Many viruses utilise common techniques which are well known within the anti-virus community.

Analysis comprises:

1. Acquisition of an active sample.
2. Logging of all information relating to the infection: unexplained activity, corrupted data files, etc.
3. Disassembly of the sample.
4. Assessment of the risk based on the disassembled virus.

In some cases where the virus appears to be destroying data or programs it may be necessary to issue warnings based purely on symptoms or initial testing of the virus under supervision. Such testing provides an incomplete picture of the virus' operation because of the complexity of the activation criteria of many viruses, an example being the Italian or Bouncing Ball virus.

The Italian virus has a small activation window during which it will display its characteristic display of a small ball (a rhombus character 07h in the IBM set) bouncing off the boundaries of the screen and moving through all text on the screen. This window occurs every 30 minutes and lasts 1 second. If a disk access occurs inside this window the effect will be activated.

Testing will normally include the accelerated advancement of the system clock to detect manipulations (possibly destructive) on fixed dates.

5.5.4.1.1 Acquisition

First, it is necessary to acquire a sample for analysis. In many cases this can be as straightforward as copying an infected program to a floppy disk. In the case of boot sector infectors it may require a series of operations to be carried out on the newly inserted sampling media before it becomes infected (e.g. directory listings, file copies back and forth between media). In the case of specialist infectors the COMMAND.COM or system files may have to be copied to the floppy disk.

If a boot sector virus is not prepared to infect the media, it becomes necessary to take an exact copy of the boot sector and any likely auxiliary sectors (the determination of which sectors should be dumped is complicated by viruses such as Denzuk which use specially formatted tracks). At the very least this should include the master boot record and DOS boot records. Ideally a complete sector by sector copy should be made of the disk (if it is an infected floppy). Such a copy must be done on a clean system (witness the camouflage attempts by Brain which involve returning the user an uninfected copy of the boot sector).

The transfer of infections by electronic means is even more complex. In the case of boot sector viruses, utilities are available which will take a complete image of a disk, compress it to save space, and store the resultant information as a standard file which can be downloaded.

5.5.4.1.2 Logging of Relevant Information

All unusual activity should be logged. This should include the determination of which files have been corrupted (if any) by the virus. A selection of these files should be copied for analysis. This is particularly the case with such viruses as "dBase" which cause corruption that can easily be reversed. Analysis of such files may permit a simple data recovery utility to be produced. Logs should include information on the detailed system configuration on which the virus was detected as being active. This should as a minimum include: machine type, memory configuration, processor type, active memory resident programs and peripheral types (disks, screen drivers etc).

At this stage it is also necessary to carefully keep track of the actions taken in sampling from, and subsequent analysis of, the infected system. Introduction of computer viruses is a criminal offence under the Computer Misuse Act. If at a later date it is decided that the company wishes to report the incident and press for a prosecution by the police, then accurate records will be required in court which indicate:

1. Which systems were infected.
2. Extent of damage caused by the infection.
3. Means used to determine the cause of the infection.
4. Loss due to the infection (including the programmer time spent in analysing the virus, and due to system downtime).

5.5.4.1.3 Disassembly

To be certain of the effects of a virus, it is necessary to disassemble the virus, and then to analyse the resultant assembly (or high level) language. To aid in this work a wide range of tools are available, including:

1. Software debuggers, which are resident in the system and permit single stepping and breakpointing during execution of the virus, the contents of the processor registers being displayed on screen.
2. Disassemblers, which will disassemble a block of code on disk or in memory.
3. Hardware debuggers, which use additional specialist hardware to monitor the activity of the processor, and permit hardware single step and breakpoint facilities by directly manipulating the processor bus.

4. In-circuit emulators (ICE), which directly emulate the execution of the processor in real time, permitting extensive tracing of memory accesses, instructions executed and processor timing behaviour.

Each of the above has its own disadvantages and advantages. These are summarised below:

1. Software debuggers. The virus is active while being debugged and can thus attempt to detect debugging activity and to combat the operation of the debugger. This includes the use of the instruction pipeline detection technique in Chapter 4, the modification of the single step and breakpoint interrupts used by the actual debugger and interference with debugger code in memory, keyboard buffers or screen displays. Software debugging is inexpensive, but can be combatted by newer viruses, the so-called "armoured" viruses.

2. Disassemblers. These can operate on static inactive copies of infected files. They thus have the advantage that no malicious activity by the virus will be invoked. The major difficulty is the extensive (often multi-level) encryption that viruses are adopting. This encryption, while aimed at frustrating signature recognition, also complicates disassembly. No plaintext instructions are visible in the infected file other than the decryptor. The person analysing the virus is therefore required to analyse the decryptor, decrypt the remainder of the virus, and then proceed with disassembly. Self-modifying viruses also slow down the process of disassembly. The decompilation stage can be taken one step further (particularly when the virus is written in a high level language) by decompiling the assembly code to produce a program in a high level language. Decompilers are complex, and apply a large variety of heuristics to determine the structure of the iterative and conditional programming constructs which generated the original virus code. Such utilities may be subject to export controls similar to those imposed on cryptographic software.

3. Hardware debuggers. These are potentially more powerful than software debuggers as they are not subject to interference by the active virus. They are, however, not executing in real time and as such are subject to detection by the virus using careful observation of external system events (such as the system clock). This technique was commonly used by software protection code to detect the use of such devices. Hardware debuggers are also more expensive than their software cousins, costing in the region of £100–£1000. Debuggers normally rely on the bus contention logic in the processor by manipulating the system bus. This permits the processor to be suspended after a single instruction or at a particular location. All address and data on the system buses are also readily visible (and recordable). The use of hardware debuggers may be subject to UK copyright legislation, preventing the availability of such devices, or restricting their use in reverse engineering code.

4. ICE. Finally, the most expensive mechanism is the ICE. This device executes the full instruction set of the processor being emulated. In fact, the device directly replaces the processor (hence the term "in-circuit"). The device may permit clocking of the emulator at a speed comparable with the target processor

on slow system architectures, thus frustrating detection using timing attacks. The emulator can accurately determine the sequence of instructions executed by the processor and permits advanced debugging. ICE devices are extremely expensive, often costing tens of thousands of pounds.

An alternative (and highly specialist) approach is to produce accurate simulations of the entire system environments (processor, memory, clocks, peripheral drivers, etc.) in software. Such simulators permit the virus code to be introduced, and its effects to be carefully monitored in virtual time through software simulation of each instruction. The virtual time concept permits the simulator to mimic exactly the timing of each system component (admittedly, a single microsecond of processor time may take milliseconds or whole seconds of simulator time). A variety of system configurations may be tested by simple modification of the software carrying out the simulation.

Simulators provide facilities for exhaustive testing of viruses: they are, however, expensive to develop and require significant time to execute the simulation. Development of such simulators is under way at the University of Queensland for the purposes of detailed viral analysis.

5.5.4.2 Dissemination of Information

Following initial detection of the virus, there is often an immediate need to react to the infection. This is particularly the case if the virus is unknown or known to be damaging or destructive. In these cases it is necessary to issue a warning within the organisation concerning the possible implications of the virus. Before issuing such a warning consider:

- What will the impact of the warning be on employees? Will they be capable of acting to combat the threat, or does disinfection require specialist technical knowledge?
- What will the effect of the warning on customer confidence be? Hand and hand goes an assessment of the risk of the infection being spread to customers
- If (and this is an assumption with large organisations) the warning is passed to the press, will it cause a loss of confidence in the company which may affect future business or current stock values?
- What is the potential loss to the company caused by damaged data, lost programs and denial of machine service?

Each of the above factors must be considered before the warning is authorised, the detailed technical information in the warning is decided, and the potential audience determined.

It is advisable to issue an immediate brief warning if the threat is significant. This warning will just note that a virus has been detected (possibly giving the strain if the user community is knowledgeable), giving symptoms and a contact point to which any possible infections should be reported. Such a warning might also re-iterate good anti-viral precautions. Initial disinfection work can begin at this point, as can tracing of possible introduction channels for the infection.

A release of a specialist signature detector for the virus may be considered at this point if the virus will potentially evade detection by the anti-virus software in use within the company.

When detailed analysis has reached the stage at which the virus can be positively identified, specialist software to disinfect this particular virus and to repair damaged or corrupt data may be made available.

In each case a balance should be struck between the level of technical information made available to the user, and that required by the user. Certainly the distribution of disassembled or decompiled source would be unwise, possibly in breach of professional codes of conduct, and open to consideration as an incitement to breach the Computer Misuse Act. Information about the symptoms, identity and procedures for the removal of the virus can normally be justified. Where the virus' identification as a particular strain would cause unjustified "panic" or ill reaction then it may be possible to suppress the identity by allocation of an in-house identifier. It should be borne in mind that virus catalogues are widely available (certainly at academic or regular bulletin board using corporate sites) and an in-house identifier will be discovered, and the correct virus strain determined.

Consideration should also be given to distribution of samples (particularly for new viruses) to the research community. If necessary, anonymous "donations" will be accepted by most researchers, although some information on the effects and extent of spread would be of use. Information on research establishments working in the area of computer viruses is given in Appendix 14.

The police force also wishes to be informed of any virus infections so that a dossier of damage caused by each virus can be compiled for future criminal proceedings.

5.5.4.3 General Containment

Finally, general containment may include segregation of infected systems, temporary suspension of network services or external gateways, temporary controls on the traffic in storage media, and the removal of computers from corporate sites.

Infected systems should be isolated immediately from other clean systems to prevent further infection. Similarly, infected networks should be isolated from other networks within the company. An assessment of the damage caused by the potential spread of the virus against the denial of service caused may temper this disconnection policy.

Backups should immediately be taken of any system with an unidentified virus or worm active. This will permit recovery of data in the event of loss or corruption due to viral activation. These backups should be marked as infected and segregated from all other backups on the system. In the case of infection by a known or easily identifiable virus, or in which the value of data is insignificant, backups may be avoided.

Network disconnection may be partly avoided by installation of filters on server or gateway machines. Such filters can flag infected code *en route* via the network and abort the transfer. It must be borne in mind that a large variety of transfer mechanisms exist, often with mutually exclusive protocols. In this case the filter can be established at:

1. Application layer: for specific applications such as networked filing systems, remote copy facilities or electronic mail services.
2. Network layer: to screen all data *en route* to external sites.
3. Data link layer: to screen all outgoing data.

The possibility of false drops should be borne in mind. The patterns should thus be sufficiently long and discriminating to minimise this possibility.

Where a high level of infection exists it may be necessary to segregate specific systems from the network, not because of infection, but because of the risk that they may become infected. Thus, high integrity systems may be isolated from the network while disinfection of general access systems is under way.

Infections should thus lead to a re-assessment of the requirements for network and physical data compartmentalisation.

As a footnote it is worth mentioning that disconnection of gateways in the face of wide area network worm propagation may significantly inhibit the flow of information from the network community on combating the worm. It is therefore preferable to offer a limited gateway service (probably restricted to email) on a system whose architecture is not attacked by the worm. Such an example might be a XENIX system during the Internet worm attack.

5.5.4.4 Tracing of Infection Source

A final component of investigation and response must be the tracing of the infection to original source, and determination of the extent of spread both within and without the organisation. The logs of software installation can be used, together with file modification date/timestamps (if these were not reset by the virus) to establish the spread within a system, and the possible source of the infection.

Normally, however, a virus will reset the timestamps on infected files. In this case recourse to the reports of unusual behaviour must be made, coupled with scans of old backups to determine the date of infection.

Once a date of infection has been determined the flow of software to and from the system can be analysed. Software installed immediately before the initial infection date is obviously a prime candidate (although bear in mind the possibility of a trojan horse releasing a virus, in which case the trojan may still be resident on the system). Systems within the organisation can be placed in a tree structure based on the date of infection, the initial point of infection forming the root of the tree. Software traffic from infected systems must be traced. This includes the location and disinfection of potentially infected backups, and the tracing of disks which have left the site or organisation.

Basically, the tracing of infection is a slow, hierarchical process, beginning with determination of the system's point of infection, and the initial file infected. It continues with determination of the organisation's point of infection, and the initial system infected.

Certain viruses can carry version numbers, generation numbers or other information which can permit determination of the order or source of infection. The Yale boot sector virus, for instance, carried a generation counter in the infected boot sector which was decremented between each generation. A noteworthy example of a virus capable of being traced to source is the "Traceback" virus.

The Traceback virus was an IBM PC direct and indirect file infector. After 5 December 1988 the virus would begin to scan the system directory when executed. If a COM or EXE file was found it would be infected. If an existing infected file was discovered then the virus would scan the current directory for a file to infect. When the file is infected by the direct search technique a buffer within the written virus code will contain the full directory path of the file being infected. However when the virus infected using the indirect method (trapping the load DOS subfunction) this string would be unaltered. Thus the infected file would contain the directory path of the file which infected it, permitting a limited tracing of infection – hence the virus' common name, Traceback.

In addition, archives created on disk as backups will normally not be subject to later infection. They can thus be unpacked and checked for infection at the time the archive was built.

Hruska provides a brief summary of the characteristics of a computer virus which may be an aid to further investigation and tracing of infection sources. His list includes:

- Characteristics of assembler used (for instance the idiosyncratic assembly instructions generated by the A86 public domain assembler were detected in the Yale virus)
- Use of hardware specific features such as processor dependent opcodes or pre-fetch pipeline characteristics
- General programming style such as register and stack use preferences, techniques to TSR, clear register blocks, etc.
- Language and spelling of text messages within the virus
- Place and time of initial detection
- Traceable ancestors using compatible signature techniques or common code blocks

All of the above can possibly point to the author of the virus, or at least establish common authorship. The most obvious indication is, however, the specific targeting of the virus (such as the Scores virus) against a product or products of a particular firm.

5.5.5 Disinfection of Viral Code

This section deals with the procedures to disinfect an infected system, and by extension an infected network. Disinfection can be achieved by system re-installation (either complete or restricted to infected components), or by the use of virus specific disinfection software.

5.5.5.1 Re-installation

Re-installation requires access to an uninfected backup or write-protected master diskette. In the extreme case where no critical data has been lost between backups, then re- installation may be complete. This consists of performing a cold reboot of the infected system using a write-protected system master disk. A copy of the format is then run from a clean master disk to reformat all connected hard disk media. All software is then restored from the original master diskettes (preferable) or from an uninfected system backup. All data is restored from the latest backup (if the virus does not corrupt data) or, if necessary, from earlier backups.

The procedure (and requirements) can be summarised as:

1. Switch the infected system off for at least 30 seconds.
2. Boot from a clean write-protected system master disk (which should include clean format, virus scanning, restore and copy programs).
3. Run the format utility from the system master disk to reformat all connected drives.
4. Re-install all software from original master diskettes.
5. If software cannot be installed from master then insert latest backup, scan for virus infection using scanner on system master disk, if clean then copy to reformatted disk, otherwise use next youngest backup.
6. Re-install data from last backup. If a data corrupting virus is present then installation from earlier backups may be necessary.

Partial re-installation to replace infected utilities may be possible. In this case proceed as above, except the master diskette should also contain a delete or remove program (preferably one which scrubs the sectors belonging to the deleted file, rather than just marking the file as deleted in the directory). At stage 3, delete all infected programs rather than reformatting connected drives. In the case of boot sector viruses use the "SYS" DOS command or equivalent (e.g. M-DISK public domain utility) to replace the boot sector on each connected drive with uninfected code.

It should also be noted that formatting occurs at two levels on most IBM PC systems, namely:

1. Low level format: all tracks on the media are erased and a new pattern of sectors laid down.
2. High level format (or logical format): a new boot sector is generated, the FAT table and root directories are cleared.

High level formatting is carried out via the standard DOS format. Low level formatting must be invoked using a device dependent call via the DEBUG or HFS commands. Execution of the DOS format command on a floppy disk carries out a low level format, followed by a logical format.

Low level formatting is expensive in terms of time, and is not required to disconnect a boot sector virus from the execution path. The DOS format command will replace the boot sector with a clean copy, and will ensure that the original data is no longer accessible from DOS. A low level format does, however, give the assurance that the data on disk has been scrubbed and erased, and thus no fragments of virus code can be read using low level BIOS calls.

5.5.5.2 Recompilation from Source

An alternative to re-installation from master diskettes or saved backups is to recompile from source. This implies that all programs in the compilation path must be uninfected, including compilers, linkers, and object manipulation utilities (such as symbol table strippers).

Recompilation from source using trusted components can provide a high level of assurance that the resultant executables are uninfected. This also has the advantage of reducing the requirement for inspection of incoming code for viruses. It becomes sufficient to screen a subset of operating system utilities together with the compilation path. This can include inspections of the programs for potentially suspect code sequences or testing on a sacrificial machine.

The trusted compiler may then be used in a clean system environment to generate clean object files (assuming of course that a source code virus is not active).

5.5.6 Checking for Re-infection

A vital part of an attempted disinfection must be monitoring for re-infection. Even with the most careful disinfection of hard disks it is likely that re-infection will occur from floppy or other removable media in the hands of users. Such media should therefore be screened (often impractical due to the large number of such floppies, although bulk loaders are available to speed the disinfection process), failing which software should be installed on the clean system to prevent re-infection from an infected floppy (a simple example might be installation at boot time of a resident monitoring utility which is known to detect the virus).

Checks should be made at regular intervals after disinfection to ensure that the protection in place is proving sufficient. This can be delegated by educating end users or junior managers in the operation of the virus scanning utilities. Utilities can be optimised (if necessary) to scan for the single virus being monitored – this will result in a significant speedup.

5.5.7 Disinfection Utilities

Finally, disinfection utilities are available both commercially and in the public domain to remove a virus from an infected file. Such disinfection utilities are useful as an emergency measure when backups or original masters are not available. Disinfection in COM files is normally possible via a general or specific technique, i.e.:

- Specific. Using knowledge of the particular structure of a virus to determine where the saved jump or first few bytes of the original host are stored within the virus. These bytes can then be restored. The infected host can then be truncated to its original length, effectively discarding the virus code.

- General. General techniques rely on analysis of the virus to determine the start of the host program. Specifically, if the original object file consists of a jump over an area of static initialisation data, then this stored jump instruction can be located within the appended virus, and restored. This can be as simplistic as scanning for a jump to the host program within the virus code.

Disinfection in EXE files tends to be more unreliable due to rounding of file sizes to paragraph boundaries, coupled with the common problem of an erroneous length specification in the EXE file header. The latter has in the past led to viruses overwriting part of the host file, and effectively causing no visible extension of the host.

Finally, the alteration of the host program may not be directly reversable because of corruption by the virus. In these case limited patching of the utility may be possible.

An important point when disinfecting an application is that the virus code should be purged from the infected file. This prevents a hostile or malicious user from reconnecting the residual virus code. Ideally, therefore, an infected file should be truncated, and the area beyond the new logical EOF but within the physical EOF scrubbed.

5.6 Recovery from Viral Infection

The final section in this chapter deals with ensuring a rapid and complete recovery from viral infection. This section is divided into three topics:

1. Backup and recovery procedures.
2. Contingency planning.
3. Remedial action.

5.6.1 Backup Procedures

Backups should be regularly taken of all systems which require data integrity or protection against denial of service. The frequency of backups may be variable, depending on the value of data stored on the system. This might include:

- Monthly backups on public access low integrity systems, or demonstration systems
- Weekly backups on casual use, general or archive sites
- Daily backups on critical development systems and line of business systems
- More frequent backups on integrity critical systems

Basically, the cost in terms of personnel (to take backups) and lost time (due to reduced system performance or downtime) together with the cost of magnetic media must be offset against the risk to the organisation of data loss (either directly via failure of system operation, indirectly via contract penalties or via litigation for failure to provide services).

The most extreme cases may be traffic control services where system recovery without data loss may be vital. Such issues are often addressed by redundancy in system design, standby machines, etc. At the other extreme, public access systems may have no requirement for data integrity, in which case the system may be restarted, the disk reformatted, and the operational software re-installed from master diskettes.

Between these two extremes lie most systems. It is worth noting that automated backup systems can take much of the time and effort out of taking backups – these included automated backing up of live systems (once a specified amount of data change has occurred), use of bulk storage WORM devices, etc.

Viruses and trojan horses introduce no further requirements in terms of frequency of data and program backup. They do, however, introduce a requirement to retain long term backups to permit fallbacks in cases where recent backups are infected, or data has been incrementally corrupted.

A number of tiered incremental backup strategies exist, including simple strategies such as:

Day	1	2	3	4	5	6	7	8	9	10	11	12
Level	1	2	1	3	1	2	1	4	1	2	1	3

in which each higher level of backup includes all files modified since the last backup at that level or above. Thus, a level 3 backup stores all changes since the last level 3 or 4 backup. A level 1 backup stores all changes since the last backup (irrespective of level). This strategy minimises the number of backups which must be retained and minimises the number of backups which must be applied to return the system to a valid state. This scheme may, for instance, be applied over a month, with a full backup at the start of the month, and tiered incremental daily backups at 5 levels over the remainder of the month. Thus, any failure would require (at most) restoration of level 5, 4, 3, 2 and 1 backups. This requires five tapes for the active month and one tape per inactive month, and provides the ability to backtrack for a minimum of 14 days using early backups.

Backups should always be verified after writing. There have been a large number of cases in which organisations have generated backups which were then carefully stored. Months later when the backup was restored it was discovered that:

1. A tape was too short for the amount of data to be backed up, no error message had been generated when the backup was aborted.
2. The head or transport mechanism on the drive was faulty and the tape had not been written.

Very high density storage media can be fairly drive specific, so while the original drive may re-read the data, other similar drives may not do so. A trial on a separate system should be attempted.

Backups should be accelerated during critical project developments or prior to important demonstrations. It is during this period that the risks from data corruption are greatest, and the impact of a disgruntled employee can be most effective.

5.7 Contingency Planning

Contingency planning addresses a wide range of issues in an organisation's response to the viral threat. Many issues, such as the organisation of a virus response team, have been addressed elsewhere in the chapter. The issues considered here are:

- Redundancy and reserve system configurations
- Insurance

- Public and media relations

The first item is concerned with making provision of continued operation of the organisation's computing facilities, the second with compensation for failure to continue operation.

5.7.1 Redundancy

Key systems should be identified within the organisation. If they are easily accessible then they may be at risk from malicious software. In this case a decision must be made whether to reduce accessibility or to make provision for reserve systems. The reserve systems can rapidly be brought up and into operation following activation of malicious software. Ideally the environments on both systems should be identical, although a lapse in software installation between the production and reserve system may be advisable. Redundancy is similar: in this case sufficient reserve capacity is provided for within the organisation to absorb the impact of isolated system failures due to malicious software. In both cases it is vital that the reserve or redundant systems be isolated in terms of access (both physical and electronic) to minimise the likelihood that both systems will be affected by such software. It is crucial to identify key points within the computing provision in an organisation and, if the possible financial loss justifies it, to make provision to reduce vulnerability.

5.7.2 Insurance

A small number of firms now offer insurance against the specific effects of malicious software. Such a firm is Lloyds of London. It is however worth noting that most computer damage policies which insure the user for damage from physical destruction (or even from intrusion) specifically exclude damage caused by malicious software. This an area of fine print which should be carefully checked.

5.7.3 Public Relations

The third item is the most complex and potentially sensitive of all issues. It is vital that a company maintains the confidence of its customers, and that enquiries from the media do not interfere with the recovery process. Many organisations choose not to report viral infection because of the danger of adverse publicity. It is worth noting that a positive and carefully worded media statement may often bring praise rather than criticism, e.g.:

> Following detection and successful elimination of a computer virus XXX today temporarily suspended network services to significantly enhance their network security by installing advanced virus detection software on all connections. This is part of XXX's ongoing commitment to improved system security.

> XXX were today forced to disconnect their network to eliminate a virus spreading rapidly throughout the organisation. XXX made no comment on this issue, other than to state that measures had been taken to prevent a recurrence.

The tone and style of a public relations statement can significantly alter the press' reaction to an incident, and may convert a major incident into a plus for the company. In large organisations it is likely that a major incident will leak to the press, and it is preferable to have informed opinion (even if misquoted) rather than uninformed speculation.

The security policy must therefore indicate whose responsibility public relations is, who decides whether an incident should be reported, and who drafts the press releases.

In large corporates it may be advisable to establish a public relations officer designate who will deal with all press queries if a major incident is under way. The technical staff of the organisation should not be bothered by press or customer enquiries if this can be avoided, as they have a vital role to perform in the rapid analysis and elimination of the threat. In the Internet worm incident the MIT press office were complemented for their handling of the incident, and the non-interference with the technical work under way.

Measures to regain customer confidence, such as the provision of disinfection software and information on the virus, should be considered, especially if there are any indications that the virus may have spread from the company.

Part of the public relations policy must address whether the incident will be reported on open networks (corporate or external such as Virus-l), and whether returns will be made to bodies carrying out surveys of such infections (e.g. the Audit Commission).

The UK Computer Crime Unit has indicated an interest in any incidents of viral infection which may occur, and is keen to have such incidents reported. This permits the construction of a dossier of damage attributable to a single malicious software component, and strengthens the case for a legal suit against an author of malicious software.

5.8 Remedial Action

Finally, punitive action may be considered against the perpetrator of any malicious software incident. This action may be contractual or legal. If an employee is the perpetrator of malicious software or has through deliberate action or negligence permitted the software to become active within the organisation, then he or she may be in breach of their contract of employment.

The contract of employment is not solely limited to the contract signed on appointment by the employee but may include either the additional codes of conduct which the employee agrees to abide by (either implicitly or explicitly), such as a statement of "conditions of use" for corporate computer equipment. It is advisable to ensure that every employee has read (and signed!) such a document.

In such cases the employee may be subject to internal disciplinary action under the corporate disciplinary codes, or may be subject to civil litigation for recovery of damages resulting from his/her breach of contract.

Alternatively, a criminal legal sanction is available under the Computer Misuse Act 1990. This Act makes it an offence to alter computer data without permission. Such an offence may with malicious intent carry a penalty of up to 5 years' imprisonment.

Chapter 6
Apple Macintosh Viruses

6.1 Introduction

This chapter examines a further personal computer system which has been heavily afflicted by computer viruses, namely the Apple Macintosh. It shows the significant differences caused by the resource based abstract structure of Macintosh object files, and the complexity of the system initialisation sequence. The other two primary targets of virus writers (the Atari ST and Commodore Amiga) are also mentioned briefly.

The University of Hamburg virus catalogue project's remit also extends to other personal computer platforms. The Hamburg June 1990 catalogue (together with the IBM PC October 1990 Homebase and Disinfectant 2.4 documentation for the Mac) give the following distribution of viruses per annum. The figures for 1990 are partial, as a result of reliance on catalogues for mid-year together with the lead time for analysis of viral samples. In general a figure of 20 Amiga, 20 Atari ST, 10 Apple Mac and 120 IBM PC viruses can be postulated, thus yielding a total for 1990 of 170 new viruses, and a grand total of 310 viruses (including four Apple II strains – "Elk Cloner", "Festering Hate", "CyberAIDS" and "Lode Runner").

Platform	Number of detected viruses during year					Total	Source
	1986	1987	1988	1989	1990		
Amiga	-	1	7	27	-	35	Hamburg
Atari ST	-	-	5	13	-	18	Hamburg
IBM PC	3	11	16	43	81	154	Homebase
Macintosh	-	6	1	3	7	17	Norstad
	3	18	29	86	88	224	

The non-IBM PC platforms undoubtedly have fewer strains of virus. It is however generally the case that existing viral strains are far more common (especially on games machines such as the Atari and Amiga). A significant number of users will have encountered "Byte Bandit" on the Amiga, "Mouse Inverter" on the Atari or nVIR B on the Mac.

In general, the characteristics of the viruses on the four platforms are significantly different. The high level support environment on the Mac permits straightforward production of link viruses, but in general discourages the low level camouflage techniques observed on the IBM PC, Atari and Amiga systems. The absence of convenient access to executable code files via directory search services on the Atari ST has severely restricted the number of non-boot sector viruses, although the software protection utilised in prevention of games piracy has developed a number of complex camouflage and anti-tamper mechanisms. Software protection mechanisms were indeed the first to exploit the "ripple" decoder technique utilised by the fourth generation of IBM PC viruses.

This chapter seeks to outline the differences in operating system environment and to detail how shortcomings of each have affected the types of virus prevalent on the system. Each system is analysed using the common methodology described in Chapter 4, namely identification of all avenues of implicit and explicit code execution and assessment of their associated vulnerability to viral infection.

6.2 Macintosh: The Abstract Operating System

The Apple Macintosh represents the highest level, most abstract and most complex operating system of any of the personal computers dealt with in this work. The Macintosh operating system and associated "toolkit" provide a wide range of services for the user, supporting a window, icon, menu and pointer environment with sound and colour support. The operating system divides into a number of clearly defined modules. Each module has a well-documented interface to its users, and a detailed description of the services it provides. The modules and their inter-relationships are illustrated below:

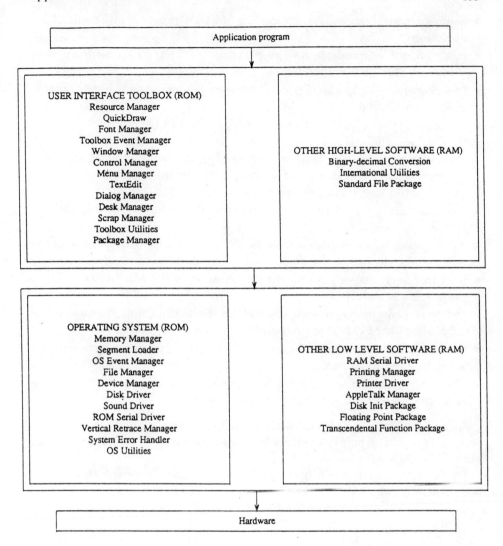

This diagram (modified from *Inside Macintosh*, volume 1) represents the firmware and software configuration for the early Mac models. A number of newer components have been added as peripheral complexity has increased. Of the traditional and newer modules, the following are of specific interest to the virus author:

- Resource manager: a vital component of the Mac toolbox which permits the user to manipulate applications as functional modules either containing executable code or parameters to routines within the toolbox which manage the user interface

- Memory manager: responsible for allocation of blocks of memory from the system heap

- Segment loader: responsible for loading of CODE modules into memory for execution
- File manager: responsible for the provision of a file based abstraction of secondary storage peripherals
- Device manager: a low level general interface to storage peripherals capable of block structured I/O
- Disk driver: the actual interface to a specific disk storage peripheral
- Vertical retrace manager: responsible for allowing the installation of subroutines to be executed during the period when the Mac is not generating part of the displayed image (i.e. the electron beam is returning to the top of the screen after completing a scan)
- Disk initialisation package: responsible for the formatting of disk storage media
- Apple desktop bus manager: responsible for handling slow speed data I/O peripherals attached to the proprietary ADB interface
- Start manager: responsible for the initialisation of the Mac and associated peripherals at startup
- Deferred task manager: responsible for permitting the installation of subroutines to be executed on return from an interrupt handler
- SCSI manager: responsible for the small computer systems interface to fast secondary storage devices
- Shutdown manager: responsible for termination of all activity on the Mac and associated peripherals before power down

Each of the above devices (plus the network services offered via the Apple proprietary LAN, AppleTalk) offers facilities which may be utilised by a virus author.

To commence analysis of this exceptionally complex hierarchy of software and firmware modules we can consider in detail the Mac initialisation sequence. This sequence is part of the functionality of the Start manager.

6.2.1 Initialisation

Initialisation comprises a number of hardware and firmware actions following the application of power. These actions are connected with the initialisation of all peripheral devices, establishment of the window environment and the location and execution of either a user specified application or the window manager. The components of the initialisation procedure are (virus critical components in bold):

- Testing of critical hardware devices such as the peripheral drivers, on-board timers and interface chips. A complete test of RAM is also carried out (although a partial test is only carried out if the machine is restarted)

- Interrupt vector table is initialised and certain system global variables instantiated. The Package manager and Time manager are initialised

- Slot manager (if present) is initialised and the ROM initialisation code on each slot device executed

- Apple desktop bus (connecting keyboard and mouse) is initialised

- SCSI, disk and sound managers are initialised

- The parameter RAM (EAROM) is interrogated to retrieve the internal SCSI drive id. A search is then carried out for a start device from which can be read various system parameters and the RAM resident component of the operating system. The search checks 3.5" drives (beginning with the specified internal drive), then the device specified as default startup device by the user is checked, then the SCSI bus devices starting with internal hard drives, and finally the remaining drives in reverse order of unit number are checked (6 to 0). The device driver for each device is read into memory

- **The configuration information in the system startup block on the selected device is read (if the block is marked as executable the code in the block is executed – this provides the Mac equivalent of a boot sector virus)**

- The resource, system error and font manager are initialised from the system file located from a "blessed" directory on the start device

- **The debugger specified in the startup block is executed, providing a Mac equivalent of a virus executed via the CONFIG.SYS file on the IBM PC (e.g. a virus masquerading as a device driver)**

- **ROM patch resources (the concept of a resource is described below) of type PTCH are installed into memory**

- **Apple Desktop bus code is loaded from resources of type ADBS and executed**

- **Tracking of mouse movement begins (this may utilise mouse tracking code)**

- Device drives read from ROMs in devices slotted into the backplane are executed

- **Initialisation code contained in resources of type INIT in the system file is executed**

- **Initialisation and driver code contained within files in the system folder (the blessed folder in which the system file resides) is executed**

- **If a startup application is specified it is launched (started), failing which the finder or multifinder is launched**

In the above list a large number of routes exist for incorporation of viral code during the system initialisation. Additional routes (described later) permit incorporation of viral code during disk insertion or application startup. Before proceeding further, it is important to understand the "resource" based structure of the system file and applications in general.

6.2.2 Resources

Within the Mac, each file (whether data or application) has two distinct components known as "forks". The two forks are the data fork which contains data used by a user application, and the resource fork. The latter is of particular interest to the anti-viral software writer. This fork contains parameters for system modules (such as a definition of a window to be displayed on the screen, a sequence of sound to be interpreted by the sound manager or the pattern of an icon or graphic), together with executable code. Each resource is identified by three features:

1. Resource type: a four-character identifying string unique to that particular format of resource – many are reserved for use by Apple.
2. Resource id: a numeric value which differentiates between different resources of the same type.
3. Resource name: an optional user specified name for an individual resource, specified as a string of characters.

A typical user application would comprise a large variety of resources (only a portion of which contain executable code), permitting the simple definition of windows, icons, pictures, sounds, menus, dialogues, alerts, colours and lists through the use of data in a format specific to the operating system component which interprets the resource. The resources of particular concern are those which contain executable code. These are a subset of all resource types, and include the following resource types:

Type	Function	Type	Function
ADBS	Apple desktop service routine	CACH	RAM cache code
CDEF	Control definition function	CODE	Application code segment
DRVR	Desk accessory or device driver	FKEY	Command-Shift-Number routine
FMTR	3.5" disk formatter code	INIT	Initialisation resource
LDEF	List definition procedure	MBDF	Default menu definition proc
MDEF	Menu definition procedure	MMAP	Mouse tracking code
PACK	Package	PDEF	Printing code
PTCH	ROM patch code	ROvr	ROM override code
SERD	Serial RAM driver	WDEF	Window definition function
NBPC	AppleTalk bundle		
atpl	Internal AppleTalk resource	boot	Boot block copy
cDev	Control panel devices	mppc	AppleTalk configuration code
snth	Sound synthesiser code		

Other code resources may have been added in later system files and ROMs. Resources may be loaded into memory as the result of the system initialisation procedure or as the result of being loaded and executed by an application or by a system utility. In the case of system initialisation, code in ADBS, CACH, DRVR, INIT, MBDF, MMAP, PACK, PTCH, ROvr, SERD and mppc resources will be executed. Through the normal actions of the user in utilising the Apple window manager "finder" or "multifinder", other resources will be loaded and executed implicitly through actions of the user. Such actions as the opening of a window, or use of a list, menu or system defined control will cause the execution of CDEF, LDEF, MDEF and WDEF resources. Further resources such as FKEY are executed as a result of a particular key sequence (Ctr-Shift-3 or 4 normally), or as the result of the use of a system function e.g. FMTR.

To locate a resource for execution the system uses a standard "search" order. This search order looks through the resource forks of a number of files in a specified sequence. First is the resource fork of the application data file which (through association) has caused launching of the application, second is the resource fork of the launched application, third is the system file, and fourth is the system ROM. (This order may be modified by a number of factors – in general it is representative. The last two items may be swapped in search order using standard resource manager calls.)

Thus, opening of a window (which causes the window manager to search for and executed a WDEF resource appropriate to the window type) may invoke code in the application or its data file, system file or ROM. It is important to note that data files on the Mac may contain resources, which may in turn contain executable code. The distinction between data and executable code is less clear than in the IBM PC environment.

Other system applications may open additional resource files which will be inserted into the search sequence. All resource files are searched in a last-opened first-searched sequence. An important example is the window manager "finder" which permits the user to manipulate files and execute programs via a window interface. This program makes use of data on each mounted disk volume. This data is used to locate a particular requested application on disk via the use of a "signature". The mapping between signature and actual file name is stored in a "desktop" file on each volume. This file additionally stores information on the location of icons and windows on the screen. It may unfortunately also include executable code resources such as MDEF, WDEF, CDEF and LDEF. These resources may therefore override the standard resources stored in the system file (since the volume desktop resource file was opened after the system file, and is thus searched before it). This is the technique used by the so-called "implied loader" viruses such as the WDEF and CDEF viruses. These viruses exist as executable viral code in the desktop on each storage volume. The act of inserting a disk will cause the finder to open the desktop on the volume, and will thus place the WDEF or CDEF viral code into the finder's resource search path. These can broadly be considered to be boot sector viruses since they are transported by movement of medium rather than application, and are an integral part of the initialisation of a storage volume. They are however extremely dangerous, as loading of viral code occurs as a result of disk insertion without the requirement to run any application.

Previously in this work the possibility of transferring large components of the operating system code into ROM was mooted. It is worth noting that the Mac has taken this approach, and includes a variety of system ROM sizes ranging from 64 K on early Mac models to 256 K on newer models. Apple has, however, included the flexibility of overriding code in the ROM. This can be achieved in a number of ways:

1. Patch resources, containing fixes to the ROM. These are loaded at initialisation time from the system file: on execution they may re-vector system traps to pass control to patch code.

2. ROM override resources, providing the ability to replace one or more ROM resources completely by a replacement resource. The system executes a ROvr resource at the time the resource manager is initialised. The function of this specialist resource (not included in the standard system file) is to locate specified resources in the ROM and to override them using system file copies.

3. Inclusion of an overriding resource in a resource file opened later (this is not appropriate for device drivers and other resident code loaded at system startup time).

Each of these routes permits a virus to bypass ROM code: each must therefore be checked for and prevented by anti-viral software.

The system ROM includes a number of standard resources which may be used by applications permitting virus free code to be executed. These include:

CDEF 0	Default button definition	CDEF 1	Default scroll bar definition
DRVR 3	Sound driver	DRVR 4	Disk driver
DRVR 9	AppleTalk driver	DRVR A	AppleTalk driver
DRVR 28	AppleTalk driver	MDBF 0	Default menu bar definition
MDEF 0	Default menu definition	PACK 4	Floating point arithmetic package
PACK 5	Transcendental functions package	PACK 7	Binary-decimal conversion
SERD 0	Serial driver	WDEF 0	Default window definition (document)
WDEF 1	Default window definition (rounded)		

Resource loaded from the system file (not contained in ROM) include:

PACK 0	List manager	PACK 2	Disk initialisation package
PACK 3	Standard file package	PACK 6	Internation utilities package
PACK 12	Colour picker package	DRVR 2	Printer driver
DRVR 18	Control panel desk accessory	LDEF 0	Standard list definition

and additionally further WDEF, MDEF, CDEF, LDEF, FKEY (3 and 4), MMAP 0, ADBS 2, KCHR and INIT resources.

6.2.3 Trap Dispatch Table Structure

In a similar manner to the vector table in an IBM PC system, the Mac utilises a central nexus known as the "trap dispatch table". This table uses a finer grained approach to that of the IBM PC vector table (in which all main DOS services are represented as functions of the main Int 21h trap), and includes separate vectors or trap addresses for all operating system and toolbox routines. Thus, a virus can intercept any facet of the Mac's behaviour via the dispatch table. Equally, an anti-viral monitor can apply a fine grained approach to the monitoring of system behaviour by intercepting only those functions which can be utilised for viral code propagation. These functions are primarily those of the "resource manager", "file manager" and lower level drivers.

The resource manager (unfortunately) offers extensive facilities to add new or modify existing resources within an application. These facilities make the production of a link virus trivial on this platform. It is however possible for a virus to undermine the abstraction provided by the resource manager and to directly access the resource fork of a file via the "file manager". Theoretically, with added viral complexity, a virus can undercut even the file manager and directly utilise "device manager" or "disk driver" calls.

In general, the key functions to monitor in the Mac environment are:

Resource	OpenResFile	Open specified resource file for IO
Resource	OpenRFPerm	""
Resource	SetResAttrs	Modify the attributes of a resource (including read only)
Resource	ChangedResource	Indicate that a resource has been modified and should be written out when convenient
Resource	AddResource	Add a new resource to the file
Resource	SetResFileAttrs	Modify resource file attributes (again read only)
File	OpenRF	Open a resource fork for direct IO
File	PBOpenRF	""
File	PBHOpenRF	"" (using hierarchical file system HFS)
Device	PBWrite	Write to file specified by parameter block
SCSI	SCSIWrite	SCSI driver low level write
SCSI	SCSIWBlink	""

In addition, remote file manipulation calls via the AppleTalk manager may allow introduction of viral code to remote systems.

The considerations described in Chapter 4 for interrupt monitors apply equally in the Mac environment. It is however somewhat easier to jump directly to a resource which is present in ROM (using resource manager calls to place the ROM resource map in front of the file based resources), and thus bypassing of interrupt monitors is a significant risk. This is a major problem with trojan horse utilities.

It is possible to invoke viral code implicitly by redirection of a number of system pointers stored as globals. These pointers are jump vectors used by specific components in the Mac operating system. If they were redirected to virus code present in memory then they would effectively cause execution of the virus under operating system control. This is one of a number of techniques which a virus or trojan horse might apply to remain resident in system memory. Others to be guarded against include:

Time manager   Use of delayed execution facilities
Vertical retrace manager   Use of execute on vertical blanking facilities
Shutdown manager   Use of shutdown procedure installation facilities

together with the usual options of redirecting system vectors, restructuring jump tables and RAM resident system code modification.

6.2.4 Non-link Viruses

The viruses which can exploit implicit loading of code by the operating system fall into a number of groups:

1. Boot code viruses: directly exploiting the ability to store executable code in the system startup block on each volume.
2. Initialisation code viruses: making use of executable code resources within the system file loaded and executed at initialisation time. These include viruses exploiting INIT, ADBS, DRVR, PTCH and ROvr resources. These also include viruses which exploit the so-called "INIT 31" mechanism. This function (provided via an INIT resource id 31 in the system file) searches all files in the system folder for DRVR and INITs: if found, they will be executed. This is a common route by which a trap monitoring anti-virus utility is started.
3. Auto-load viruses: making use of the facility to load a debugger or startup application specified via the system startup block on the volume.
4. Implied loader viruses: loaded indirectly via the execution of finder which causes the execution of certain window system definition resources.

To protect against such non-link viruses it is vital to continuously monitor or trap alterations to the system startup blocks (block 0 and 1) on each volume, to the system file and to all files within the system folder.

6.2.5 Link Viruses

Applications on the Mac comprise a number of executable code segments of maximum size 64 Kb. Each segment is relocatable in memory. Inter-segment jumps are made via a centralised segment jump table. This jump table permits dynamic loading of segments on an as-required basis. It also permits the simple restructuring of modularised programs to introduce viral code.

A typical application on the Mac comprises a number of code segments which are loaded from code resources of type "CODE". The jump table is stored in its initial form in a special "CODE 0" resource. When an application is executed the segment loader loads the jump table from the CODE 0 resource into memory. Each entry (describing a procedure entry point for a procedure which may be invoked from outside its home segment) is initially in an "unloaded" state.

A jump to the table entry will automatically invoke the segment loader, which will load the segment into memory and then rewrite the jump table entry to a direct jump to the procedure entry point (the loaded state). Should the segment be unloaded the jump table entries will be returned to their unloaded state.

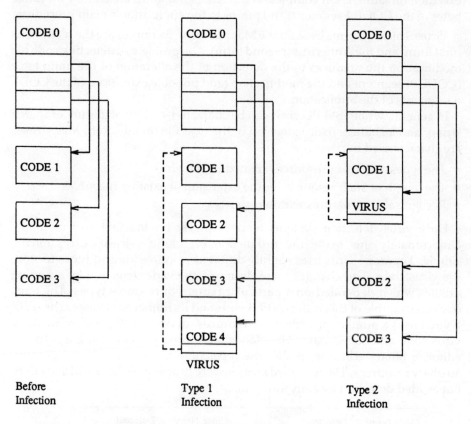

Before Infection

Type 1 Infection

Type 2 Infection

Dotted line represents restoration of original jump entry for the CODE 1 resource

In type 2 an intra-segment relative jump may be used to pass control to the original CODE 1 resource

A link virus normally operates by one of two methods:

1. Addition of a new viral resource of type "CODE" to the resource fork of the application. The initial jump table entry is modified to point to the viral CODE

resource, the original being stored by the virus. The launch of the application thus causes the viral code resource to be run. On completion, the virus restores the original application's jump table entry and jumps to the application via the entry.

2. Modification of the application's CODE 1 main procedure. In an analogous manner to the link viruses in traditional IBM PC COM files, the virus may append its code to the procedure. The jump table entry is then modified to point to the start of the virus (alternatively the initial part of the CODE 1 segment is replaced by a intra-segment jump to the virus). The virus is thus executed on launch. On completion it restores the jump table entry (or initial bytes of the CODE 1 segment) and jumps to the application's main procedure.

Viruses of both forms exist on the Mac platform. Examples are the nVIR virus (first form) and the Anti-virus (second form). The problem of detecting code file modification thus reduces to the detection of the alteration of the jump table (CODE 0) segment and the modification (and possible extension) of the CODE n segments of the application.

In general, while IBM PC virus can be characterised by a signature or search string, and a characteristic extension of the host file on infection, Mac viruses are characterised by:

- The types and ids of resources created by the virus
- The length of such resources or the extension of existing resources
- Recognisable signatures within resources

Early virus detection systems tended to rely on the first two methods. Unfortunately this made the production of "clone" viruses exceptionally simple. The clone virus uses slightly different resource ids and types to store the virus code. The changes were designed to evade detection by scanning utilities which depended on a particular pattern of resource types. The most obvious example of this is the nVIR B virus and its numerous clones. The nVIR B virus uses a number of additional resources (of type nVIR) to store auxiliary virus code and saved data. The clones were produced by using a resource editor or binary editor to modify the types (and in one case the id) of these auxiliary resources. The modified viruses were functionally identical to nVIR B, but evaded detection by early anti-viral software.

Clone Name	Detected	Clone Name	Detected
Hpat	Dec 1988, Arizona	AIDS	Mar 1989, Netherlands
MEV#	Apr 1989, Belgium	nFLU	Aug 1989, Minnesota
Jude	Nov 1989, Switzerland	fuck	Jan 1990, USA
MODM	Nov 1990, USA	zero	Nov 1990, USA

The zero strain has a resource name which consists of four null hex bytes.

Later software uses "generic" detection algorithms which recognise either specific signatures or patterns of flow within an application. In the latter case, we can look for potential anomalies such as an initial jump to a non-CODE 1 resource. This may be indicative of a virus having modified the host. The public domain "Interferon" product applies a number of such heuristics, including:

1. A CODE 0 resource jumping to the last CODE resource (id = n) when resource CODE n−1 does not exist.
2. A CODE 0 resource jumps to the last CODE resource.
3. A CODE resource exists in a data or system file.
4. Existence of INIT resources in user applications.

The search for executable virus code can be further restricted by considering only those files within the Mac file system which have a "file type" which indicates that they contain executable code (or code that will be implicitly loaded and executed as part of system initialisation). These file types are:

APPL	Application	cDev	Control panel device
		FNDR	Finder
INIT	Initialisation code	PRER	Non-serial printer driver
PRES	Serial printer driver	RDEV	Other device driver or desk accessory
ZSYS	System file		

6.2.6 Notes on Keyboard Sequences

Before completing this section on Apple Macintosh viruses, it is worth mentioning a number of keyboard sequences which, like the "Ctrl-Alt-Del" sequence on the IBM PC, carry out special functions.

Firstly the Command-Option key combination will cause the desktop file on the media being mounted to be rebuilt. The rebuilding operation involves scanning the hierarchical directory structure for all applications. The bundled resources for the application are added to the desktop – including icons and signatures. This operation will also remove (by overwriting) any implied loader virus in the desktop. This sequence can be held down at system boot time to rebuild the desktop on the startup volume, or when inserting a floppy disk to rebuild the desktop on the floppy.

Secondly, the Command-Option-Shift key combination when opening the control panel desk accessory will cause the system parameter RAM to be reset to its default values. This can avoid the specification of a non-standard startup volume in the PRAM.

6.2.7 Summary of Mac Protection

Macintosh anti-viral products divide into trap/interrupt monitoring utilities, which are normally small "INIT" resources placed within the system file or folder (the latter loaded via the INIT 31 mechanism described earlier), or signature scanning programs existing as applications or desk accessories. A range of checksum utilities is also available, some of which are tailored to generate checksums of critical system areas on disk (such as the startup blocks) as well as checksumming a restricted range of resources types (only those which are executable). The list of functions to be monitored includes:

1. Addition (or modification) of executable resources to applications, desk accessories, device drivers or desktop.
2. Addition (or modification) of executable resources to components of the boot sequence (system file, files in the system folder, startup blocks).
3. Relocation of an existing file into the system folder (where it will become a part of the startup sequence).
4. Direct manipulation of the resource fork of a file via the file manager.
5. Modification (via lower level device drivers or direct hardware manipulation) of the volume boot blocks, directory structure (possibly moving executable code blocks into the system folder, or adding blocks of executable code to existing files).
6. Actions to disable the file change monitoring facilities such as modification of the trap dispatch table, direct overwriting of the utility in memory, etc.

In general, the level of technology exhibited by Mac viruses is approximately 18–24 months behind that of the IBM PC virus field. There has been little indication of the development of self-modifying and encrypting virus techniques, the use of low level system access to undermine protection or the inclusion of extensive anti-debug routines. There have, however, been examples of viruses directly calling routines in ROM (such as the WDEF virus) to bypass anti-viral utilities monitoring the trap dispatch table.

Chapter 7

Mainframe Systems: The Growing Threat

7.1 Introduction

Previous chapters have concentrated on the spread of viruses on personal computer platforms. This chapter examines (first in theory and then in fact) the threat posed by viruses within the formal security models implemented by high confidentiality or high integrity mainframe and mini computer systems.

While such environments do inhibit the propagation of viral code, there is little doubt that viruses can successfully circumvent most existing protection mechanisms. This chapter also examines the introduction of the concept of data and code "integrity" and its incorporation into existing security models and protection mechanisms.

7.2 Hardware Architectures

All mainframe and mini computers now include hardware support for the concepts of segmentation and paging to provide a user virtual memory space (as discussed previously with regard to the 80386 chip), together with some form of support for privileged operations by trusted software components. As with the 80386, these privileged operations normally include:

- I/O to external peripherals
- Modification of the virtual to physical memory translation
- Interference with privilege level flags

The significant change is that the hardware compartmentalisation facilities are utilised and integrated with the access control modules embedded in the host operating system.

7.3 Software Architecture

The principal features of the software access control system are:

- Authentication of the user
- Establishment (and enforcement) of a set of access rights for that user
- Propagation of access rights to all processes activated by the user

Significantly, the third point applies to a virus or trojan horse utility executed by the user. The system confidentiality (and, as will be seen later, integrity) control functions operate to restrict the spread of viral code or the execution of hostile trojan code.

Two principal classifications of access control mechanisms exist (described in the DoD Orange Book, and its associated Discretionary Access Control Handbook):

- Discretionary access control (DAC) – at levels C1/C2
- Mandatory access control (MAC) – at levels B1– B3

These two classes reflect significantly different approaches to the ownership of information, namely:

- DAC – user ownership
- MAC – corporate or state ownership

The concept of ownership dictates which body places the primary restrictions on the security of the information.

7.3.1 Discretionary Access Controls

DACs may be placed on access to data created by a user. The user normally has full rights to control access to the data (possibly subject to the inheritance of a default set of system access rights). Access rights can be specified in a number of ways, including:

- Access control lists (ACLs) or matrices
- Capability based systems
- Cryptographic techniques

ACLs permit the user to specify a list of users, groups of users, or processes which are permitted access to his data (or executables) and to specify the constraints on access to the data by such users. The reverse form (specifying which users shall be denied access) is often also available.

A simplistic example of an ACL is the UNIX protection mechanism. UNIX associates three sets of permissions with each file (executable or not) in the file system. These are:

- Owner access rights
- Group access rights
- World access rights

The term "owner" refers to the creator of the file, "group" to his peer group, and "world" to all other users with logins to that system. Each set of permissions includes 3 bits:

R   Read permission
W   Write permission
X   Execute permission

Thus the full permission set is 9 bits long, and consists of:

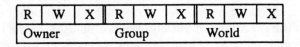

R	W	X	R	W	X	R	W	X
Owner			Group			World		

These permissions permit the owner coarse control over access to his data.

To aid consideration of the operation of a virus or trojan horse within such a DAC framework, the following scenarios are presented:

Scenario 1: infection by the instigator   User A wishes to infect as many users as possible with his virus or to install his trojan horse in their filespace. The access controls on user B's directory (RWXR-XR-X) prevent user A writing into it, and thus prevent the virus writing to his files or the insertion of a trojan horse. User C's directory may be (RWXRWXRWX), in which case user A can insert a trojan horse, or replace one of user C's files by the virus or trojan horse. If user C's executable code files are writable, the virus can infect the file directly. Even if they are non- writable, but readable, user A can copy the file, change its permissions (since he is owner of the copy), infect and re- install the infected file in place of the original. Thus for security against direct insertion of viral or trojan horse code a user must:

- Deny write permission on all directories containing executable code (this definition is examined later)
- Deny write permission to the executables themselves

Scenario 2: infection by the target   User A realises that he cannot directly write to user B's executable code files. He therefore moves his trojan or virus to a public software area on the system and announces the presence of an "all singing, all dancing" utility. A possible examples might be a trojanised or virus-infected virus scanning utility (such as the numerous incidents of the Homebase virus scanner being converted into a trojan horse by an unscrupulous user). User B notices this utility and decides to try the program out to see what it can do. At that point the utility is running with user B's permissions, and can thus easily infect his files and executables.

DAC techniques are vulnerable to attacks via Scenario 2, and by user default to attacks via Scenario 1.

The definition of what constitutes a directory containing executable code is particularly crucial. This is defined as:

Any directory searched automatically for executable code as a result of a direct or indirect action of the user

UNIX specified a "PATH" (similar to DOS) which consists of a list of directories which will be searched when the user requests execution of a code file. Thus if any branch on this PATH is writable, a direct infection by insertion of viral or trojan horse code can occur, similarly if an executable in any branch is writable, a direct replacement by viral or trojan horse code can occur.

The corresponding file technique mentioned in Chapter 4 can be exploited both in UNIX and DOS to allow infection even if the user does not have write permission on the executable. Basically, the hostile user inserts his viral code earlier in the search path, in a file of the same name as the user wishes to run. The user then executes this code (unintentionally) in place of the intended utility. No change to the original utility can be detected (this is comparable to the EXE/COM corresponding file virus in DOS).

In UNIX a standard search PATH might be:

.:~/bin:/usr/local/bin:/usr/ucb/bin:/usr/bin:/bin:/usr/et c:/etc

Thus a utility in the system binary directory "/usr/bin/" can be overridden by a viral utility in the system local directory "/usr/local/bin" or the user's own bin directory "~/bin", or even the current working directory ".".

In summary, for UNIX DAC, trojan horse or viral code can be insinuated by:

- Direct inclusion if the target user has: (i) a writable directory in his search path; (ii) a readable directory in his search path with a writable executable file; or (iii) a searchable directory in his search path with a writable executable file. The difference between (ii) and (iii) is that in (ii) the attacker can read the directory to discover the names of all files in the directory, in (iii) the filenames are unknown and must be probed for by guesswork or exhaustive search.
- Indirect inclusion if the target user runs a virus or trojan horse utility.

It may be possible using an extension of DAC to limit the propagation of viral or trojan horse code via restrictions on data flow. We can associate a flow limit with each executable file or data file, which determines a limit on the propagation of such data or code within the system, e.g.

A data file is created by user A and is tagged by the system as having maximum spread 3. User B uses his access right to open the file and read data into a program. This program inherits a spread factor of 2 (actually the minimum of the spread factors of all opened data files − 1). Any data written by this program to a file inherits the minimum of the spread factor for the data file and the spread factor of the writing program. Thus, user B writes data with spread 2. This process continues until the spread factor becomes 0, at which point the system prevents writing by any utility reading spread 0 data.

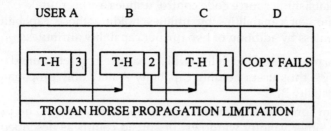

This approach will constrain viral or trojan horse propagation if the spread factor is mandatorily assigned by the system when an executable or data file is created, e.g.

In the absence of spread limitations DAC can, if carefully controlled, establish compartments within the user space. They are, however, vulnerable if a user can be tricked into malicious software execution.

Other DAC systems include extensions to UNIX ACL mechanisms, adding general ACL schemes such as:

- Per user access right specifications
- Rights to "append", "modify access rights", "propagate access rights", etc.
- Time or login channel restriction

The most general technique (and one which can utilise embedded viral or trojan horse code detection) is the specification of an access control or gatekeeper program which is invoked whenever access to an object is requested. This program can then use complex user defined criteria to determine whether access should be permitted. This may include verification that the program requesting access does not contain recognisable viral or trojan horse code, or that it does not attempt to execute certain damaging system functions.

Capability based systems operate by associating one or more "capabilities" with each data item. Any program possessing a matching "capability" is permitted access. The capabilities may be distributed by the owner of the file, or an agent acting on his behalf.

Thus the writer of a virus might associate a null or widely distributed capability with this virus, and then publicise his utility. His virus may however lack (because he himself lacked) capabilities which permitted access to object/ executable files. In fact these capabilities may be restricted to utilities in compilation route, e.g. compilers, assemblers and linkers. This technique may prevent viral code propagation by effectively installing a trusted channel via which object code may be modified. This channel approach prevents both self-modifying and non-self-modifying code, and effectively centralises trust in the compilation route, operating system and hardware (rather than in all executable programs). Naturally this does not inhibit source virus propagation, although similar measures can be taken to establish editors as the trusted route to modify source files (or indeed to enforce software configuration management by establishing source code control utilities as this route).

Propagation of capabilities by utilities holding those capabilities is not restricted unless by addition of two further capability attributes:

- Ability to propagate a capability (which may itself be determined by a further capability – thus users holding capability A may only propagate it if they hold capability B)
- Maximum spread of capabilities – capabilities may be aged on propagation carrying either validity windows, or spread counts as described for ACLs

Capability based systems have been implemented in hardware via association of a capability (or capabilities) with each segment of virtual memory maintained by the memory management subsystem.

The capability system suffers from similar problems to ACL based systems, namely:

- Propagation of access rights
- Inheritance of access rights from the user by his utilities
- Implementational rather than model base technique (this issue is addressed later)

Finally, cryptographic techniques may be applied, such as the use of "DES" to implement data confidentiality. Thus, in place of a capability to access data, the user has access to the secret key for the data. This scheme can compensate for shortfalls or absences of access control in the host operating system, although a requirement for key submission and handling to be secure still exists. In terms of avenues for viral infection or trojan horse attack this scheme is identical to other DAC schemes.

7.3.2 Integrity Versus Confidentiality

The above implementational schemes for security mix two separate components, those of:

- Data Confidentiality: ensuring that data is not read by parties not authorised to receive it
- Data Integrity: ensuring that data is not modified by parties not authorised to change it

The DAC scheme controls both data confidentiality and data integrity in a single scheme. A functional separation could be achieved by controlling read access to affect confidentiality, and write access to affect integrity.

Malicious code propagation relies on defeating data integrity mechanisms, and is thus primarily a system integrity issue. Viruses which rely on embedding of code into an application or system also raise data confidentiality issues for two reasons:

- They require read access to the host executable to determine the necessary modifications (unless the structure of the executable is sufficiently standardised to allow inference of such characteristics)
- They may attempt to compromise data as part of their manipulation task

The functional split between confidentiality and integrity can be clearly identified in the following public key encryption scheme:

1. A user has a private key with which he encrypts (signs) all executables before storage – anyone can decrypt his programs using the public key. No one can, however, forge a signed executable as this requires the user's private key. Integrity of the program is thus ensured.
2. A user has a public key with which he encrypts all executables before storage – only those users with a matching private key can decrypt the executable and examine or run its contents. Confidentiality of the program is thus ensured.

Approach 1 permits anyone to read the contents of the executable and affords no confidentiality. Approach 2 permits anyone to alter the contents of the executable and thus affords no integrity.

Thus a DAC can be extended to implement discretionary confidentiality and discretionary integrity using either ACL, capability or cryptographic techniques.

In this environment integrity controls will inhibit viral infection or trojan horse introduction; security controls will inhibit link virus infection or data compromise by viruses.

7.3.3 Mandatory Access Controls

The Bell-LaPadula security model is an example of a MAC based on the military classification scheme. This classification scheme is based on assessment of the threat to national security caused by the potential compromise of data by an enemy. The UK and US military classification hierarchy is given below:

US	UK	Damage potential
Top secret	Top secret	Expected to cause exceptionally grave damage
Secret	Secret	Expected to cause serious damage
Confidential	Confidential	Expected to cause damage
Sensitive	Restricted	
Unclassified	Unclassified	

The "sensitive" classification is informal, based on an exemption for release under the Freedom of Information Act in the US.

The user is required to classify all data at the point of introduction to the system environment (this may require the consent of multiple users). Two criteria are applied to control data flow:

- No Read-Up (simple security property): a user cannot read data classified higher than his "clearance"
- No Write-Down (*-property): a user cannot declassify data by writing it to an object of lower classification

The model is implemented as a series of protection rings, thus:

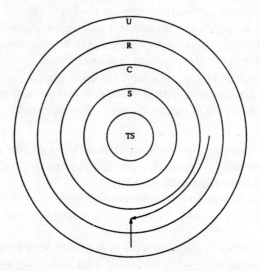

Data flow is restricted to be within a classification ring, or to be to a more restrictive classification ring. A virus cannot propagate its code to lower classification levels and is thus restricted under Bell-LaPadula to propagate:

- Within a classification
- To a more restrictive classification

Thus a virus existing at a "restricted" classification may rapidly propagate to the executables at "top secret" classification. When run by a user with a "top secret" clearance the virus may then compromise data at this classification or at any lower classifications. This compromise is restricted by the security model to covert channel techniques. This restriction may be insufficient when attempting to contain high security data (often with implied integrity requirements).

Trojan horses can similarly be copied from a lower to higher classification by:

1. A user cleared at the lower classification (absence of Write-Up restriction).
2. A user cleared at the higher classification (absence of Read-Down restriction).

The Bell-LaPadula model has been extended in two ways. First, compartments have been added within classifications to further restrict data flow based on a coarse "need to know" principle. This does not fully inhibit viral or trojan horse code propagation – viruses can still propagate to the highest classification and strictest compartments. It does however prevent infection of data which is not marked as being part of the infected compartment.

Second, integrity controls (Biba extensions) have been added to this model to address the issue of malicious and untrusted software. This addition has taken the form of integrity classifications analogous to confidentiality classifications. Two criteria are applied to data in the Biba model, namely:

- No Write-Up: a program running in a low integrity environment cannot write to executable or data files in a higher integrity environment
- No Read-Down: a program running in a high integrity environment cannot read data or execute code in a lower integrity environment without affecting its own integrity level

The second point requires a limited amount of explanation, namely reading of data may modify the control flow of a program in a manner which may compromise its integrity, particularly the case when major assumptions are made by the reading program about the structure of the file.

Viruses normally exist in "low" integrity software – such viruses are inhibited from:

- Propagation to high integrity software
- Modifying the behaviour of high integrity software via modifications to configuration files

Integrity compartments may be added in a similar manner to confidentiality compartments, with extended criteria:

- A program may only write to equally or less restrictive integrity compartments
- A program in a restrictive compartment may not read data from a less restrictive compartment

Thus when a user introduces an executable into the system he (or the system tools used to introduce the program) must:

- Specify a confidentiality classification and compartment
- Specify an integrity classification and compartment

The assessment of integrity may be based on distributed trust via restrictions to specific sources of software, and internally to software developed using specific tools or techniques, or by specific programmers. Thus in the same manner as users are cleared to handle data at a specific classification, programmers or data preparation staff are cleared to generate data and executables at a specific integrity level.

Integrity "locks" can thus be created which permit the introduction of executables to a specific integrity level. Such locks may require the use of "trusted software" components, thus a route to an arbitrary integrity level 4 may require:

- Use of a compiler, assembler and linker certified at level 4 or above
- Clearance of the user to integrity level 4 based on an assessment of his programming skills and professional responsibility
- Application of certain internal inspection and quality control criteria

A possible list of software integrity classifications (based on Pozzo and Gray) might be:

Origin	Credibility	Risk
User files	0 - Lowest	0 - Highest
User contributed software	1	.
S/W from bulletin boards	2	.
S/W from system staff	3	.
Commercial application S/W	4	.
S/W from OS vendor	5 - Highest	5 - Lowest

To maintain integrity, distributed trust is still in evidence. We must still trust the compiler, linker, assembler, operating system and hardware. This requires the extension of the integrity model (either formally or informally) beyond the boundaries of our own system.

The integrity and confidentiality classifications and compartments can be visualised as a two-dimensional structure in which the X axis represents the movement from high confidentiality to low confidentiality, and the Y axis the movement from low integrity to high integrity. The system access controls therefore prohibit movement away from the origin along either the X or Y axis, and constrain viral flow towards the centre of the model both in terms of confidentiality and integrity.

Within the model can be placed various "locks" or "tunnels" permitting the transition from one confidentiality or integrity level to another. Such tunnels include routes for declassifying information via human intervention, or routes for increasing software integrity as a result of applying a specific test. One such integrity tunnel might be the use of a virus or malicious code detection system which might permit the movement of code from low integrity to medium integrity. Such tunnels permit carefully defined localised violations of the generalised confidentiality and integrity policy to occur.

Without such tunnels all programs carrying out mass data aggregation would eventually migrate to the highest confidentiality and lowest integrity compartment.

Two systems operating the Biba extensions to Bell-LaPadula may be coupled via the use of communications channels with cryptographic assurance of trust, i.e. use of encryption to prevent data compromise of confidentiality data, use of digital signature to prevent data corruption of high integrity data.

7.3.4 Commentary on Security Standardisation

The previous sections have concentrated primarily on the DoD Orange Book standard "Trusted computer system evaluation criteria", and have in summary indicated that:

1. Viruses are primarily an integrity rather than a confidentiality problem, and can propagate in the absence of strict DACs to the highest confidentiality ring and most restrictive compartment of the MAC model.
2. In the absence of MACs the virus can compromise data across all confidentiality levels and compartments.
3. In the presence of MACs but absence of covert channel restriction the virus can compromise data via covert channel mechanisms.
4. In the presence of covert channel restrictions or auditing the virus is restricted to covert channel propagation beneath the threshold bandwidth indicated in the covert channel guideline (Orange Book, Section 8.0).

In terms of viral propagation and subsequent data compromise according to the Orange Book classification, it follows that:

- Class D: minimal protection. Complete propagation and full data compromise, no auditing of spread or compromise available
- Class C1: discretionary security protection. Active propagation restricted by DAC, passive propagation by running of malicious software unrestricted, data compromise unrestricted, no auditing of spread or compromise available
- Class C2: controlled access protection. As above. Audit trail available to trace spread and data compromise
- Class B1: labelled security protection. Propagation prevented to security classifications below point of infection, or to compartments less strict than point of infection. Data compromise restricted to covert channel mechanisms
- Class B2: structured protection. Compromise restricted to covert channels below threshold (0.1 bit/sec) which may be subject to auditing
- Class B3: security domain. Propagation or data compromise may be subject to evaluation of suspicious activity by the security kernel
- Class A: verified design. No new specifications

The maximum damage resulting from data compromise caused by viral infection can be estimated by considering the Yellow Book requirements for use of specific Orange Book protection classes. This yields the following table of possible compromise (assuming an open security environment):

Class	Risk rating	Compromise assessment
C2	0	Unrestricted
B1	1	Restricted to non-bandwidth limited covert channel
B2	2	Restricted to bandwidth limited covert channel
B3	3	Subject to expert system analysis to determine suspicious activity
A1	4	as above
*	>4	Beyond state of art

The risk index is based on the difference between the highest classification of data in the system and the lowest level of user clearance. The maximum data sensitivity gives a risk value of 0 (Unclassified), 1 (Sensitive), 2 (Confidential), 3 (Secret) and 5 (Top Secret). The minimum user clearance giving a risk modifier of 0 (Unclassified), 1 (Authorised to access sensitive information), 2 (Confidential), 3 (Secret), 4 (Top secret – current background investigation), 5 (Top secret – special background investigation).

The risk index is given by: Risk value – Risk modifier. Thus secret material (risk 3) stored on a system used by users cleared to confidential (modifier 2) would attract a risk factor of 1, and require a B1 system.

Therefore, in a scenario in which a multi-level secure system was connected to a public network the permitted risks would include:

Unlimited covert channel compromise of data at the "not classified but sensitive" classification, restricted < 0.1 bit/sec compromise of data at the "confidential" classification and possible limited compromise of data at the "secret" classification.

The connection of systems holding "top secret" data to public networks (inferring the adoption of the open security environment criteria) is forbidden. The issue of malicious software penetration of trusted systems is addressed in Appendix C of the technical rationale behind the Yellow Book.

The Orange Book is one of a group of national security criteria. These include the Red Books published by the Communications and Electronic Security Group at the Government Communications headquarters in the UK, the Green Books published by the Department of Trade and Industry Commercial Computer Security Centre in the UK, and the new proposed "Information Technology Security Evaluation Criteria" (ITSEC). The ITSEC is the result of the merging of the national evaluation criteria of France, Germany, The Netherlands and the United Kingdom.

The ITSEC is based on an abstract specification of the security philosophy to be adopted at each level of system trust, together with specifications of security criteria applying to configuration control, startup, operation and development security. Thus the criteria are far wider reaching than the original Orange Book, but they do not address implementational issues such as the specific access control mechanism which will be implemented within the system. Thus the ITSEC would define a level E3 access mechanism as being:

1. A translation or mapping from a well-defined functional specification.
2. Required to possess a clearly defined interface with other components.

3. Subject to analysis of side effects and unjustified functionality.

4. Subject to testing at the object code and source inspection levels.

The ITSEC does include a number of draft functionality classes, F1–F10, which are functional descriptions of controls which might be appropriate to a system whose design and implementation had been certified as being trusted at a specified evaluation level E1–E6. These functional classes are broadly based on the German information security agency criteria which are themselves modelled on the Orange Book. These classes are:

Functional class	Orange book class	Definition
F1	C1	-
F2	C2	-
F3	B1	-
F4	B2	-
F5	B3/A1	-
F6	-	High integrity
F7	-	High availability
F8	-	High integrity communications
F9	-	High confidentiality communications

A system can have one or more functional classes implemented, such as: F5 kernel, with F6 high integrity support and F8 high integrity communications support. Of these functional classes, F6 and F8 are of particular interest. These classes specifically address the integrity of the system and associated data communications.

Class F6 is summarised as:

Each object within the system is typed. Access to a particular type of object is constrained to be via a specified process or processes (gatekeeper, as mentioned in the DAC section). Objects may only be introduced into the environment by authorised users. All communications between users and the security kernel is via a trusted path (which is immune to spoofing by a virus or trojan horse). A full audit trail of object access attempts shall be maintained.

F6 would constrain the introduction of a virus or trojan horse into the system environment and would further constrain attempts by a virus to modify executable objects. Sole authority to modify such executable objects would be vested in the system compilation utilities, which might require authentication from the user before generating or modifying an executable. To satisfy this criteria it is implied that the security kernel is resistant to tampering and maintains its own integrity.

F6 is not an implementation of the Biba integrity model, but relies instead on the creation of arbitrary groups of objects with associated access/modification routes. Thus text files are under the control of system editor utilities, executables under the control of system compilers, spreadsheets under the control of spreadsheet programs, etc. These are the only routes by which the object can be created or modified. Thus the filesystem is compartmentalised by usage (rather than by confidentiality or integrity).

Data communications integrity is the subject of functional class F8. This class specifies that peer authentication will occur on all data exchanges, and that all data (and protocol control blocks) will be subject to error detection and correction. This will apply both in the case of inadvertent corruption due to datacomm problems or to deliberate manipulation.

7.4 UNIX: A Viral Risk Assessment

The previous section concentrated on the access control mechanisms available in UNIX, and indicated possible MAC frameworks for confidentiality and integrity of data. Commercial UNIX systems are available at a wide range of Orange Book certification levels, most falling in the range C2–B3. Commercial UNIX systems can be approved at level C2 with minimal modification (audit and shadow password system incorporation).

This section considers the assessment of the risk posed by a computer virus on a C2 secure UNIX system based on the Berkeley Software Distribution release 4.3 (BSD 4.3), in this case Sun OS 4.0 with the security software option.

The methodology established previously can easily be extended to a complex operating system such as UNIX. The techniques require the identification of all routes via which viral code can be executed, either directly or indirectly as a result of user action, system initialisation, termination or network activity.

To commence this analysis we will consider the UNIX boot/startup process, with a view to identifying each component in this sequence.

7.4.1 System Startup

Initial execution commences with the location of a system boot block on the root file system or from a media specifically designed to be read at system startup. This boot block is the "primary bootstrapper" and is located at a fixed offset on the storage media. The bootstrapper is responsible for locating and loading a secondary bootstrap program from the filesystem.

The secondary bootstrap can be a standard UNIX file with data blocks scattered throughout the file system, as against the sequential primary bootstrap. The location of each block of the secondary bootstrap is stored as part of the primary bootstrap program to avoid the overhead of interpreting the complex structure of the UNIX filesystem (earlier versions were able to do this and thus located the boot program by name within the root directory).

The secondary bootstrapper initialises the system hardware in a machine dependent manner – such as setting up a stack, initialising the memory management system, and creating a hardware context for the initial process. The bootstrapper then loads the kernel binary from the file "vmunix" in the root directory on the startup volume, and jumps to the function entry point "main" within the program.

The kernel then creates the heart of the UNIX multitasking environment – the scheduler process (process id = 0). The kernel then proceeds to carry out further configuration of the memory management system, device and hardware driver configuration and creation of two further processes: the initialisation or init process (process id = 1) and a swap space manager (process id = 2).

The initialisation process "/usr/etc/init" carries out the next stages in system initialisation. These are:

1. Run all commands in the command interpreter "shell" script /etc/rc.boot: this file configures the network interfaces and checks the root filesystems.
2. Run all commands in the shell script /etc/rc: this file runs a wide variety of daemon (background) processes and system services; it also runs the script /etc/rc.local containing local service initialisation information.
3. When initialisation scripts have completed, init commences multi-user operation by running the programs specified in the file /etc/ttytab on each connected terminal line.

The normal command specified for each terminal in the ttytab file is /usr/etc/ getty. This command writes the system banner on to each terminal and then awaits user login.

The daemon processes started from a typical series of /etc/rc files include:

File	Daemon	Function
rc	rwhod	Propagation of information on users to other network machines
rc	inetd	Spawns internet protocol service daemons on request
rc	lpd	Line printer spooler daemon
rc	update	Daemon to flush IO buffers at regular intervals
rc	cron	Timed command execution service
rc.local	portmap	Provide remote procedure call address mappings
rc.local	keyserv	Key management system
rc.local	named	Domain name server (DNS)
rc.local	biod	Block IO service daemon (used in NFS)
rc.local	syslog	System logging daemon
rc.local	auditd	Security audit trail daemon
rc.local	sendmail	Electronic mail handling daemon
rc.local	ndbootd	Network disk daemon
rc.local	nfsd	Network filing system (NFS) daemon
rc.local	mountd	Remote procedure call (RPC) - file system mounter
rc.local	rarpd	Reverse address resolution protocol daemon
rc.local	bootparamd	Client boot parameter provision service
rc.local	statd	Network status monitor
rc.local	lockd	Network file locking service
rc.local	pwdauthd	Shadow password authentication service
rc.local	x29	X29 terminal login service

All of the above daemons are run with root privilege before full multi-user operation completes with full root privileges. Thus it is vital that all daemon binaries are fully protected from infection by viruses or modification to incorporate trojan horse code. Of particular importance are the "cron" and "inetd" daemons, since these permit execution of further UNIX commands specified in their respective configuration files.

Cron provides the "clock daemon". This daemon reads a number of files in the directory "/var/spool/cron/crontabs". Each user may establish his own crontab file which contains commands run under his user id at timed intervals. The file format permits specification of the month, day of week, day of month, hour and minute fields (with limited wildcarding) at which the user command will be run. Obviously, the spool directory and individual crontabs must be protected to prevent indirect execution of malicious or harmful code.

The cron daemon also supports the batch command execution system provided by the UNIX "at" command. This command stores command scripts in the subdirectory "atjobs" for execution by the cron daemon. Similarly, introduction of viral or trojan horse code into the scripts in this directory must be guarded against.

The inetd provides a similar command execution function, in this case in response to a request by a remote system for a network service. Such network services include file transfer, remote login, remote shell, time and user id services and various RPC services. Each service is attached to a specific network address or port on the local system. A call to this port will cause inetd to invoke the appropriate UNIX command to handle the request. Thus the file /etc/inetd.conf (which contains details of these commands) must be protected against writing.

Finally, as previously mentioned, the file /etc/ttytab which contains the programs to be run on completion of initialisation by init must also be protected. In summary, therefore, the components of the UNIX initialisation sequence are:

1	ROM bootstrap code
2	Primary bootstrap code at fixed offset in startup filesystem
3	Secondary bootstrap code in /boot
4	VMUNIX operating system kernel in /vmunix
5	/etc/rc and /etc/rc.boot UNIX command scripts
6	all daemons run from these command scripts
7	cron daemon's crontab and "at" batch files
8	inetd daemon's configuration file and daemons
9	ttytab configuration file and daemons

At this point the startup sequence has completed and multi-user operation has commenced.

7.4.2 Login and User Commands

The getty program (run by init on each terminal line) displays the login banner for the system. When a user supplies his user id, the getty program overwrites itself with the standard login command "login". This program is responsible for prompting for a password from the user and for verifying the supplied user id and password combination. This verification may include the use of the pwdauthd if the shadow password facility is operating.

If the password is correct then the login program overwrites itself with the "shell" specified in the /etc/passwd (system password) file for the user. This program commences operation and may then read one or more initialisation files prior to providing the command interpreter/shell prompt to the user.

The initialisation files depend on the type of shell specified in the passwd file, these include:

Shell	File	Function
sh	.profile	Sequence of command executed at login time
sh	/etc/profile	System supplied sequence of initial commands
csh	.cshrc	Sequence of command executed whenever a shell starts up
csh	.login	Sequence of command executed at login time (after .cshrc)
csh	.logout	Sequence of command executed on logout

The files .profile, .login, .logout and .cshrc are found in the home directory for the user (a directory specified in the user's entry in the /etc/passwd file). All of these files must be write-protected to prevent malicious software being inadvertently executed by the user via his command script. The file /etc/profile is even more sensitive as it is executed by all users logging in to the system who have specified the bourne shell "sh" as their command interpreter.

After shell initialisation has completed, the user is prompted to enter commands for execution. This provides the final opportunity to invoke malicious software – either by direct execution of a trojan horse or viral utility by a careless user or by incorporation of the utility earlier in the user's search path. Modification of the user's shell initialisation files may permit the PATH variable (which controls the search for executable files by the shell) to be altered to include viral or trojan horse code in the search path.

Even if the user explicitly specifies the path to an executable file (using an absolute pathname commencing at the root of the filesystem, e.g. /bin/test), he may still be open to spoofing. The shell has no hard wired concept of what constitutes a separator in command sequences. This is specified by another shell variable, the inter-field separator list, IFS. This variable may be altered to make the shell interpret the pathname separator "/" as a space. Thus the command "/bin/ls -la" which is an attempt by the user to specify an absolute path to the list directory command, may be interpreted by the shell as "bin ls -la", causing the execution of the command "bin" in the home directory.

This, together with general security principles, suggests that the PATH of super-users (normally with login id root, who can bypass all file system security and have full privileges on the system) should not include the home directory.

A final twist in the search path technique is the observation that users frequently make spelling mistakes when invoking basic commands. Thus a viral code may be incorporated in an executable with a name closely related to a common system function such as ps, ls, mv or cp. Thus possible names may be:

    px ks lx ld pd mc mb nc nv xp co

all differing by one keyboard place from a standard two letter UNIX command.

Thus any checksumming of commonly used utilities as part of a security scan must address the inclusion of new or modified utilities with similar command names.

7.4.3 Bugs and Loopholes

In an operating system as complex as UNIX there are a number of bugs and loopholes in the user interface. Such bugs often permit the user to gain root/super-user privilege. It is possible for a virus, worm or trojan horse to probe for such known bugs in order to upgrade its privilege level before attempting to infect other systems or executables, or to execute damaging privileged system functions. Such bugs divide into two categories:

1. Configuration errors – related to erroneous configuration of the UNIX access control and user authentication mechanisms.
2. Software errors – bugs in the operating system and programs which comprise the trusted computer environment.

A variety of utilities such as the "COPS" expert system package exist to verify the correctness of a system configuration. Such packages typically operate by assuming user privileges and then attempting to trace a path (via modification of the initialisation or user command environment) that permits super-user status to be gained.

Software errors are loopholes in the environment which permit the assumption of higher privilege levels. It is vital to realise that such errors can occur in the operating system, startup files, bootstraps, daemons (both local and network service) and authentication mechanisms. The user interface in UNIX is extremely complex and diverse due to a design decision to limit the complexity of each software component, by providing a flexible toolbox of simple utilities. Thus user login is handled both by the getty and login programs, and a separate command shell is then run.

Any loopholes in a program running with "root" privilege is critical – this includes the initialisation utilities and the authentication mechanisms, as well as a wide variety of administrative tools run directly by the root user (as against those which are run automatically by the system).

A number of such loopholes have unfortunately been detected. The Computer Emergency Response Team (CERT) (described in Appendix 12) provides short descriptive reports on such loopholes and the appropriate bug fixes. A sample list of CERT advisories is included in Appendix 13.

7.4.4 Mechanics of UNIX Viruses

7.4.4.1 Batch Viruses

The previous sections have dealt with the means by which a hostile user can invoke viral code, and have provided a description of the various avenues for the introduction of a UNIX boot virus. This section addresses the remaining two areas of concern, namely the UNIX batch virus and the UNIX link virus.

The two command shells offer extremely powerful batch programming environments which permit access to iterative and conditional branch constructs, as well as access to the full range of UNIX command utilities. Thus, construction of a batch virus is unfortunately straightforward. Both the UNIX bourne shell and csh provide iterative, conditional and limited subroutine call facilities, together with access to the external file system via the "cat", I/O redirection and "echo" operations.

Hybrid viruses can be produced which exploit the macro or initialisation files used by a number of common utilities. Many of these files permit either specification of alternative search paths for common functions (such as the default system pager and editors in the case of news software) or permit direct execution of shell commands on utility startup. One particularly serious case is the .exrc initialisation file used by the "vi" and "ex" editors. This initialisation file can cause the shell command to be run. Worse, the editors also check the text file being edited for lines of the form "ex: command:" or "vi: command:". If these occur within the first five lines then they will be directly executed. Thus the act of editing a text file may permit a virus or trojan horse to become active. The editor initialisation commands might also include commands to delete themselves from the text file, so remaining unnoticed.

7.4.4.2 Link Viruses

Object code viruses can also be produced – witness Fred Cohen's early work on UNIX platforms. The structure of a UNIX object code file varies depending on the architecture of the system concerned. The example below is based on the AT & T Bell system V common object file format (COFF). In this case the object file comprises:

File Header

UNIX system header

Section 1..n headers

Section 1..n data

Section 1..n relocation information

Section 1..n line number info

Symbol table

String table

The file header identifies (using a magic number) the structure of the executable file, records the number of sections of data or executable text, and contains a pointer to the symbol table within the object file.

This is followed by a system specific header containing a further magic number, total size of the initialised data segment, total size of the uninitialised data segment, entry point for the executable and base address for loading text and data section (broadly equivalent to a segment in DOS).

Each section is described by a section header containing:

Section name

Virtual address of section in process memory

Size of section

Pointer to raw data for section

Pointer to relocation table for section

Pointer to line number info for section
Size of section relocation table
Size of line number table

When an executable is processed by the UNIX link editor (ld) all symbol references between executable modules are resolved to absolute pointers within the virtual memory space of the process generated by the executable. At this point the user may request the relocation table and line number information to be deleted from the executable (the action of stripping an executable).

The "exec" system call in UNIX loads the executable into memory, establishing three (or possibly more) areas of memory:

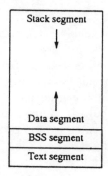

The text and BSS segments contain executable code and initialised data (respectively) loaded from sections defined in the executable file. The stack segment grows downwards in process virtual memory and is extended automatically. The uninitialised data segment grows upward from the end of the BSS segment through the use of the "sbrk" system call.

Depending on the system, a virus may either amend the object file to add a new viral section, or alternatively append itself to the existing text section. These options are comparable to the two distinct forms of link virus of the Macintosh; those which add new CODE resources, and those which append to existing CODE 1 resources.

In the first case the virus creates a new object file which consists of the header information, section headers, a new section header for the viral section, the original BSS and text sections and finally the new viral code section. This viral section can be placed anywhere in the process virtual memory space which would not be subject to overwriting either by stack or uninitialised data section extension.

In the second case (which is generally applicable to non-COFF systems) the virus must directly modify the main program text section. In many cases this can be simply achieved *in situ* by exploiting the fact that text segment sizes in UNIX are rounded to multiples of a minimum section size. This minimum size is often a function of the underlying system page size – in the case of the Sun 3 system it is 8 K. Thus, on average, approximately 4 K is available without restructuring of the object file.

If the virus finds sufficient space it adds its code directly to the end of the text segment and amends the entry pointer in the file header to point to the viral code. If insufficient space exists the virus is forced to restructure the object file by extending the text segment by a multiple of the minimum section size, adding its code and amending the entry pointer. This restructuring operation may require the movement and copying of relocation, line number and string table information in unstripped binaries.

7.4.4.3 Dynamic Loading

A final possible mechanism available for viral initialisation in newer UNIX systems is via the dynamic library loading mechanism. Because of the considerable size of newer UNIX libraries (particularly graphics and communications libraries), a mechanism has been developed whereby entry points to library files can be resolved at the time the object file is run (rather than statically at the time the file is linked). A virus can be incorporated into such a dynamic library and will be activated by any program exploiting the dynamic library. Thus a virus added to the standard "libc" library will potentially be run by all programs using this dynamic library (thus all programs compiled in the language C). This compares with the effects of deliberate addition of a virus to a static library. In this case the viral code will be linked whenever a program is re-linked (or compiled), and non- retrospective infection will occur.

7.4.4.4 Other Considerations

Virus operation in a UNIX environment is constrained by the operation of the memory management system. This effectively restricts the ability of viral code to remain active in memory when its host has terminated. To do so a virus must explicitly create a new process containing the resident portion of the virus, or delay termination of the host process. In general both techniques are available on UNIX.

Process creation is achieved using the UNIX "fork" command, which will generate a new exact copy of the original program. The copy will commence execution immediately after the point in the original at which the fork command was executed. Thus a virus can fork, create a new process, and then permit the continued execution of the original host program. The copy is capable of recognising the fact that it is a copy (using the return value from the fork system call) and of acting accordingly.

Process delayed termination is achieved by interception of the "exit" C library routine. This can either be done directly by modifying the address of the call to the exit function, or indirectly by the installation of a termination handler via the "on_exit" library call.

Delayed termination can normally be detected for interactive processes, but may be invisible for background or server processes.

The virus can unfortunately conceal its identity by overwriting the argument vector (a data structure used to pass command line arguments to programs, the first element of which is the name of the program). This structure is displayed by "ps". It may also exploit the "fork" when resident for a certain time – the technique that the Internet worm exploited. In addition processes running at sufficiently high privilege levels can directly modify the system accounting files (to delete references to the process) and active process table (to modify the process control structure).

Indeed, processes with access rights to /dev/kmem and /dev/mem (two special files in UNIX which allow direct access to kernel and physical memory) can arrange to directly infect processes in memory (including special processes such as init, and the standard daemon processes); relocate the virus code segment into the kernel address space (from where system interrupt and UNIX system calls can be redirected to the virus code); or a wide range of system data structures such as password buffers, disk I/O buffers, etc.

In general, once /dev/kmem write permission has been gained a virus has the potential to modify or alter system operation in a manner comparable to PC viruses.

A further vital channel which must be protected is the raw or block disk files which provide a low level direct access route to the peripheral devices. Such files permit a complex virus to directly bypass the UNIX filesystem and thus modify individual sectors on the storage media.

With regard to the signatures utilised by a resident UNIX virus, many possible channels are available (fewer on systems which inhibit covert channel data transfer, such as B2 or above) which can be exploited, including:

1. Files created in public filespace.
2. Ports created in the network space.
3. Processes with special names.
4. Shared memory or semaphores in the System V IPC package.
5. Use of advisory locking on existing files.
6. Timing channels such as processor, network and memory behaviour.

Finally, the principal technique for identification must be considered to be direct search of the file system (in general, indirect infection is exceptionally complex because of the requirement to directly intercept kernel system calls). A wide range of library functions are available to make directory search trivial.

7.4.4.5 Protecting Against UNIX Viruses

The principal techniques for protecting against UNIX viruses are:

1. Careful use of the standard UNIX DACs to prevent access to object, shell script and system initialisation files.

2. Correct setting of the PATH and IFS shell variables to prevent corresponding file attacks.
3. General controls on software installation including curtailing use of automatic archiving systems without integrity verification facilities.
4. Use of regular checksumming on system object and initialisation files.
5. Checking of system audit trails to flag potentially subversive program behaviour.
6. Scanning of incoming code files for suspect code which indicates trojan horse functions.
7. Fixing of known bugs and loopholes which permit root status to be gained.
8. Use of a shadow password system to prevent exhaustive search of the password space.

Expert systems are under development to help with each of these tasks, and include the COPS system, which carries out a check of file system permissions to detect potential channels for acquiring root privilege within the system.

7.4.4.6 Cohen: Early UNIX Viruses

As a final word on the UNIX virus risk, it is worth considering some early work completed by Dr Fred Cohen on virus propagation within the UNIX environment. These experiments began on 3 November 1983 and consisted of a trial using an infected system utility on a VAX 11/750 system. The availability of the utility was advertised on a system bulletin board, and five infection trials were carried out. Root privileges were gained in all cases, normally within an hour, although in one case within 5 minutes. This is a clear example of the DAC weakness which permits a program to inherit the permissions of its user. At that point the virus had considerable potential for infection of available object files. The significant difference is that the careful administrator who tried out the program using his/her usercode rather than "root" would infect a number of his own binary files. When he/she later ran one of the infected binaries as "root" full system privileges would be granted. In this respect virus attacks under DAC are much more insidious in that they can incrementally penetrate the DAC permission hierarchy, rather than trojan horses which must directly gain "root" permission to be globally destructive (other than direct denial of service attacks).

Cohen's virus was written in 8 hours and infected within half a second. The reaction of the systems administration was to prohibit any further testing of viral material, including installation of virus tracking utilities and augmented password security controls.

Later, in July 1984, Cohen was involved in an experiment to test virus propagation under the Bell-LaPadula model. This experiment, based on a UNIVAC 1108 system, used a clumsy virus (due to inexperience of the authors) which was 200 lines of Fortran code, 5 lines of assembler and 50 lines of command script. Nevertheless the virus infected within 20 seconds. The trial clearly indicated that penetration to higher security levels in the model was occurring.

In August 1984 trials began on tracking the incidence of code sharing (and potential viral spread) on a UNIX VAX system. Initial results reported that a clear pattern existed in code sharing. Specifically, a few users shared widely, a moderate number occasionally, and the bulk of users rarely. Cohen noted that systems administrators tended to try all new programs, leading to rapid penetration by viruses infecting such programs. Normal users were content with a small subset of standard UNIX utilities.

Cohen presents the results of his infection trials in a summary table:

	Unix-C	Bell-LaPadula	Unix-Shell	VMS	Basic	PCNet
Write in(hours)	8	18	0.25	0.5	4	8
Infect in (s)	0.5	20	<1	<1	10	0.5
Code (lines)	200	260	1	9	100	100

Chapter 8

Network Viruses: The Worms

8.1 Introduction

The rapid expansion in wide area and local area networking has led to the establishment of a global internetwork linking millions of systems. Through this network, which interlinks many diverse hardware architectures, a limited range of basic network functions are available – normally restricted to electronic mail and file transfer. The component networks within the global internetwork often use standardised protocols and architectures (thus avoiding the extensive protocol conversion carried out by gateway systems). Within these networks many "closely" coupled services are available. Such services include remote login, remote execution of code and transparent file systems across numerous machines.

As an, example electronic mail is now possible from a Joint Academic Network (JANET) host at a UK university to:

- Internet: DARPA Internet in USA, Canada and Europe. Mainly university, government and commercial contractors
- UUNET: an early (but now extensive) network connecting UNIX systems using dial up or leased line circuits
- BITNET: a tree structured international network linking university and research sites
- Fidonet: a diverse worldwide dial up network of bulletin board systems
- MILNET: US unclassified military network
- HEPNET: high energy physics network run by NASA
- SPANET: space physics analysis network run by NASA

In addition, there are many regional or national networks such as the Japanese University network (JUNET). The DARPA Internet consists of 3200 interconnected networks, including the networks of many vendors, government organisations and laboratories. A typical network might include hundreds of local systems connected on one or more LANs. Fidonet consists of approximately 10 000 bulletin boards spread from Alaska to Zimbabwe. Interconnected commercial bulletin boards include BIX, CONNECT, Genie and Prodigy, each with many thousands of users.

The number of interconnected hosts (loosely – for email purposes) is certainly in the millions. The global network offers incredible potential for information interchange. With such information comes the risk of malicious software replication – either self-replication or via human intervention.

To place the risk in context it is necessary to differentiate between various degrees of "coupling" between networked systems, namely:

Loose   Electronic mail transfer only
                               Limited file transfer facilities

                        Reliable "virtual" circuit data links
                               Remote login facilities

                           Remote command execution

Tight   Networked transparent access to file systems
                        Distributed processing and load balancing

As the degree of coupling increases (from loose to tight) so the risk of self-replicating code becomes greater. In loosely coupled systems worms or viruses are restricted to propagation by electronic mail techniques which normally require the intervention of a human user to start execution of the received virus or worm.

Into this category fit the trojan horses copied by users and the chain letters which are bulk mailed and then run on receipt by a user. Unfortunately, even email may allow remote command execution – the uudecode alias security loophole in UNIX is a typical example. The risk in a well designed mail system is normally minimal. Gateway mail systems may filter (using techniques such as permitting only ASCII text transmissions), and pad (by adding padding characters in column 1 of a message which will prevent its execution by a system command interpreter such as the UNIX shell) messages.

Intermediate systems permit establishment of a reliable data connection between two processes via the network. This includes remote login with all the related problems of distributed trust and electronic password search. This is normally sufficient to allow copying and execution of viral code under remote control.

Finally, and most dangerous, are the systems which support close coupling. Such systems normally have an exceptionally complex network interface composed of many separate applications. These include network transparent file systems and remote procedure call facilities. Worms and viruses can utilise these systems to copy code to hosts under remote control.

8.2 Standardisation

At the moment communications protocols are effectively at the "Tower of Babel" stage, with a large number of proprietary and network specific protocols. This has led to the construction of complex gateways between networks, such gateways carrying out protocol conversion at the application level (e.g. email relay or ftp-ftam file transfer relays). Such gateways have resulted in loose coupling between networks, reducing the risk of viral or worm code spread. An example is the restriction of the Internet worm to the DARPA Internet due to the email-only gateway between the Internet and JANET.

In the near future two streams of standards are likely to predominate, namely:

1. The *de jure* Open Systems Interconnection (OSI) standards promulgated by the International Organisation for Standardisation.
2. The *de facto* Internet Protocol standards promulgated by the Internet Engineering Task Force (IETF).

This standardisation will lead to tighter coupling between networks and will unfortunately lead to increased risk of worm or virus propagation. There is little doubt that the benefits from such close coupling are considerable. However, security must be considered. It is only now with the maturity of both protocol suites that initial work is under way on security functionality. It is likely that the incorporation of confidentiality, integrity and access control in a standardised and consistent manner will not occur for a number of years. At this stage network applications such as FTAM, SMTP, MHS, etc. are expected to provide their own access control facilities, often in an *ad hoc* manner.

A further problem evidenced in the Internet worm and DECNET worm incidents is the inertia of such large networks to update and change. Thus patches fielded to security loopholes take a considerable time to achieve significant penetration of the network hosts. Even now it is likely that a large number of Internet hosts (and indeed some software vendors) still contain the loopholes used by the Internet worm.

This chapter considers the Internet Protocols, DECNET and OSI protocols and assesses their vulnerability to virus/worm activity. Examples of previous worms are also given.

8.3 History of Network Pests

8.3.1 Early Work: Pre-1980

The earliest network worms were reported in 1970 – the Creeper and Reaper programs described in Chapter 2. These early experiments in distributed computation introduced the concept of migrating computation, and counterworms.

Early experimenters at Harvard then integrated the Creeper with a distributed flight simulation package under way. This produced a distributed self-replicating flight simulation with various distributed components representing each component of the flight space.

Xerox worm research built upon these initial experiments to investigate the concept of self-distributing computation. This work included research into:

1. Initialisation of worm binaries.
2. Location of idle machine units.
3. Use of multicast addressing (only recently incorporated into the IP suite) to communicate between worm components.
4. Distributed and centralised worm control algorithms.

The Xerox work reported by Shoch and Hupp in 1982 was far in advance of the technology incorporated in the malicious worms in terms of the complex worm control algorithms used to detect and correctly compensate for:

- Fragmentation of the network
- Unexpected termination of a worm segment
- Changes in network configuration and utilisation

During the development phase a number of problems were encountered, including one instance of a worm segment being corrupted during migration. The corrupted segment then crashed each machine it attempted to spread over.

8.3.2 Recent Benign and Malicious Worms

Since 1987 there have been a significant number of incidents during which worms were released onto public access networks. The target networks included BITNET, DECNET and Internet. A summary of these incidents is given below:

Network	Date released	Description
BITNET	9 Dec 87	CHRISTMA EXEC chain letter replicating on IBM CMS systems on VNET, BITNET, EARN
INTERNET	3 Nov 88	Internet worm replicating on Sun 3 and VAX UNIX
BITNET	5 Dec 88	CHRISTMA EXEC re-released on BITNET
DECNET	22 Dec 88	HI.COM Christmas worm replicating on DECNET/SPANNET/HEPNET
BITNET	8 Mar 89	BUL EXEC released on Turkish EARN node
BITNET	5 Apr 89	ORGASM EXEC released from PSUVM BITNET node
BITNET	8 Apr 89	HEADACHE EXEC found at Ottawa BITNET node
DECNET	16 Oct 89	WANK worm replicating on SPAN network
DECNET	30 Oct 89	OILZ variant of WANK worm on SPAN network
BITNET	25 Nov 89	DIR EXEC replicating on BITNET
BITNET	24 Sep 90	Source of CHRISTMA EXEC sent to alt.hackers newgroup
BITNET	8 Oct 90	TERM EXEC replicating on BITNET

The outrage of the Arpanet on 27 October 1990, despite being cited by a number of writers as a worm incident, was attributable to a hardware fault on an Interface Message Processor (IMP) coupled with vulnerabilities in the distributed routing algorithms used on the network.

In the case of BITNET each "worm" was actually a chain letter written in the REXX command language. It relied on the recipient of the chain letter to run the resultant file, which purported to print a Christmas tree on his/her screen. The Christmas EXEC was modified to produce the BUL, DIR and TERM exec modules.

The Internet and DECNET worms were, however, self-propagating and did not rely on any intervention by the user. They represent the first true incidents of malicious worm propagation on their host networks.

A description of the DECNET and Internet worms is given later in this chapter, together with information on the protocols and features which permitted these worms to spread.

In the meantime a brief look at the CHRISTMA EXEC program (infamous) will show that the term "chain letter" is appropriate.

8.3.3 CHRISTMA EXEC Chain Letter

The term "chain letter" is chosen because the program spread by way of an electronic mail message sent to a number of users. This message contained a program script which purported to be benign and entertaining. In fact, when run by the user, it replicated by sending copies of itself by email to a large number of addresses.

The Christmas chain letter was written in the command language REXX used by the IBM mainframe CMS operating system. The chain letter circulated widely amongst BITNET, the European Academic Research Network (EARN) and IBM's internal network (VNET). Infection commenced at 1300 GMT on Wednesday 9 December and originated from EARN node (DCZTU1) at Clausthal-Zellerfeld in West Germany. From here the chain letters spread rapidly through most of BITNET, and successfully crossed via a gateway site onto IBM's internal VNET network. The chain letter was apparently written by a student to send Christmas greetings to his friends. One of the recipients, unaware of its nature, ran the received greeting and started the bulk infection.

Within BITNET, infection was cleared by 14 December, although within IBM a major network shutdown occurred on 11 December to clear the infection.

The REXX command script when run:

1. Displayed a message and Christmas tree on screen.
2. Checked that the current year was 1988 or earlier, and that the month was December, January or February.
3. If this was the case the script examined two CMS files – NAMES and NETLOG. NAMES is a CMS file which contains mappings between mail

aliases used by the user and full email addresses. NETLOG is an audit trail of users whom you have sent or received mail or files from. Together these files provided the script with a rich collection of mail addresses.

4. Mailed a copy of itself to each address in the NAMES and NETLOG files.
5. Deleted itself.

An important point is that the NAMES and NETLOG files contained users whom the person running the script regularly communicated with, and this made it likely that the recipient (seeing that the chain letter originated from a known colleague) would run the script. The script was also structured to include the innocuous tree printing code first:

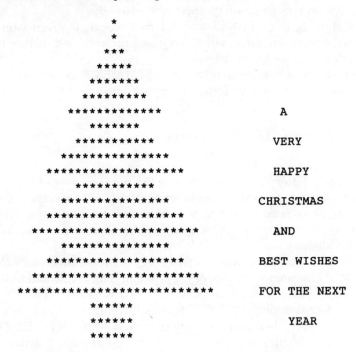

followed by a message that:

Browsing this file is no fun at all, just type CHRISTMAS from CMS

Thus many users (who might be unfamiliar with the REXX command language) neglected to read any further, and ran the script.

The script was published by a number of sources (as well as being widely available), including the book *Computer Viruses: A High-tech Disease*. The CHRISTMA EXEC has since been modified on a number of occasions and was re-released onto BITNET on 5 December 1988 (possibly accidently sent from Louisiana State University). Modified versions included the BUL EXEC released from the EARN backbone site in Turkey on 8 March 1989 (it was found because of a warning from its author within 10 minutes of release), and the DIR

EXEC released on 25 November 1989 (which purported to produce an MS-DOS format directory listing of CMS files) and detected at BITNET node TECMTYVM.

Other CMS chain letters have included the ORGASM EXEC released from Pennsylvania State University on 4 April 1989, which spread to the University of Central Florida; the HEADACHE EXEC found at the University of Ottawa on 8 April 1989, and TERM MODULE, originating from Turkey (a REXX exec to pretty print the CP QUERY NAMES command), which spread to the USA and Canada.

8.3.4 Chain Letters on UNIX

The CMS exec chain letters above can be placed in the same category as transmission of shell scripts by UNIX email. The latter is now a significant problem because of the large number of automated archiving sites which receive source code postings from USENET electronic news groups. At the least, such archiving utilities will store the shell script for later request and execution by other users; at the worst the archiver will attempt local unpacking of the shar (shell archive), which may result in trojan horse code being executed.

UNIX source news groups are countering this risk by adding checksumming to transmitted archive files. Until the advent of extensive digital signature utilisation such automated distributed archiving via an untrusted electronic mail channel will be vulnerable.

8.4 Internet Protocols

The first of the popular suites of network protocols to be considered in this chapter is the Internet Protocol (IP) stack. This suite was developed by the Defense Advanced Research Project Agency (DARPA) network user community. This community is spread across the military, research and commercial sectors. The protocols are specified by a series of "request for comments" (RFC) documents available via the network itself. Since the original network has now expanded to embrace gateways to thousands of other networks, it is generally referred to as the Internet. The protocols used on this network are now an integral part of BSD UNIX and have been adopted by many other vendors. It is true to say that the Internet Protocols represent the *de facto* standards in the UNIX community, as against the *de jure* standards being promulgated by the ISO.

The Internet Protocols provided the carrier medium for the Internet worm of November 1988. Before examining the case history of this incident, it is necessary to consider briefly the protocols and their vulnerability to virus/ worm attack.

8.4.1 Architecture

The IP stack comprises a number of layers of protocols, each responsible for some component of the two abstractions provided by the suite, namely:

- A reliable error-free data stream between two application programs
- An unreliable packet delivery service (the datagram)

The stack includes the following elements:

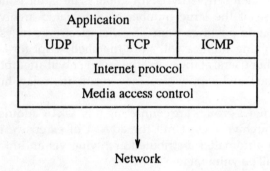

The media access control layer interfaces to the underlying network drivers, supplying packet headers and trailers appropriate to the underlying network.

The IP provides a network layer which supports an unsequenced, unreliable packet transmission service between two host systems carrying out routing and fragmentation services. Each host is identified by a four byte Internet address.

Above this layer are two separate transport layers – the user datagram protocol (UDP) which supports unreliable, unsequenced packet transmission between two host applications, and the transmission control protocol (TCP), which supports the abstraction of a reliable data stream linking two application programs. Each program executing within a host is allocated a separate "port" address for each network connection. Thus a program may have two connections open: "port 5122" and "port 5123" on Internet host "192.9.201.23". Thus a message at the transport layer is addressed using the host address, and the port on that host. The communications software will then deliver the message to the application "listening" on the specified port.

The IPs are extremely open due to their developmental environment. Only now are security features being incorporated to protect data confidentiality and integrity.

8.4.2 Peer Authentication

Each host on the network is trusted to identify itself correctly by supplying its Internet address. Hosts may masquerade as other systems by forging the source IP address of a transmitted packet. Gateways amd the hosts being imitated may flag security warnings when being impersonated. Since the IP layer is unreliable the real host may be tricked into ignoring the dummy packet by a deluge of valid packets (this may cause the buffer space on the host to be exhausted, causing received packets to be dropped).

Equally, by using the dynamic network redirection facilities provided in the Internet Control Message Protocol (ICMP – a network management and error reporting protocol), it is possible for a hostile system to intercept traffic destined for a valid system. This is achieved through the host of the ICMP redirect message. Receipt of such a redirection request causes a system to update its routing tables according to the information in the request. Thus host A can be tricked into sending all traffic intended for host C, to host B; by host B sending a redirect message to A. This message then causes A to update its routing table.

Used in conjunction the two techniques allow host B to redirect all traffic from host A to C via itself, and then to impersonate host C during accesses to host A. If host B and C are not on the same physical network then the masquerade may never be detected. This technique potentially undermines the concept of trust between posts based on peer authentication.

By masquerading, a host may initiate services on a destination system which would normally be restricted to the host being impersonated:

1. Host B sends a redirect request to host A that indicates a shorter route to host C.
2. Host A then begins sending all traffic to host C via host B.
3. Host B sends a forged request appearing to come from host C to host A.
4. Host A performs the trusted function based on the forged message.
5. Host A sends the results via the shortest route to host C; this route is via host B.
6. Host B captures the reply and fails to forward the packet to host C.

Equally it is possible to forge the original source port id. This will ensure that the message appears to originate from a trusted application or daemon.

Of crucial importance are two concepts in the Berkeley IP implementation:

- Trusted ports which only the super-user or administrator may allocate, they have port numbers < 1024.
- Fixed port id used by standard services such as mail, file transfer and remote login

The ability to forge host and port ids permits a worm to spread by copying its code via trusted network services, and then to execute such code remotely.

8.4.3 Access Controls

Access controls depend on two features at the transport level:

- Source host id (trusted host id)
- Source port id (trusted or known port id)

As previously mentioned, both can be forged. Thus Internet access control is susceptible to a breach of trust by any host connected to the network (or dependent on gateways to the local network).

This major difficulty can be overcome by the new extensions to application protocols which incorporate authentication via cryptographic techniques, e.g. privacy enhancements for electronic mail – RFC 1113.

8.4.4 Data Stream Integrity

An established data stream using TCP is highly reliable, providing recovery facilities for lost or duplicated packets or data. This layer is however susceptible to a number of well known attacks, first described by Robert Morris (father of the author of the Internet worm) in 1985. These weaknesses centred around the implementation of the initial sequence number (ISN) generation used in the TCP transport protocol in Berkeley systems.

The sequence numbers are used to order all packets in the TCP session and to permit recovery from lost packets. When a connection is established the initiator transmits its ISN to the destination. The destination system then replies with its own ISN.

A foreign host may masquerade as a trusted host using TCP. This is achieved by sending a connect request to the destination alleging to have originated at a trusted host. This connect request carries the ISN to be used by the foreign host. The destination system will then acknowledge this request, sending its own ISN to the trusted system. If the masquerading host can successfully predict the pseudo-random ISN generated by the destination host, it may inject data or commands that purport to have originated at the trusted host. This attack does not require manipulation of routing tables, since the foreign host is relying on its ability to "predict" the contents of the acknowledgement packet being sent to the trusted host. This attack permits:

- Injection of malicious code into code being transmitted by applications (e.g. into remote copy requests (RCP))
- Insertion of malicious command into login, file transfer or remote execution sessions

It is worth noting that one of the most common remote filing system protocols (NFS) uses UDP as its transport layer, and is thus subject to trivial manipulation by hostile (or infected) systems on the local network.

8.4.5 Daemons and Servers

Above the transport layer are placed the numerous application services of the Internet, each of which listens on a special fixed port for incoming service requests. These services if spoofed allow remote copying and execution of viral or worm code.

Port Id	Remote Copying	Execution	Service Description
21	X		File transfer protocol (FTP)
23	X	X	Telnet remote login protocol
25	X	(X)	Simple mail transfer protocol (SMTP)
69	X		Trivial file transfer protocol (TFTP)
79		(X)	Finger protocol
111		X	Remote procedure call (RPC)
512		X	Remote execution service (REXEC)
513	X	X	Remote login service
514	X	X	Remote shell service (RSH)

In the above table, X indicates that remote execution may be possible through bugs in the daemon, rather than through a design feature.

The remote procedure call facility also allows a range of special functions to be executed which include the rexd (remote execution service).

Each service carries out its own user authentication and access control functions, possibly using the standard system login procedures. The services of particular note are those with known bugs or loopholes which could be exploited by a worm to gain access:

- Sendmail: numerous bugs, e.g. CIAC advisory A-13, BSD Fix 1.67, CERT Advisory 9001 including the DEBUG option loophole exploited by the Internet worm
- Rsh: BSD Fix 1.36
- Rlogin: BSD Fix 1.36, BSD Fix 1.60
- Telnet: BSD Fix 1.60
- Ftpd: BSD Fix 1.65
- Tftpd: absence of security checking for read access to filesystems
- Rcp: BSD Fix 1.82, CERT Advisory 8907
- Fingerd: BSD Fix 1.69

The samples above indicate that the majority of the applications forming the network interface have known bugs or loopholes which as a minimum permit reading of system password files, and thus allow remote cracking of passwords stored in encrypted form.

8.4.6 Distributed Trust

Of particular interest are the "r" series protocols provided by BSD UNIX as extensions to the IP application layer. These are "rlogin", "rsh" and "rexec" (remote copy makes use of rsh). To simplify the tedious process of remote login and program execution, Berkeley introduced a way for trusted hosts and users to login directly without supplying a password. The extent of the "distributed trust" was specified by the administrator of the system, and could be extended by individual users.

The local system could specify a list of "trusted" hosts in its /etc/hosts.equiv file. Each user on a remote trusted host could login to an account on the local system with the same user id. Thus user "fred" on "helios" could login without supplying a password to the local system "solaris". This implies that the mapping of user name to user id must be the same on both systems. If this was not the case user Fred Alexander who has user id "fred" on helios and user id "alex" on solaris, could log into Fred Smith's account (user id fred) on solaris.

If host helios is compromised, a route immediately exists to login or remotely execute commands on host solaris. The only exception is the "root" user who is forced to explicitly specify a list of trusted hosts (who would be permitted password-less login) in the file /.rhosts. The /etc/hosts.equiv file is ignored for the root user.

Had this been the extent of trust, then it is arguable that it might have been manageable. However, each individual user could also specify additional trusted hosts and users in the file .rhosts in his/her home directory.

Thus, user fred on solaris might specify in his .rhosts file:

- ormazd = user fred on ormazd is trusted to login as user fred on solaris
- osiris james = user james on osiris is trusted to login as user fred on solaris

A complex graph of trust was thus established which was impossible to administer, and led to complex routes of vulnerability, such as:

	solaris	oberon	loki
fred	.rhosts = oberon	.rhosts = oberon nigel	
nigel		.rhosts = loki	.rhosts = solaris nasty
nasty			

In the above case, user nasty on solaris could login as nigel to loko, then from loki to oberon, change user to fred on oberon and finally login as fred to solaris. Fred certainly does not trust nasty, but he trusts nigel, who does.

8.4.7 Trusted Ports

Finally, as previously mentioned, there exists in the "r" protocols the notion of trusted ports. Machine solaris will accept a remote login originating from oberon on trusted port 513. It will then expect the remote system to send the user id of the remote user, together with the user id he wishes to login as on the local system. If oberon is compromised then the remote user can link to the login server via a trusted port (he is root and can thus originate a call from a trusted port) and send any user id he wishes as his local user id. This problem was made even more severe by a bug in rsh/rlogin which caused these processes to accept "trusted" connections from any port whatsoever.

8.4.8 Problems and Solutions

Thus, in summary, worms can attack the IPs by:
• Masquerading or forging IP or port addresses at network and transport layers
• Injection of malicious code or commands via faults in transport protocols
• Bugs in server/daemon processes implementing application layer
• Utilising distributed trust in "r" protocols to suppress access controls

MIT has addressed the issue of an untrusted workstation being connected to a LAN and has redesigned BSD UNIX to incorporate authentication, data confidentiality and integrity services. The environment developed at MIT is known as "Kerberos", named after Cereberus, the three-headed dog which guarded hell in Greek mythology.

The environment is based on the concept of centralised trust in a number of authentication servers. These authentication servers support a large number of untrusted networked workstations. Thus when a user logs into such an untrusted workstation, the workstation will communicate with the central authentication server to establish the user's identity and network credentials.

The connection of untrusted hosts to the network also means that the authentication mechanisms in Kerberos must be resilient to impersonation and replay attacks by other hosts. Kerberos supplies support for centralised rather than distributed trust.

Kerberos may become an integral part of the BSD 4.4 operating system release. For further details of the key management facilities incorporated in this secure distributed communications environment the reader is referred to the paper from the MIT Athena project cited in the further reading section.

8.4.9 Internet Worm: Black Thursday – 3 November 1988

On the 2 November 1988 at around 1800 EST, Robert T. Morris, a Cornell student and son of a senior scientist at the US National Computer Security

Centre (NCSC) executed a binary image of a UNIX worm program on a public access machine at MIT – prep.ai.mit.edu. This machine was used for the storage and distribution of shareware – in this case the widely used gnu software packages.

This worm was to spread across the USA and infect an estimated 6000 computer systems.

8.4.9.1 Internals

The worm exploited a number of features and bugs in the daemon processes that implement the applications layer in the IP suite. These included:

1. Fingerd: The fingerd bug, mentioned previously, allowed the worm to overwrite an I/O buffer in the program, corrupting the stored program counter in the stack frame. Thus, when the daemon executed a procedure "return" instruction it was tricked into execution of a series of instructions causing it to overlay itself with a copy of the UNIX shell. This shell remained connected to the original network connection which had invoked the fingerd. The shell ran with the permission of the fingerd which had invoked it – i.e. root! The buffer overrun bug potentially exists in programs which make use of a wide range of UNIX library calls, including gets, scanf, fscanf, sscanf, strcat and strcpy. The inclusion of such library calls (whose existence has been perpetuated via the POSIX international UNIX standards) has been a frequent source of UNIX software bugs.

2. Sendmail: The sendmail mail handler daemon in standard BSD UNIX had been distributed with debugging code enabled. Sendmail listens on port 25 for a series of commands in the SMTP protocol. These commands take the form of:

MAIL FROM: davidf@cs.hw.ac.uk	Sender address
RCPT TO: fred@anywhere.org	Recipient address
DATA	
.....	Text of letter
QUIT	Close connection

The address is restricted to a valid email address. By issuing the command "DEBUG", the worm placed the mail daemon in a debugging mode which would permit the destination address to be a UNIX command. This command would receive the text message as its input. The command started by the worm was the UNIX shell.

3. Rsh: Not a bug, but a feature. The worm utilised the distributed trust features in the Berkeley "r" protocols to spawn a remote shell on the target system.

4. Passwords: Finally, the worm would attempt to spread using the accounts of other users on its local system. The worm used a variety of brute force

techniques to break the password of a user on the local system. If the attack was successful the worm would attempt to use the remote execution service "rexec" to start a shell on a target remote system using the cracked user id and password. If this failed the worm started a command under the cracked user id and password locally, and then attempted to use the "rsh" protocol to start a shell on the remote system.

On UNIX passwords are stored in encrypted publicly readable form in the file /etc/passwd. The encrypted form consists of using the password as a key to encrypt a fixed constant. The worm did not try to invert the cipher, but attempted a brute force technique which consisted of trying large numbers of passwords and comparing the encrypted constant with the value in the password file. This search of the plaintext domain was accelerated by selecting obvious choices of password for testing:

1. No password.
2. User id used as password.
3. User id appended to itself and used as password.
4. A nickname from the GECOS field in the password file.
5. User's surname from the GECOS field in the password file.
6. Reverse of the user's surname.
7. A 432 word built in dictionary of likely passwords.
8. Full UNIX on-line dictionary of 24 474 words.

The worm appeared to use an optimised DES encryption routine, which appeared stylistically distinct from the remainder of the worm, and was significantly faster than the DES encryption routine distributed with UNIX.

When the worm had successfully obtained a shell on a remote system it proceeded to transfer a small vector or carrier program, together with the shell commands to compile and execute the carrier. It is worth noting that the carrier was essentially architecture independent since it was written in the C high level language, and was compiled and executed using high level commands in the shell command language.

The carrier opened a network connection to the infected source host. Over this connection two executable modules were transferred (actually the worm had facilities to transfer up to 19 such executable modules. Only two were used – modules for the DEC VAX and Sun 3 systems). If either of the transferred modules executed successfully it caused repetition of the infection process on the remote system – the worm had spread. In summary the worm:

- Exploited known bugs in fingerd and sendmail
- Exploited distributed trust in Berkeley "r" protocols
- Attempted exhaustive searches for encrypted passwords
- Used an architecture independent carrier/vector program to transfer two executables for the VAX and Sun 3 architectures

8.4.9.2 Action and Reaction

The brief chronology below gives an illustration of the spread of the Internet worm, and the reaction of the community to the worm. It is important to realise that at this time the community was unorganised and relied primarily upon the "old- boy" network to co-ordinate its response. With the advent of the Computer Emergency Response Team (CERT), which was directly attributable to the Internet worm incident, it is likely that any future event will be dealt with rapidly. (All times below are in Eastern Standard time (EST).)

Date	Time	Site and event
		Epoch
29 Oct 88	-	Cornell: extensive testing of sendmail - probably attempting direct binary transmission of worm modules
2 Nov 88	1702	Cornell: infection of a Cornell system by the worm
	1926-2100	Massachusetts Institute of Technology: infection of PREP.AI a public access shareware repository
	2100	Stanford: infected
	2124	Rand Corporation, Santa Monica: infected via University of Pittsburgh
	2130	MIT: Project Athena workstation infected
	2130	University of Minnesota: infected
	2204	University of California: Berkeley infected
	2234	Princeton University: infected
	2240	University of North Carolina: infected
	2248	SRI International: infected
	2252	Carnegie Mellon University: attacked by worm
	2254	University of Maryland: infected
	2255	Cornell University: attacked by worm
	2259	Pennsylvania University: attacked by worm
	2345	Dartmouth College and Army Ballistic Research Lab: infected
	2349	University of Utah: infected
3 Nov 88	0007	University of Arizona: infected
	0033	University of Delaware: infected
	0100	University of Michigan: attacked
	0105	Lawrence Livermore National Laboratory: infected
	0130	University of California: Los Alamos site infected
	0200	University of Harvard: infected
		Black Thursday: first warning and reaction
	0228	A message is sent by Peter Yee of UCB to the tcp-ip mailing list warning of extensive infection
	0315	University of Chicago: infected
	0334	An anonymous posting is sent by Andrew Sudduth warning of the worm, apparently at the request of Robert Morris the author
	0400	Colorado State University: attacked
	0400	Purdue University: attacked
	0700	Georgia Institute: infected

The chronology of initial infections (of which these are a selected subset) shows that the worm rapidly spread during the early evening of Wednesday 2 November, infecting many sensitive sites (including the Lawrence Livermore National Laboratory). The worm appears to have been under development on a Cornell system since mid-October 1988. The authorities at Cornell successfully retrieved and decrypted (because of the use of crypt, an insecure UNIX encryption tool) a number of versions of the worm, including:

1. An early source code version dated 15 October 1988.
2. An almost completed version dated 2 November, 1213 EST.
3. A completed version dated 2 November, 2026 EST.

The early version has comments which indicate that the fingerd bug was known, and that additional bugs were to be exploited, including a fault in the "yellow pages" directory service daemons. It is significant that the early version makes no mention of the sendmail DEBUG attack technique. Testing of this may have commenced on 19 November, although the Provost's enquiry at Cornell notes that Morris visited Harvard between 20 and 22 November. After this point, the Cornell enquiry notes that backups of the worm files included this attack technique.

After the release of the worm, Robert Morris made a phone call to Paul Graham of the Aiken Computational Laboratory, Harvard. Paul, who was at the time (2300 on 2 November) conversing with Andrew Sudduth, also of Harvard, mentioned to him that "something big was up". On being pressed by Andrew he mentioned that Robert Morris had released a virus which was overloading computers at Cornell and might spread all over the country.

Robert Morris (after a prompting mail message from Andrew Sudduth) called him at 2330 and told him that "something was going on", but did not admit releasing the worm. At 0230 on 3 November he again called Andrew and asked him to send a letter of apology across the network. The anonymous letter (using a common sendmail forgery technique) was sent out at 0330, and included the text:

A possible virus report:
There may be a virus loose on the internet.
Here is the gist of a message I got:
I'm sorry.
Here are some steps to prevent further transmission:

1) Don't run fingerd, or fix it to not overrun its stack when reading arguments.

2) recompile sendmail w/o DEBUG defined

3) don't run rexecd

Hope this helps, but more, I hope it is a hoax.

This message was trapped at an overloaded relay site (relay.cs.net) before reaching the distribution point for the tcp-ip mailing list. In the absence of these crucial warning the community was forced to disassemble and analyse the worm from scratch.

The initial message from Peter Yee to tcp-ip flags an initial warning to the entire community:

Date: Wed, 2 Nov 88 23:28:00 PST
From: Peter E Yee
Subject: Internet VIRUS alert

We are currently under attack from an Internet VIRUS. It has hit UC Berkeley, UC San Diego, Lawrence Livermore, Stanford, and NASA Ames. The virus comes in via SMTP (ed. Simple Mail Transfer Protocol is the mail protocol used by the TCP/IP based Internet, which includes ARPAnet, MILNET, and a whole slew of others all over the world), and then is able to attack all 4.3BSD and SUN (3.X?) machines. It sends a RCPT TO that requests that its data be piped through a shell. It copies in a program, compiles and executes it. This program copies in VAX and SUN binaries that try to replicate the virus via connections to TELNETD, FTPD, FINGERD, RSHD, and SMTP (ed. these are the standard background tasks, or daemons, that run on TCP/IP equipped machines; the tasks performed by them include remote login sessions, file in them. They appear in /usr/tmp as files that start with the letter x. Removing them is not enough as they will come back in the next wave of attacks. For now, turning off the above services seems to be the only help. The virus is able to take advantage of .rhosts files and hosts.equiv. We are not certain what the final result of the binaries is, hence the warning.

Work was under way at the University of California at Berkeley, resulting in an initial fix posted at 0558 by Keith Bostic. This fix suggesting recompilation of the sendmail program without the DEBUG option, and the stopgap of renaming the standard C compiler (cc) which the worm required to compile itself. A second bug-fix message was posted at 1112 and suggested the use of the UNIX "strings" command to search for the string "debug" in the sendmail program – a test of whether a site was vulnerable. The Berkeley group was joined by the MIT telecommunications network group, who successfully captured VAX and Sun worm binaries. The fingerd attack was discovered at 1921 by the University of Rochester (although MIT claims to have discovered the bug at about the same time).

The bulk of disassembly and analysis work took place on the evening of 3 November when work was under way in the Student Information Processing Board (SIPB) at MIT to disassemble the worm. This work included recognition of the encoded form of text strings in the worm (using a basic XOR technique). The phage-l mailing list was established by Eugene Spafford of Purdue. This electronic mail list was to be the first formalisation of the old boy network, and was to act as a crucial focal point for discussion and information exchange. One of the first messages was posted at 2120 as a result of the analysis work under way at Purdue, it was the so-called "condom": a simple fix to prevent infection by creating a directory "/usr/tmp/sh". The worm tries to use the file "/usr/tmp/sh" to store temporary code: this condom prevented successful creation of the temporary file.

At 2218 Keith Bostic made the first bug fix for the fingerd bug, including new source code which utilises fgets, rather than gets. Decompilation of the worm was completed in the morning of 4 November due to an incredible overnight effort at a number of sites. Decompilation went hand-in-hand with direct testing of captured worm binaries on isolated systems. The use of the rexec/rsh attack was noted at 0422 on 4 November. The MIT group finally exchanged code with the Berkeley decompilation team at 0545. Decompilation work at UCB finished at 0900.

The MILNET responded to the Internet worm by disconnection of its mailbridges (hosts gatewaying between the public internet, and the unclassified but sensitive MILNET) at 1130 on 3 November. The two networks remained disconnected until 1100 on 4 November. It is questionable whether the approach of disconnection to avoid infection (of which this was but a single case) inhibited the distribution of bug fixes and interchange of information between analysis staff.

Finally it is worth noting that the worm did incorporate primitive camouflage and concealment measures, including:

1. Renaming the executing worm "sh" to imitate one of the many command shells normally running on an active system.
2. Removing the original binary from the filesystem and killing of its parent task.
3. Using the UNIX fork system call to create a new copy of itself whenever its elapsed processor time reached a critical value, thus avoiding the obvious indicator of a system shell with excessive elapsed processor time.
4. Trivially encrypting the strings and password dictionaries used within the worm.
5. Attempting to detect the presence of other copies of the worm on the local system, and to negotiate their termination.

There was little doubt therefore that Morris was actively trying to conceal the presence of the worm.

8.4.9.3 The Aftermath

When the dust had settled from this incident Robert T. Morris was indicted under the US Computer Fraud and Abuse statute and found guilty on 4 May 1990 by US District Judge Howard Munson in Syracuse, New York. He was sentenced to 3 years' probation, a $10 000 fine and 400 hours of community service.

The Provost's report from Cornell University concluded that Robert Morris had:

1. Probably not intended to destroy data or other files or to interfere with the functioning of the computers that were penetrated.
2. Intended the worm to spread widely but to remain undiscovered. It was uncertain whether an announcement of its existence would be made at a later date.
3. Clearly violated the Cornell computer science department's "Policy for the use of the research computing facility".
4. Made minimal efforts to halt the worm once it had propagated, nor did he inform a person in a position of responsibility of his actions.
5. That it was an uncharacteristic act for the student who was normally concerned to protect against abuse of computers.

Cornell University, acting on its commission's report, suspended Robert Morris for a minimum of one year, the faculty to consider re-admission after this time frame.

The damage caused by his creation has been variously estimated as being:

- $97 million: John McAfee, President, Computer Virus Industry Association
- $10 million: Cliff Stoll, security consultant and author of Cukoo's Egg
- $250 000: Cost of reacting to worm at Los Alamos National Laboratory
- $200 000: Gene Spafford's personal estimate of cost
- $100 000: Cost of reacting to worm at Lawrence Livermore National Laboratory
- $72 500: Cost of reacting to worm at NASA's Ames Research Center

- 8000: Gene Spafford's estimate of personnel hours lost battling the worm
- 6000: NCCD's estimate of number of these hours which were not compensated
- 6000: Most common estimate of number of hosts infected

The actual figure of loss due to the worm will never be exactly known. There is general agreement, however, that it lies in the region of $100 000 to $10 million. The figure quoted by McAfee has been widely criticised as being excessive. However, the cumulative loss figure for the three government laboratories quoted together totals $422 500. It is likely that of 56 000 connected hosts, a significant proportion were infected. One site alone (MIT) quotes an infection rate of 10 per cent (200 hosts out of 2000 infected). This statistic has been extrapolated to produce the widely quote statistic of around 6000 infected hosts.

Infection reports from apparently active worm instances continued to be detected until early December 1989.

There is little doubt that the legacy left in the aftermath of the worm will continue to significantly influence the entire computer security community. In its aftermath the CERT organisation was born, an organisation now being extended worldwide. The bugs exploited by the worm still exist on some hosts despite the patches being globally available. The potential for a repeat of the incident still looms over the Internet, a network which developed in an open academic environment and is only now beginning serious consideration of the issue of network security.

8.4.10 DISNET: A Child of the Internet

As a brief aside, I would like to consider the planned architecture of the Defense Integrated Secure Network (DISNET) which forms the classified backbone service provided by the Defense Communications Agency in the US. This network relies on extensive end-to-end encryption (E3) at the network layer.

The network is designed to permit the carriage of secret, top secret and compartmented top secret data over a physical network classified at the secret level.

DISNET provides extensive support for data confidentiality and traffic flow analysis prevention. Data integrity is the responsibility of the host system with support from the network service. The access constraints appropriate to the secret classification of DISNET will substantially reduce the probability of malicious software introduction by direct physical access to the network. All data in transit is also encrypted, complicating the insertion of malicious code (to insert useful commands or data it is necessary to determine the encrypted form of the malicious software – this knowledge of the private key component, insertion of random garbage or corruption of data is of course less difficult). Support for the detection of data integrity violations will be provided.

The DISNET effectively extends the Orange Book MAC protection model by offering network support for security classifications and compartments, together with support for access identification of a user community's classification and compartment permissions. The interface between DISNET and the unclassified MILNET segment will be TCSEC B-2 level systems. Such systems could be subject to bandwidth limited covert channel attacks at < 0.1 bit/sec by malicious software exploiting possible bugs in the network applications layer on the gateway. The only form of communication supported by the gateway is electronic mail store and forward – this restriction should severly limit the size of the applications interface and permit extensive verification of mail handling software.

Such a mail bridge (also including traffic limitations to prevent denial of service attacks) would however still permit chain letter attacks and the exploitation of bugs on destination system email servers. The MILNET to Internet backbone links would be via TCSEC B-1 level systems, again restricting service to email forwarding.

The E3 encryption system (Blacker) is front-ended by a filter (BFE) which implements the mandatory access control requirements of the DoD security policy. Use of strict filtering at the BFE would minimise the trust placed in the mail gateways and would prevent covert channel compromise as a result of trojan horse introduction via chain letter, mail server access or direct posting.

In summary, the proposed DISNET is protected due to its loose coupling to public access networks, simplification of the application layer interface on gateways, and backbone support for data integrity and confidentiality. The network is still vulnerable to chain letter attacks and electronic mail handling server bugs causing possible data compromise at low bandwidths, and possible corruption of data on connected host systems not implementing integrity extensions to the basic Bell-LaPadula model.

8.5 OSI: Security in the Making

The International Organisation for Standardisation (ISO) has standardised on a seven layer model for data communications – the open systems architecture (OSI) model. This is formalised in the international standard ISO 7498-1, and comprises:

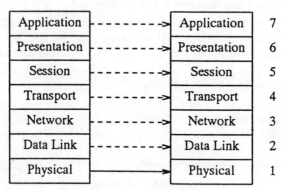

Confidentiality and integrity services are located at a number of levels in the OSI hierarchy including:

	OSI Model Level						
	1	2	3	4	5	6	7
Data origin authentication			Y	Y			Y
Connection integrity with recovery				Y			Y
Connection integrity without recovery			Y	Y			Y
Selective field connection integrity							Y
Connectionless integrity			Y	Y			Y
Selective field connectionless integrity							Y
Access control			Y	Y			Y

The principal layers involved in information integrity are the network, transport and application layers. The level of data integrity is indicated to the network and transport layers by a protection quality of service (QOS) parameter supplied as part of the connection process. The OSI Security Management Information Base (SMIB) maps the protection levels required to each module level, thus an application requesting support for a particular combination of security services may cause specific values of transport protection QOS and network protection QOS to be requested. During connection establishment a negotiation process takes place between the requester and responder. This negotiation process attempts to derive a common QOS based on the requester's requirements and the services available from the responder. Unfortunately, at this time (November 1990) the QOS can only be negotiated towards less restrictive or secure protection. Facilities are under discussion to allow the responder or network service to require a stricter protection QOS. Thus a remote host which implements a high integrity environment may require all incoming network connections (over untrusted networks) to be negotiated to use the "connection integrity" protection QOS.

At the application layer users can select from a variety of OSI communication security and integrity services, including the provision of connection integrity using checksum and cryptographic signature algorithms. By selecting an appropriate set of OSI security modules the user can establish a checksummed or signed data transfer session with positive authentication of data origin or communicating peer identity. Access control facilities can then permit the establishment of a mapping from transmitted data integrity identifier to local data integrity levels.

The OSI security model is still at the specification stage with the implementation of many of the security features being deferred. Any implementation may still be open to similar problems to the BSD implementation of the data integrity feature in TCP, namely an implementational flaw.

8.6 DECNET: Insecurity Through Default

The proprietary DECNET protocols were the subject of two well- known virus attacks, namely the HI.COM (Christmas) and the NETW (WANK) worms. Both of these worms spread worldwide across the SPAN and HEPNET sponsored by NASA. Both worms exploited a number of poorly configured network services to propagate.

DECNET, like its Internet cousin, permits transfer and remote execution of code files to occur. This facility is implemented through the use of the "TASK 0" remote execution service, and via a default DECNET account which is comparable to the anonymous ftp service in the Internet (allowing downloading of public file without user authentication). Together, these facilities permitted the worms (both using similar techniques) to copy their code to a remote system and to trigger its execution.

In general, the problems on DEC systems were caused by lax security installation procedures. On many sites the DECNET account password remained its default value on system setup of "DECNET". This, coupled with the numerous examples of users possessing the same password as their login name, led to a fertile breeding ground for worms.

8.6.1 HI.COM: The Christmas Worm

The HI.COM DECNET worm was released from a European HEPNET node (20597::NEDCU2) at 2152 (Swiss time) on 22 December 1988. The worm originated in a widely used group account (PHSOLIDE) at the University of Neuchatel, Institute of Physics in Switzerland. The account itself was shared by 15 scientists, and the password was therefore well known around the campus site. Login records for this account indicate that except for a number of logins from terminal servers all logins originated from hard-wired terminal lines or trusted remote nodes.

The timing of these terminal server logins is crucial. The actual logins are given below and may have originated either on campus or via a connected modem line:

Date	Login	Logoff
22 December	2109	2114
	2116	2157
	2246	2324
23 December	0658	0723

The worm was placed in the batch queue on the system at 2152 and terminated at 2316. SPAN reports that a minimum of 47 of its hosts were infected by the worm during the period 2214 on 22 December to 0820 on 23 December.

The Christmas worm operated in the following manner:

1. The infected node copied a DCL command procedure named "HI.COM" to the target node to the default DECNET account.

2. It then attempted to start remote execution of this procedure via the TASK 0 facility, or via the batch submission facility of the DECNET account (using the string "DECNET" as its password).

3. If execution is successful the worm runs on the target node, modifies its process name to "MAIL—178DC" (attempting to conceal its process as an innocuous mail service) and deletes the HI.COM procedure from the directory.

4. Sends the system announcement banner (containing the system name) to the PHSOLIDE account on node 20597.

5. Checks the system time and if between 0000 and 0030 on 24 December 1988 sends a Christmas greeting by mail to all authorised users of the system and terminates. If the system time is after 0030 the worm exits, otherwise it remains active in the system.

6. The worm randomly generates a node number in the range 1..63K and attempts to copy the HI.COM file to the target node using the technqiues above. This continued until midnight on Christmas Day arrived.

The greeting message sent by the worm contained the text:

> **Hi,**
>
> **how are ya ? I had a hard time preparing all the presents."**
> **It isn't quite an easy job. I'm getting more and more"**
> **letters from the children every year and it's not so easy"**
> **to get the terrible Rambo-Guns, Tanks and Space Ships up here at"**
> **the Northpole. But now the good part is coming."**
> **Distributing all the presents with my sleigh and the"**
> **deers is real fun. When I slide down the chimneys"**
> **I often find a little present offered by the children,"**
> **or even a little Brandy from the father. (Yeah!)"**
> **Anyhow the chimneys are getting tighter and tighter"**
> **every year. I think I'll have to put my diet on again."**
> **And after Christmas I've got my big holidays :-)."**
>
> **Now stop computing and have a good time at home !!!!"**
>
> **Merry Christmas**
> **and a happy New Year**
>
> **Your Father Christmas**

During the last login to the PHSOLIDE account at 0723 on 23 December all received banners were deleted, and mail forwarding was set up to forward all incoming messages to the account "STOP".

8.6.1.1 Reaction of the DECNET Community

Eight minutes after its release, the worm was noticed at the Goddard Space Flight centre. At 0312 (Swiss time) a warning message was sent by the network security manager at the NASA jet propulsion laboratory to the administrator of the node NEDCU2 and other security administrators on SPAN/HEPNET. This message was followed by a detailed analysis of the attack at 0456 (Swiss time). A formal warning was sent to site managers by the SPAN security manager at 2030 (Swiss time). The worm was reported as having been purged from SPAN by the evening of 23 December.

The NEDCU2 system was separated from the main backbone by scheduled maintenance of the interconnection to the CERN routing centre. This isolation occurred at 0841 (Swiss time) and effectively fragmented the worm into a local component and a network-wide component. The former continued to run until 1820 (Swiss time).

The worm was thus killed within 24 hours of its activation by the combined action of the JPL, SPAN, HEPNET security and site management. In the event, the worm successfully managed to infect a number of systems during this period. A record of the infections occurring in each hour time slice is given below.

Time slice	Hosts infected during time slice
2200–2300	6
2300–0001	10
0001–0200	7
0200–0400	6
0400–0600	6
0600–0732	2

These figures indicate that the rate of new infection peaked rapidly at about 2330 (Swiss time). Because of the removal of the mail records at 0732 it is impossible to definitely identify the hosts which did send announcement banners to PHSOLIDE. In the period from 0732 until network disconnection at 0841 a total of 12 hosts sent their banners (which were discarded due to mail forwarding).

The security bulletins clearly identified the weaknesses which the worm exploited, including advising the disabling of TASK 0, changing of the DECNET account password, and inhibition of remote batch submission privileges for other user accounts.

8.6.1.2 Worms Against Nuclear Killers

On the 16 October 1989 at around 0430 (EST) a further worm was released on the SPAN network. This worm spread slowly and was reported as having infected approximately six machines by mid- afternoon. The worm ironically exploited the same weaknesses as its predecessor.

The WANK worm operated in the following manner:

1. The worm checks that no other instances are active (by checking for a process with name "NETW_"), otherwise it ceases execution. This check is restricted to checking for worm processes which the user can view using the GETJPI service. Thus the worm may not detect copies running under other usercodes.

2. The worm changes the default DECNET account password to a random character string.

3. The infected node, together with the new DECNET password, is mailed to the user GEMPAK on SPAN node 6.59.

4. The process name is changed to "NETW_" followed by a random numeric string.

5. If the worm is running with "SYSPRV" it changes the system announce-ment banner to the banner illustrated below, disables mail to the SYSTEM account, and modifies the standard login procedure to apparently delete all user files.

6. The worm then searches for any command procedures within the directories specified in the logical name table. If the procedure is world writable trojan horse code is inserted to change the FIELD account password and account permissions. This would allow the original author to login remotely to this account.

7. Next, a node is picked at random, the PHONE service used to determine the active users, and each active user sent a "fortune cookie".

8. The RIGHTSLIST file is then read for usernames. The worm then attempts to access a random remote system using the usernames found in the RIGHTSLIST file (together with a list of 82 built-in usernames). A password which is the same as the account name is tried. All successful probes are recorded.

9. If the worm finds an account with access to the SYSUAF.DAT file it is copied to that account and executed, otherwise a non-privileged account is chosen.

10. The worm goes back to step 7 and continues to probe systems.

Depending on the version of the worm, it attempted to use additional password values in the probe. Examples included DIGITAL, PSIPAD and MANAGER. The author had originally intended to probe for the null password, but a bug in the worm prevented this code operating correctly.

If the worm successfully penetrated a privileged account the system banner was set to:

W O R M S   A G A I N S T   N U C L E A R   K I L L E R S

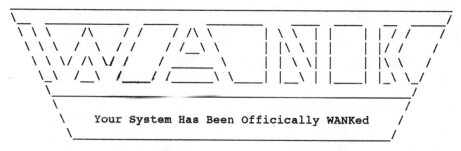

```
              Your System Has Been Officially WANKed
```

You talk of times of peace for all, and then prepare for war.

A CERT advisory (dated 17 October 1989 at 1546 local time) once more gave the official advice to disable TASK 0, change the default DECNET password and use passwords which are not identical to the account name. Administrators were also advised to disable BATCH, REMOTE, INTERACTIVE and DIALUP access methods on the DECNET account.

Had this advice been followed by all nodes on the network, then the replication of the WANK worm would have been considerably restricted. A variant of the WANK worm was restarted on DECNET on 30 October 1988. This worm renamed itself to "OILZ_" and a random numeric string. This variant changed the password of the account it penetrated irrespective of privileges, and thus caused severe denial of service to network users.

Chapter 9

Reactions of the IT Community

This chapter is concerned with a review of the organisation of the IT world to combat the threat of computer viruses and malicious software in general. It will consider the establishment of rapid response centres to provide advice, the formalisation of discussion and debate, the ethical and moral pressures on virus writers and finally the legal sanctions in place within the UK.

9.1 Discussion and Advice

The world has reacted in a comparatively *ad hoc* manner to the risks of malicious software, driven particularly by major incidents such as the Internet worm of November 1988. Each identifiable user community has reacted in its own, and often uncoordinated manner, leading to the establishment of a number of organisations with similar aims and objectives.

The principal sub-groups can be identified as:

- Bulletin board and casual computer users
- Academic establishments
- Government research establishments
- Military organisations
- Commercial organisations
- Criminal investigation organisations
- Professional organisations

Each community is discussed briefly in turn, followed by a discussion on the moves afoot to co-ordinate the overall response to malicious software.

9.1.1 Bulletin Board and Casual Users

Casual users of computers and software are served by a network of bulletin boards around the world. The bulletin board community relies on a network of "trusted" bulletin board sites which carry information on new anti-virus products, general advice, discussion and information on discovered viruses. Many of the boards are run by authors of public domain anti-virus products, including:

Author	Product	Bulletin board
Tjark Auerbach	AVSearch	+49 7542 52110
Rich Levin	Checkup	+1 215 333 8275 (Mother Board)
Ross Greenberg	Flu Shot	+1 212 889 6438
Eric Newhouse	Dirty Dozen	+1 617 492 0892 (Crest)
Alan Solomon	Dr Solomon's Antivirus	+44 494 791090 (S&S)
John McAfee	Virus Scan	+1 988 4004 (Homebase)
Patricia Hoffman	Virus Summary List	+1 408 244 0813 (Excalibur!)
John Norstad	Disinfectant	CompuServe 76666, 573
George Woodside	VKiller	CompuServe 76537, 1342
Jeff Shulman	Virus Detective	CompuServe 76136, 667
ICVI	-	+1 503 488 2251

The principal bulletin board in the IBM PC world must be considered to be the CVIA bulletin board (Homebase) on which updates of the extensive range of shareware anti-virus products can be obtained. The board also has an area for the uploading of discovered viruses, and a number of restricted areas on which CVIA anti-virus workers can share disassemblies and samples.

In general, the latest release of each product can be obtained direct from the author's board with a clear guarantee of receiving an unaltered product. By its very nature the bulletin board community tends to be loosely organised; the possible exception to this structure is the Fidonet network of boards. These boards are networked via dialup telephone links (in a similar structure to the UNIX community's USENET) over which file transfer and electronic mail discussion forums are carried. In particular Fidonet supports a VIRUS echo discussion list.

A number of principal magazines provide anti-viral software services, including disks of shareware products. An example is the *MacUser* magazine which offers disks with John Norstad's Disinfectant program.

9.1.2 Academic Establishments

The academic community is organised via an *ad hoc* combination of global and regional network administration services coupled with user groups. The principal academic networks are the NSFNET (National Science Foundation Network) which provides the backbone of the DARPA Internet, the BITNET/CREN (Corporation for Research and Education Networking), the NASA-administered HEPNET and SPAN, and various other regional networks.

Because of the incidence of network worms or chain letters (coupled with general security concerns) on all of the above networks, the administrative authorities have established network security centres and approved conditions of use.

Each network has specified its own contact and incident reporting procedures. These procedures, together with extracts from the codes of conduct, are given below.

9.1.2.1 CREN/CSNET

CREN provides a network to "facilitate the exchange of information consistent with academic, educational and research purposes". Four principles govern the administration and use of the network. All use must:

- Be consistent with the purposes and goals of the networks
- Avoid interfering with the work of other users of the networks
- Avoid disrupting the network host systems (nodes)
- Avoid disrupting network services

The acceptable use statement then proceeds to specifically prohibit the sending of "messages that are likely to result in loss of recipients' work or system", and requests all users to be responsible in their use of chain letters or broadcast messages. The BITNET chain letter incident can clearly be seen to have influenced this policy. The loosely coupled nature of BITNET and CSNET have not forced detailed prohibitions on worm propagation over the network.

On BITNET/CSNET, network co-ordination is provided by the Co- ordination and Information Centre (CIC) which can be reached by email as "cic@cs.net", or in an emergency by telephone on +1 617 873 2777.

9.1.2.2 NSFNET

The backbone of the DARPA Internet is provided by the high speed interconnections between super computing centres in NSFNET. An interim acceptable use policy has been published for NSFNET, which includes a statement of categories of message traffic which are deemed to be acceptable. The issue of malicious software propagation is not directly addressed, other than by authorising the NSFNET project office to at any time determine that a particular use or uses of the network are not consistent with the purposes of NSFNET.

The DARPA Internet in general is controlled by the Internet Activity Board (IAB), whose roles include the formation of Internet communication standards, strategic planning for the Internet, and management of the Internet Engineering and Internet Research Task Forces (IETF and IRTF). The IETF has an active interest in the development of security and data integrity standards for the Internet, including a variety of electronic mail privacy standards (RFC 1113-1115). The IAB has issued a statement on ethics and the Internet (RFC 1087), which endorses the view of the division advisory panel of the National Science Foundation division of network, communications research and infrastructure, which described as unacceptable any activity which:

- Seeks to gain unauthorised access to the resources of the Internet
- Disrupts the intended use of the Internet
- Wastes resources (people, capacity, computer) through such actions.
- Destroys the integrity of computer based information.
- Compromises the privacy of users.

Within the Internet community the principal centre for the monitoring of network security incidents, and the provision of advice and information on the prevention of such incidents, is the Computer Emergency Response Team. The CERT organisation, based at the Software Engineering Institute at Carnegie-Mellon, has a broad remit (summarised in Appendix 12) to assist the research community in responding to emergency situations. In its initial press release, part of CERT's role is explicitly cited as being "response to computer security threats such as the recent self-replicating computer program that invaded many defence and research computers". Certainly, the Internet worm must be considered as one of the main driving forces behind the establishment of the initial CERT group. CERT's role is also cited as providing a focal point for the identification and repair of security vulnerabilities; it is in this role that CERT has issued advisories on a wide range of issues (summarised in Appendix 13). These CERT advisories are regularly re-issued by other similar organisations.

CERT maintains an extensive electronic mailing list for warnings, including the publication of warnings in the "comp.security.announce" newsgroup on USENET. A central archive of tools and general security information is maintained at the "cert.sei.cmu.edu" host on the Internet. A mailing list for security tools is maintained by CERT, requests for membership are sent to "cert-tools-   request@cert.sei.cmu.edu",   submissions   to   "cert-tools@cert.sei.cmu.edu".

CERT has a 24-hour hotline service for the community on +1 412 268 7090 for reports of security incidents on the Internet.

9.1.2.3 HEPNET/SPAN

These two NASA sponsored networks were attacked during the DECNET worm incidents. Both networks have established acceptable use statements and have a security co-ordination and response structure in place. In the HEPNET case the acceptable use statement restricts traffic to particle physics related issues, with non-particle physics traffic accepted under specific closely controlled arrangements. Such traffic must be of a scientific nature, and must be subject to national and international HEPNET rules (which include restrictions related to network security).

SPAN JPL site rules discourage uploading of files into public directories and the use of TASK 0 inter-node communication. The use of procedures designed to remotely execute DCL commands is considered an attempt to penetrate security on the remote node, and has been prohibited by NASA/SPAN and HEPNET managements.

9.1.2.4 General Community Responses

The academic community has established a number of moderated (controlled) mailing lists dealing with aspects of system security and integrity. These lists serve an information, discussion and warning function. The lists consist of a central mail address (normally on the moderator's host) from which the submitted message will be bulk mailed to all readers of the list.

The electronic mailing lists have established a *de facto*, rather than officially sponsored, role in warning of security incidents. Nevertheless they are a crucial component of the IT community's response (particularly due to the wide redistribution that these lists receive).

In the area of general system security, the main mailing list is the UNIX system security list "zardoz", distributed by the "cpd.com" host under the management of Neil Gorsuch. This mailing list has a number of mail aliases including:

- General security postings: security@uninet.cpd.com
- Emergency alert postings: security- emergency@uninet.cpd.com
- Requests for membership: security- request@uninet.cpd.com

Membership is restricted to system administrators of UNIX systems. Postings are unencrypted, although sites are strongly advised to encrypt before archiving

This mailing list is redistributed via the "uk-unix-security" mailing list located at Imperial College in the UK. This list also carries copies of the CERT-tools list.

Unmoderated discussion forums also exist for security issues, including the USENET newsgroup "alt.security" and "misc.security", the latter being available as the mailing list security-l on BITNET.

In the virus field the principal mailing list is the Virus-l BITNET list. This list is moderated by Ken Van Wyk at CERT and discusses all aspects of computer viruses (stopping short of technical details which might aid the writing of potential viruses). The list includes information on new viruses, discussion and social commentary on the virus problem, updates on availability of commercial and public domain anti-virus software, and details of anti-virus techniques. Many of the authors of anti-virus software products regularly monitor this list. The list is gatewayed to the UK via Heriot-Watt University as UK-VIRUS-L.

The Virus-l list also has a large number of archive sites which carry clean copies of anti-viral software and general information on protective techniques. A summary of the archive sites and means of access is given in Appendix 17.

Virus-l also maintains an emergency virus alert list (Valert- l), which is also moderated by Ken Van Wyk. The contact points for both lists are:

- Submissions: virus-l@ibm1.cc.lehigh.edu
- Membership requests: listserv@ibm1.cc.lehigh.edu
- Alert messages: valert-l@ibm1.cc.lehigh.edu

9.1.3 Government Research Organisations

Within the US, the Department of Energy has established a Computer Incident Advisory Capability (CIAC). This organisation has provided advice on a large number of issues (the list of issued bulletins is given in Appendix 13), including general security measures, known loopholes and personal computer security. CIAC is based at the US Lawrence Livermore national laboratory and can be contacted by email via the address "ciac@tiger.llnl.gov".

The principal responsibility for the security of classified computer systems within the US is vested in the National Computer Security Centre (NCSC) based at Fort George G. Meade in Maryland. This organisation has produced a series of guidelines for trusted computer security evaluation based on the Department of Defense's Orange Book standard.

The security of sensitive and unclassified military and commercial systems falls within the responsibility of the National Institute of Standards and Technology (NIST), based at Gaithersburg in Maryland. This organisation has had a high profile and crucial role in the organisation of the US security community. NIST has two current initiatives, namely:

1. A proposal for an industrially-backed computer virus research consortium. This consortium would have an extensive remit, marshalling expertise and resources to "facilitate finding and sharing of solutions to the problem of computer viruses and related threats". It is seeking industrial funding of $1 000 000 for its first year (1991). The activities proposed for the consortium include the provision of:

(i) Virus protection guidance
(ii) Virus prevention, detection and recovery information
(iii) Anti-virus product information
(iv) A virus signature, nomenclature and technical characteristics database
(v) Research activity database and information exchange mechanisms
(vi) Virus disassembly and research sample database
(vii) Incident statistics gathering and reporting
(viii) Alert notification mechanisms
(ix) Threat analysis and standards research

2. A move to unify the range of computer emergency response teams which exist within different user communities, and to provide a communications and

information exchange infrastructure between CERTs. The proposal includes establishment of a steering committee, CERT system operational framework and unified code of conduct for member CERTs. The CERT system would embrace a number of US CERTs (such as the Internet CERT at Carnegie-Mellon and the Department of Energy CIAC).

At this time, no comparable government-backed initiatives exist within the UK to combat the malicious software problem in the IT community.

9.1.4 Military Organisations

Similar CERT structures exist within each US arm of service, and for the Defense Data Network (the DDN security co-ordination centre). The latter organisation publishes a number of public security bulletins available from the DDN network information centre by anonymous FTP (nic.ddn.mil).

9.1.5 Commercial Organisations

A number of specialist corporates offer a wide range of consultancy and software services to facilitate control of malicious software. A selection of contact addresses are given in Appendix 14. Most management and IT consultancy firms now include the provision of specialist advice on malicious software control within their portfolios. This book does not explicitly seek to market the products of any particular organisation. I have therefore provided a general list of (UK) contact points from which consultancy and information services can be obtained.

9.1.6 Criminal Investigation Organisations

Within the UK a small Computer Crime Unit (CCU) has been established by the Metropolitan and City of London Police at New Scotland Yard. This team has expressed an interest in reports of all malicious software incidents, to permit compilation of dossiers on the damage caused by known computer viruses, and to gather accurate information on the level of crime related to malicious software. The CCU can be contacted on +44 71 725 2409.

9.1.7 Professional Organisations

Each professional organisation has adopted a code of conduct which regulates the actions of its members and provides a reference framework for the

members' professional conduct. The various codes of conduct were summarised by C. Dianne Martin and David H. Martin in the paper "Professional
codes of conduct and computer ethics education". The codes include the
common theme of professional dignity and high standards. Examples are the
canons of the ACM, which state that each member shall:

- Canon 2   Strive to increase competence and prestige of the profession
- Canon 4   Act with professional responsibility

and the IEEE code of ethics which states that its members shall:

Article I.e   Advance the integrity and prestige of the profession

The British Computer Society code of conduct specified that its members
shall:

1. Uphold the dignity, reputation and good standing of the profession.
2. Shall not by unfair means do anything that would harm the reputation,
   business or prospects of another member.
3. Shall have proper regard to the public interest...

It seems certain that the release of malicious software would be in violation of
the maintenance of the dignity of the computing profession, and in particular
could be noted as being detrimental to the interests of other members of the
profession. The argument that the Internet worm incident was beneficial to the
community (through its publicity of the lack of security within a major
network) has been widely contested. The worm was explicitly condemned by a
statement made by the organisation of Computer Professionals for Social
Responsibility (CPSR) as:

being an irresponsible act that cannot be condoned. The internet should not be
treated as a laboratory for uncontrolled experiments in computer security.

The value of open networks depends upon the good will and good sense of
computer users. Computer professionals should take upon themselves the responsibility to ensure that systems are not misused.

While the codes of conduct of such institutions generally condemn the
release of malicious software, the involvement of such bodies in organising the
community to combat malicious software has been low level. A number of
independent (mixed academic and commercial) initiatives are, however, under
way.

Within the general IT community moves are currently under way to establish
a European Institute for Computer Virus Research (EICVR), which will
embrace the various commercial and government organisations researching
into computer viruses. The outcome of this proposal is not known at this time.

A second proposal is to establish a European International CERT organisation (ICO) encompassing the work of the German CERT teams (Hamburg –

virus/anomaly test centre, Karlsruhe – MicroBIT virus centre, IBM Stuttgart and Siemens Munich), a proposed UK CERT team and that of the US CERT system organisation.

1990 has seen the beginning of a large number of (often independent and uncoordinated) moves to form a worldwide malicious software analysis and response infrastructure. Such an organisation, when operational, would permit rapid response to new viruses or trojan horses before they spread across international boundaries. In the modern world of global data transfer to restrict legislative or reactive responses to national boundaries is to significantly restrict the ability of the community to respond to malicious software.

9.2 Legislative Issues

Within the UK two comprehensive surveys of computer legislative requirements have been carried out, namely:

- The Scottish Law Commission (report 106, on computer crime) in July 1987
- The English Law Commission (report 186, on computer misuse) in October 1989

The latter report formed the basis of the text of the Computer Misuse Act 1990, which received royal assent on 29 June 1990, and entered into force on 29 August 1990.

The two reports differ significantly in their recommendations and in particular in their treatment of casual hacking. The Scottish Law Commission recommended that casual hacking should not be *per se* a crime, but only where there was a demonstrable intent to:

- Procure an advantage for himself or another person; or
- Damage another person's interests

Both Law Commissions agreed that alteration or erasure of computer data should become a crime. Again, a difference in emphasis was clear, with the Scottish commission recommending that the crime should require the establishment of an intent to damage another person's interests, while the English commission defined intent in broader terms of:

- Impairing the operation of a computer
- Preventing or hindering access to any program or data held in any computer; or
- Impairing the operation of any such program or the reliability of any such data

The Law Commission reports are interesting in their extensive coverage of existing legislation which is applicable to computer crime. Before analysing the extent and application of the new computer misuse legislation, it is useful to review the state of the existing legislation.

9.2.1 Scottish Law Commission

The Commission identified eight categories of computer misuse, specifically:

1. Erasure or falsification of data or programs so as to obtain a pecuniary or other advantage.
2. Obtaining unauthorised access to a computer.
3. Eavesdropping on a computer.
4. Taking of information without physical removal.
5. Unauthorised borrowing of computer disks or tapes.
6. Making unauthorised use of computer time or facilities.
7. Malicious or reckless corruption or erasure of data or programs.
8. Denial of access to authorised users.

The report then proceeds to summarise the applicability of existing Scottish legislation. The report's findings relating to malicious software incidents are summarised below.

With regard to the erasure or falsification of data or programs so as to obtain a pecuniary or other advantage, the Scottish law of fraud was found to be capable of extension to cover incidents where the subject of the false pretence was a computer system. The definition of fraud given by Macdonald (Criminal Law of Scotland) is:

> A false pretence made dishonestly in order to bring about some definite practical result

The applicability of the concept of a false pretence in the absence of a human mind was questioned, although the Commission considered this concept to be more flexible than the concept of "deception" required in the English law Theft Act 1968.

The Commission agreed that it was not a crime under existing legislation to obtain unauthorised access to a computer.

The taking of information without physical removal was also considered not to be covered by existing legislation (except when covered by national security interests under the Official Secrets Act), due to the fact that Scots law did not recognise information as being property, and thus information cannot be the object of theft. The taking of information does not deprive the original user of the use of the information, and thus the only change has been in the exclusivity of the information.

The unauthorised use of computer time or facilities was not considered to fall within the scope of existing legislation (since no physical removal of the computer system was involved). The Commission noted that civil or internal disciplinary action for breach of contract may be an appropriate recourse in the case of an employee making such unauthorised use of computing facilities. The possibility of prosecuting for the crime of theft of electricity was noted but felt to be inappropriate due to the artificial and intangible nature of the crime.

The malicious or reckless corruption or erasure of data was felt to fall within the scope of the Scottish common law offence of malicious mischief or the statutory offence of vandalism. The former offence (triable on indictment) is restricted to deliberate damage, the latter offence (only tried summarily) is restricted to reckless damage. The Commission thus noted the inappropriateness of the vandalism offence to punish substantial destruction of programs or data.

Finally, the Commission decided that denial of service implied the occurrence of one or more of the above offences, and thus constituted either vandalism or malicious mischief, depending on the intent of the perpetrator.

In summary, therefore, prior to the Computer Misuse Act coming into force, the insertion of malicious software into a computer system with intent may constitute an act of malicious mischief or vandalism depending on intent. The insertion of software designed to compromise data security was not a crime (due to the absence of a casual hacking offence coupled with the insubstantial nature of information). Thus, a significant requirement existed for the creation of a crime of unauthorised access to a computer system with a view to the compromising of data or programs.

9.2.2 English Law Commission

The Commission summarised the available legislation relating to malicious software in the following manner:

- *Theft* Manipulation of a computer system to dishonestly obtain property or money is a crime under the Theft Act 1968 punishable on indictment by up to 10 years' imprisonment.

- *Obtaining property by deception* The applicability of the Theft Act 1968 to the acquisition of property by the act of deceiving a computer was questioned on the basis that deception required the existence of a human mind (rather than the more general Scot's law requirement of false pretence).

- *Falsification of accounting records* The Theft Act also includes an offence of falsification of accounting records to cause a gain or loss to one or more persons. This offence was considered to be applicable to a wide range of computer manipulations, including manipulations where the records involved were not maintained solely for the purposes of accounting.

- *Obtaining unauthorised access to a computer* The House of Lords has ruled that the Forgery and Counterfeiting Act 1981 may not be applied to the transitory storage of electronic impulses in the memory of a computer system, as this does not embody the concept of information storage for an appreciable period, nor the concept of the information being stored for subsequent retrieval or recovery. Thus no tangible instrument could be identified in the Prestel hacking case which was forged to obtain entry. The definition of a forgeable instrument as including "any disc, tape, soundtrack or other device on or in which information is recorded or stored by mechanical, electronic or other means" was not felt to be capable of being extended to the electronic memory of a computer system.

The charge of abstraction of electricity (Theft Act 1968) is again disregarded because of the obvious artificiality of application of this statute, and the difficulty in proving that the computer system has indeed consumed additional power during the period of the external manipulation.

• *Destruction of data or programs* The Criminal Damage Act 1971 has been applied to the destruction of data on a "smart" card used for circular saw control. The future application of this Act requires that the concept of property be extended to embrace the general destruction of information (including those incidents in which the information is stored in the insubstantial form of magnetic flux on a storage media, or transitory electrical impulses in memory). This extension is expected in cases in which the alteration takes place within a tangible media (such as a magnetic disk), and thus a general charge of criminal damage may lie. The Commission acknowledges this Act will not be applicable in instances where the hacker merely gains access to the system and does not modify data.

• *Offensive or indecent communications* The offence of sending a message that is grossly offensive or of an indecent, obscene or menacing character over a public telecommunications network is triable under the Telecommunications Act 1984. This form of offence may be applicable to incidents such as the WANK form (although indecency may be questionable). Where the communications media is a private circuit then this offence will not be applicable.

• *Unauthorised copying or acquisition of data* Copying and acquisition of data will not generally be a crime under the Theft Act due to the intangible nature of the data, and indeed the fact that when data is copied no deprivation of use occurs. Naturally such coping may be in violation of specific statutes addressing copyright and intellectual property rights.

Thus the introduction of malicious software may lay the author open to a charge of criminal damage (until the enactment of the Computer Misuse Act specifically excluded this possibility) due to the software, or alternatively a charge under the Theft Act if the software alters or amends accounting records with a view to the causing of financial gain or loss. In general the offence of obtaining access to the computer system does not appear actionable under the Forgery and Counterfeiting Act. Where the software contains copyright or offensive material additional charges may be laid against the author.

9.2.3 Computer Misuse Act

The Computer Misuse Act created three new offences, namely:

1. An offence of unauthorised access to computer material. This offence carries a maximum 6-month period of imprisonment and/or a fine at level 5 on the standard scale. This offence is a summary offence triable by a magistrate's court in England and Wales, or by a sheriff in Scotland. A person is guilty of the offence if: (i) he causes a computer to perform any function with intent to secure access to any program or data held in the computer; (ii) the access he intends to secure is unauthorised; and (iii) he knows at the time when he causes the computer to perform the function that this is the case.

2. An offence of unauthorised access with intent to commit or facilitate commission of further offences has also been created which carries a maximum sentence of 5 years' imprisonment and/or a fine not exceeding the statutory maximum if tried on indictment; or a maximum of 6 months' imprisonment and/or a fine not exceeding the statutory maximum if tried summarily. A person is guilty of the offence if he commits an offence under section 1 (described above) with intent: (i) to commit an offence to which this section (section 2) applies; or (ii) to facilitate the commission of such an offence (whether by himself or by any other person). The above offence applies only where the offence which is committed or facilitated is one which would normally attract a fixed sentence, or a sentence of five years' imprisonment (if not previously convicted and over the age of 21).

3. Finally, an offence of unauthorised modification of computer material is created which carries the same penalties as the section 2 offence above. A person is guilty of the offence if: (i) he does any act which causes an unauthorised modification of the contents of any computer; and (ii) at the time when he does the act he has the requisite intent and the requisite knowledge.

The Act also includes provision for the issuing of search warrants by circuit judges, permitting constables to enter and search premises where there are reasonable grounds to believe that a section 1 offence has been or is about to be committed.

The territorial scope of section 1, 2 and 3 offences may extend beyond national boundaries where the computer which is the object of the hack or unauthorised modification exists within the national boundary. In these cases, where the hack is being initiated from another country, the prosecutor may apply for extradition proceedings to be initiated for section 2 and section 3 offences under the 1870 Extradition Act.

The Act also resolves the issue of the applicability of the Criminal Damage Act 1971 to damage caused to computer data, by specifically excluding modifications to the contents of a computer "unless its effect on that computer or computer storage media impairs its physical condition" (section 3 (6)).

The Computer Misuse Act was specifically intended to apply to the insertion of malicious software (this is an incident which the Law Commission had intended the unauthorised modification offence to address). The author of such malicious software (self-replicating or otherwise) can thus be charged with causing of unauthorised modification to the content of the computer which he infects (or, indirectly, which his virus infects due to its replication or spread). The question of whether, and to what extent, the author can be held responsible for the action of his virus or trojan in violating section 3 may prove interesting. The non-retrospective nature of the Act (specified in section 18(3)) must raise a possible defence that the initial date of the virus' or trojan horse's release predates the date on which the Act comes into operation.

The requisite intent expressed in section 3(2) requires that the introducer of the alteration must intend to impair the operation of the computer, prevent of hinder access to any program or data held in any computer, or impair the operation of any such program or the reliability of any such data. In this regard a user who writes a benign virus may be able to question his intention to materially affect or impair the operation of the computer system.

The Computer Misuse Act is extremely sweeping in its wording of the unauthorised access and alteration offences, and thus a body of case law can be expected to define the limits of the applicability of the Act.

Finally, despite effectively removing the offence of criminal damage, a number of sanctions still remain under the Theft Act, Telecommunications Act and Copyright Act.

9.2.4 Summary of Legislation

The legislative measures now specifically address the question of unauthorised access to computers and the issue of damage or alterations to computer data. There are, however, a number of open questions relating to offences which may constitute incitement to breach the Computer Misuse Act, specifically:

1. Is publishing the source code of a virus an offence?
2. Is the creation and uploading of viruses for research purposes an offence?
3. If such a research virus escapes can its writer be held responsible for damage caused?
4. Does the uploading of benign viruses constitute an offence?
5. If the user is unaware of potential bugs in his virus does he commit an offence?

The answer to many of these questions must lie within the scope of case law under the Computer Misuse Act. Certainly, in most of the above cases the establishment of the requisite intent under section 3(1)(b) can be questioned.

Second, the principal difficulty must lie in the tracing of authorship of a computer virus to a particular person or persons. The intangible coding style differences must be considered to be insufficient to prove authorship "beyond a reasonable doubt". Thus it seems unlikely, unless the author specifically targets a virus against a firm or organisation, or unless he is caught in the act of releasing a virus, or with access to original source code, that authorship may be proved.

9.3 Professionalism and Software Development

Finally, to complete this chapter I would like to consider a number of issues relating to the ethics and professional responsibilities of software developers. It seems clear that software developers (despite many disclaimers to the contrary which normally accompany commercial software) have a general obligation to ensure that to the best of their knowledge their product is free of trojan horses, viruses or destructive bugs.

This obligation must extend to any organisation carrying out the bulk copying or distribution of software. Certainly, the instances of shrink-wrapped and publisher-distributed infected software cause an unacceptable risk to the IT community.

Generally, the lack of ethics in the software development field has been commented on by Thimbleby et al. Specifically, the high level of bugs in distributed software (often distributed with the knowledge of the vendor) is unacceptable. There is a need to encourage the adoption of software development metrics and formal development routes (possibly integrated with the Biba integrity mechanisms detailed in Chapter 7). The establishment of the legal responsibilities of developers to their customers is vital (the AIDS trojan horse test case should prove interesting in this regard).

Thimbleby cites a scenario in which software development is granted a professional status comparable to the medical profession, with illegal software development being punishable. While this represents an extreme situation, moves towards requiring safety critical software legally to comply with development standards is vital. In such carefully controlled and verified environments we can have a degree of assuredness in the trust we place in the operating system (and indeed hardware) of the system.

Chapter 10
Conclusions: The Future Ahead

In summary, this book has attempted to provide a broad view of computer viruses and the general problem of malicious software. In particular, we have covered:

- History of computer viruses
- Operation of computer viruses
- Defences against computer viruses
- Community's reaction against viruses

It is clear that a considerable potential for mischief exists in the form of malicious software, and it seems clear that such software is not adequately prevented by the open architectures of today's personal and mainframe computer systems.

The issue of malicious software has raised the much more general question of software integrity, and its incorporation in the security architectures and models of future generations of computer systems. The specification of formal development routes and controls to ensure such integrity are a necessary part of the extension process.

The book has also indicated the reliance on trust which is vital to the correct operation of our computer systems, and has indicated the requirement for a clear analysis of the relative risks and costs involved in restricting such trust to prevent the spread of malicious software.

The theory of computer viruses has been seen to be at an early stage, with initial undecidability proofs. Theoretical studies have the potential to provide information on the minimal set of restrictions in the open architectures of computer systems to limit virus propagation, and may prevent the throwing out of the baby (of networked global computing) with the bathwater (of system abuse).

The global internetworks are vulnerable to malicious acts and, despite the moves now under way to address data confidentiality and integrity, will always be vulnerable to breaches of trust by the user community.

The ethical and moral codes which should be promoted to prevent such breaches of trust have been described, together with the extensive legislation now in place to permit prosecution of such breaches. It is now up to the community as a whole to take effective action in terms of organisational structures to combat the malicious software threat, in terms of education in the responsibilities of the professional, and in terms of the willingness to enforce the ethical, moral and legal obligations of the community.

A number of on-going (potentially fruitful) areas of research have been identified, including the concept of software integrity and its incorporation into security architectures, the formalisation of distributed trust using public key digital signatures, and the theoretical studies on the minimal restriction on functionality required to combat the threat.

Finally, at all times, remember that computer viruses have only highlighted a number of traditional issues of security and professional integrity, and that they are only one small (if widely publicised) security issue. As with any other security or integrity issue it is vital that the costs of counteracting the threat never exceed the potential damage caused by the threat.

DOS Filestore Structure

1.1 Introduction

The DOS filesystem is described in this appendix, which should be read in conjunction with the lower level disk structure description in Appendix 2.

The BIOS provides a low level interface to the underlying physical devices. This interface presents a view of the device which consists of sectors, tracks and heads. Thus, a user may request n sectors starting at sector 2 on track 14, side 1 to be read from drive 1. This low level interface is the basis for the DOS filesystem abstraction.

DOS permits a physical drive to be divided into a number of logical drives (each identified by its own letter). Each logical drive may have a DOS filesystem (or indeed may be used by a foreign operating system such as UNIX). The mapping between physical disk drive and logical disk drives is determined by a special table known as the partition table. This table, which "partitions" a physical disk into logical disks, is part of the master boot record stored at head 0, track 0, sector 1.

1.2 Master Boot Record

The master boot record contains 1BEh bytes of executable code followed by a 40h partition table, followed by a 2-byte sector checksum. The executable code is jumped to by the BIOS during the initialisation procedure for the IBM PC. It is responsible for the location (by interpretation of the partition table) of a boot sector on a logical drive which can continue the initialisation procedure.

Each entry in the partition table (of which there can be four in the table) is 16 bytes long and comprises the following fields:

Field Offset	Field Length	Description of field
0	byte	Boot indicator (80h = bootable, 0 = non)
1	byte	Head on which partition starts
2	byte	Sector on which partition starts (bits 6-7 are the MSBs for the start cylinder)
3	byte	Cylinder (track) on which partition starts
4	byte	System ID (0=unknown, 1=DOS 12bit FAT, 2= DOS 16 bite FAT, 3= DOS extended disk 16 bit FAT)
5	byte	Head on which partition ends
6	byte	Sector on which partition ends (bits 6-7 are the MSBs for the end cylinder)
7	byte	Cylinder on which partition ends
8	long	First partition sector
C	long	Sectors in the partition

This table delimits the extent of each logical drive. The boot indicator also determines whether the BIOS will look for an executable boot sector on the first sector of the logical drive. It is worth noting that many hard disks contain nothing on head 0, track 0 other than the master boot record. The system id determines the File Allocation Table (FAT) structure on the partition.

1.3 DOS Boot Sector

The boot sector on each media (which is the first sector in each partition, or the first sector on a floppy disk) also contains executable code. This code is executed by the master boot record in the case of a hard drive, or directly by the BIOS in the case of a floppy disk. The boot sector is organised as:

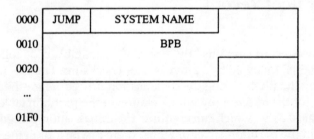

The sector commences with a jump instruction which passes control to the executable code after the BIOS parameter block (BPB). The jump instruction is followed by an 8-byte system name, which is in turn followed by the BPB. The BPB is used to determine the structure of the disk partition. It includes details of the size of each disk sector, size of the root directory and FATs, etc. The structure of the BPB (which varies depending on the DOS release) is given below. This structure is echoed in the BPB on an Atari ST PC, except for those fields marked •, which are not interpreted or have null values.

Field Offset	Field Length	Description of item
0	word	Bytes per sector
2	byte	Sectors per cluster
3	word	Reserved sectors starting at sector 0
5	byte	Number of FATs
6	word	Number of root directory entries
8	word	Total number of sectors (if < 65536)
A	byte	•Media descriptor
B	word	Sectors per FAT
D	word	Sectors per track
F	word	Number of heads
11	long	•Hidden sectors
15	11 bytes	Reserved in DOS versions prior to 3.0
15	long	Total number of sectors (if >= 65536)
19	7 bytes	Reserved in DOS versions prior to 4.0
19	byte	Physical drive number
1A	byte	Reserved
1B	byte	Signature byte for extended boot record
1C	long	Volume serial number
20	11 bytes	Volume label
2B	8 bytes	Reserved

Atari ST boot sectors use a system-generated serial number (at offset 8h in the sector) in place of the system name, otherwise the sector appears to be a standard pre-3.0 PC-DOS IBM boot sector.

The reserved sector field indicates the number of sectors before the start of the first file allocation table, in this case one (the boot sector itself). Other values may indicate that a virus has reserved space for its own code prior to the FAT.

1.4 File Allocation Table

Following the reserved sectors comes the FAT (or rather two identical copies). This contains one entry for each cluster (group of sectors) on the disk, the number of sectors per cluster being specified in the BPB. Each entry records whether the cluster is part of a file, unallocated or bad (i.e. corrupt on the media).

The root directory (described later) contains the number of the first cluster allocated to a file. If this is the only cluster allocated to the file then its entry in the FAT will contain the special value in the range FFF8–FFFFh. This value indicates that it is the last cluster in a file. Otherwise it will contain the cluster number of the next cluster allocated to the file. The FAT entry for that cluster will either have this special field or the number of the next file cluster, and so on. Thus, a linked list of clusters is formed in the FAT, representing each file.

Additional special values exist for free (unallocated) clusters – 0h – and a bad cluster – FFF7h. DOS maintains both FAT copies when an update is made. Thus, the second FAT can often be used to reconstruct a damaged first FAT. It is worth noting that certain viruses which manipulate the first FAT directly do not correctly update the second copy. DOS itself (other than maintaining it) does not utilise the information in the second FAT.

The FAT is often manipulated by viruses to conceal code (by using a cluster then marking it as bad to prevent DOS re-use) or as part of their destructive manipulation task (cross- linking or breaking of FAT chains, or random marking of clusters as bad). Examples include the Icelandic and 4096 viruses.

1.5 Root Directory

The next area on disk is the root directory. This is the heart of the filesystem and it is from here that all subdirectories branch. The maximum number of entries is specified in the BPB. Each entry has the following format:

Field Offset	Field Size	Description
0	8 bytes	File name
8	3 bytes	File extension
B	byte	File attribute
C	10 bytes	Reserved
16	word	Time of update
18	word	Date of update
1A	word	First disk cluster
1C	long	File size (bytes)

The file name and extension, together with an implied "." between them, form the standard name of a DOS file. The first character of the file name has special significance and if given the value E5h indicates that the file has been erased. 00h indicates an empty directory entry. Erasure of the file using DOS file deletion, i.e. delete command, only sets this first character. The cluster chain is left intact, and it is therefore possible to restore the file by setting the first character in the filename to a valid value. When deleting a virus-infected executable the file must be scrubbed be zeroing all component clusters (or at the very least all clusters in the chain should be unlinked and marked as free).

The directory entry is commonly used by viruses as a signature marker which can be rapidly verified without the overhead of opening the executable code file. All fields (including the reserved field) are possible candidate signature markers and should thus be part of any checksum operation.

The file attribute field contains bits indicating whether the file is read-only, hidden, a system file, a volume label, has been recently updated, or is a subdirectory. Two bits are unused in the attribute field. The hidden attribute will suppress the file entry in any directory listings. Unfortunately it can also be set for a directory entry which will suppress listing of the directory, but still permit a "cd" to the hidden directory.

Low Level Disk Layout

This appendix gives details of the internal layout of a floppy disk formatted via the Western Digital WD1772 disk controller chip. This chip (used in the Atari ST) is typical of such controllers, and is compatible with previous WD179x and WD279x series controllers.

The controller offers a high level interface, permitting retrieval and storage of block structured data on disk. Data is located by a head, track and sector specifier.

IBM PC disks are laid out in one of a number of fixed formats, depending on the capacity of the disk, namely:

Disk type	DOS FAT ID	Sides per disk	Tracks per side	Sectors per track	Capacity Kilobytes
3.5" High Capacity		2	80	18	1440
3.5" DSDD		2	80	9	720
5.25" High Density	F9	2	80	15	1200
5.25" DSDD	FD	2	40	9	360
5.25" SSDD	FC	1	40	9	180
5.25" DSDD	FF	2	40	8	320
5.25" SSDD	FE	1	40	8	160

On Atari ST systems, the media description byte in the BPB is unused, as all 3.5" floppy disks are normally of 9 sectors per track, 80 tracks per disk.

The general structure of the disk is as follows: data is laid out in a number of concentric circles (tracks) on both sides of the floppy disk. Tracks are numbered from the outermost track (0) to the innermost track. Depending on drives, the innermost track may be 79 to 83. Thus, additional tracks in excess of the 80 track limit can often be formatted. Such additional tracks are accessible via the BIOS interface. Each track has a format-dependent number of sectors from 8 to 18, numbered commencing at 1. Macintosh computers depart from the standard PC format in a number of ways, including using a variable number of sectors per track, which decreases as track number increases (and physical size of sector decreases since the head is moving towards the centre of the disk).

Each track conceptually consists of data sectors laid out in sequence: in fact, two deviations from this logical abstraction occur:

1. Data sectors are "interleaved" so that logical sectors are spaced out over the track. This permits a program to read a stream of sectors without data loss. If this were not the case the program would read sector 1 and then after a brief pause try to read sector 2. By this time sector 2 has already passed the disk head (due to the rotation of the disk), thus the user must wait until this sector returns. By interleaving, we increase the likelihood that the user will request the next sector before it has passed under the read head.

2. The disk controller requires further "hidden" synchronisation information. This information permits the reading logic to detect the start of the next sector without error and then to reconfigure internally before the actual start of the sector data commences.

This synchronisation information is the subject of this appendix, which seeks to indicate how a sophisticated low level virus might conceal additional data in unused portions of the disk, or within the gaps used by the disk controller.

The physical structure of a track on a magnetic disk is as follows:

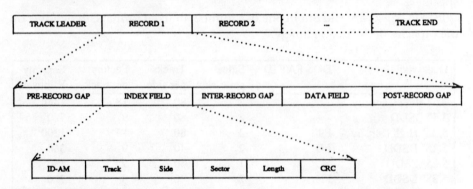

The track leader consists of a minimum of 32 bytes of 4Eh characters followed by a number of records, each containing a data sector together with its own headers and trailers. The last record is followed by a track end which consists of a minimum of 16 bytes of 4Eh characters. In fact, on a typical Atari ST disk with 9 sectors the gap left for the track end is 644 bytes; on a typical 10 sector format 50 bytes remain.

Each record comprises a pre-record gap of minimum size 8 bytes of 00h characters followed by 3 SYN (A1h) characters. This is followed by the index field containing the index address mark (FEh) followed by a byte track id, byte side id, byte sector id and a byte length field. The length field has the value 02 for a 512 byte sector, 03 for a 1024 byte sector. The index field is followed by a 2-byte CRC check. This is then followed by the inter-record gap of 22 4Eh characters, 12 00h characters and 3 A1h SYN characters. This gap is then followed by a data address mark (FBh), a data sector and a 2-byte CRC check. Finally the record finishes with the post record gap of 24 bytes of 4Eh characters.

An important issue is that the Atari ST (and other PCs) tend to be highly conservative in their use of gaps. Specifically, the track leader, track end, and pre- and post-record gaps are significantly larger than the values which will permit reliable operation of the disk controller chip.

The table below summarises these values:

Gap	Atari ST length	Minimum length
Track leader	60 bytes	32 bytes
Track end	~664 bytes	16 bytes
Pre-record	12 bytes	8 bytes
Post-record	40 bytes	24 bytes

The implication of this is that a sophisticated virus could exploit this residual space. A typical conservative 9 sector per track format leaves 648 bytes free space, a minimal gap format leaves 865 bytes free space.

In general, the implication is that if we wish to ensure complete protection from viral or trojan horse code we must consider the possibility that potentially hostile code may be concealed in non-standard formatted tracks.

The precedent of using tracks beyond the normal limit for data storage has already been demonstrated by the Denzuk virus. This virus uses the BIOS to format track 40 (one beyond the normal maximum range for 40 track disks of track 0–39), and then uses this formatted track for storage of auxiliary viral code.

This technique can be extended to use of non-standard numbers of sectors or use of smaller inter-record or track leader/end gaps. It is debatable whether the complexity of such code makes the creation of such a virus extremely unlikely.

Finally it is worth noting the interface provided by the WD1772 controller as an indication of the difficulty of directly manipulating such secondary storage controllers. The WD1772 provides the following command set:

- Restore: Move head to track 0
- Seek: Move head to track specified
- Step: In various forms to move one track in or out
- Read sector: Read sector *n* from current track
- Write sector: Write sector *n* to current track
- Read address: Read next id field on disk
- Read track: Read a complete image of a track
- Write track: Write a complete image of a track

Thus the controller presents an interface at a similar level to the BIOS absolute sector I/O facilities. Naturally, the disk controller is hardware specific, but in general with the limited variety of controllers on PCs this is not a significant restriction.

Interception of direct disk controller manipulation is impossible without memory management or I/O space protection facilities in hardware. It is, however, possible to monitor the controller status to detect possible viral or trojan horse manipulation. This may be indicated by changes in chip status register values. It is unlikely that link viruses will directly drive hardware (except as static auxiliary storage) since there are considerable costs in interpreting the structure of the DOS file system to determine the actual disk sector/tracks to be modified. This is not the case with boot sector viruses, which normally operate on absolute disk addresses as a matter of course.

EXE File Format

The format of an IBM EXE file is moderately complex, consisting of a standard header followed by a relocation table. The relocation table consists of a series of pointers to segment overrides within the program itself. These segment overrides are modified to reflect the actual allocated memory segment by the DOS loader. Thus code segment "2" may be loaded into physical memory segment "23", in which case all segment references to segment 2 will be modified by the loader to be references to segment 23.

The EXE file header contains the following information:

Offset	Field size	Description
0	word	.EXE file signature "MZ"
2	word	length of file modulo 512
4	word	size of file in 512 byte pages
6	word	number of entries in relocation table
8	word	size of header in paragraphs (16 bytes)
A	word	minimum number of paragraphs of memory required
C	word	maximum number of paragraphs of memory required
E	word	displacement of stack segment in paragraphs
10	word	SP register offset
12	word	checksum of program (not normally used)
14	word	IP register offset
16	word	code segment displacement
18	word	first relocation item displacement
1A	word	overlay number (0 = program)

Within the EXE file structure there are two areas of reserved space, namely immediately after the EXE file header and immediately after the relocation table structure. The relocation item displacement field in the header is the offset from the start of code file at which the relocation table begins.

Mac Filestore Structure

The Apple Macintosh uses two filestore structures, namely the Macintosh File System (MFS) and the later Hierarchical File System (HFS). This appendix concentrates on the latter (and now more common) structure.

An HFS volume is formatted in logical blocks of 512 bytes. Each allocated file has space allotted in "allocation blocks" which are multiples of the logical block size. Thus a significant amount (normally up to 1023 bytes) may exist which is beyond the logical end of file, but within the physical end of file (i.e. space unused by the file but allocated to the file).

A typical 800K double sided floppy disk HFS volume is laid out as follows:

Logical Block 0	System startup
Logical Block 1	information
Logical Block 2	Volume information
Logical Block 3	Volume bit map
Logical Block n	
	File contents

The system startup information (which is null if the disk is not a startup volume) is stored in logical blocks 0 and 1 on the volume. This information comprises details of the location of the system file, debugger, startup application, finder and certain system configuration parameters. Additionally, a version field id of 44h indicates that the block is followed by executable boot sector code.

Offset	Size	Function
0	word	System startup information id
2	long	Entry point of boot code (offset)
6	word	System startup version id
8	word	NULL
A	16byte	Name of system file
1A	16byte	Name of system shell
2A	16byte	Name of debugger
3A	16byte	Name of debugger
4A	16byte	Startup screen name
5A	16byte	Application to be launched
6A	16byte	Scrap file name
7A	word	Number of file control blocks
7C	word	Number of events in event queue
7E	long	System heap size for 128K system
82	long	RESERVED
86	long	System heap size for 512K system

The startup information blocks (and associated executable initialisation code) are followed by the volume information block stored in logical block 2. This block contains information (equivalent to the IBM BPB) used to interpret the structure of the remaining blocks on the volume. Specifically, it contains the volume attributes (including read-only), modification dates, media allocation blocks size and details of the number of blocks utilised by the volume bitmap and following extent and catalogue trees.

Factors to be noted from the point of view of low level access to a formatted media volume are:

1. Executable code can be stored in the startup information block.
2. Selection of alternative applications and debuggers is possible.
3. Residual space exists on disk at the end of the startup information block, volume information block and volume bitmaps.
4. Allocation of blocks for concealment of viral code is straightforward via manipulation of the volume bitmap.
5. Manipulation of directory entries is more complex due to the b-tree structure of the catalogue and extent trees. This may restrict the scope for direct manipulation of filesystem by non-boot sector viruses.

Appendix 5

PC Virus Relationship Chart

The following chart, reproduced from "Virus Information Summary List" by Patricia Hoffman with additional information provided by Fridrik Skulason, indicates the inter-relationships between computer viruses on the IBM PC platform.

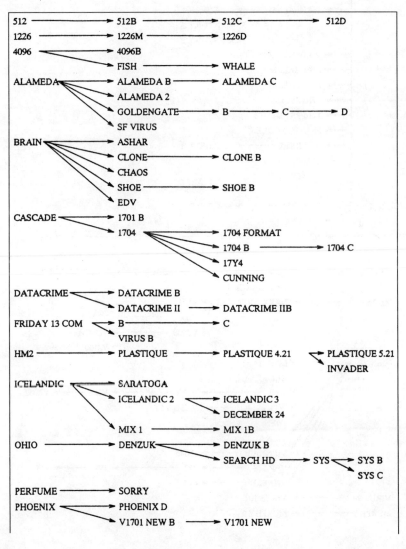

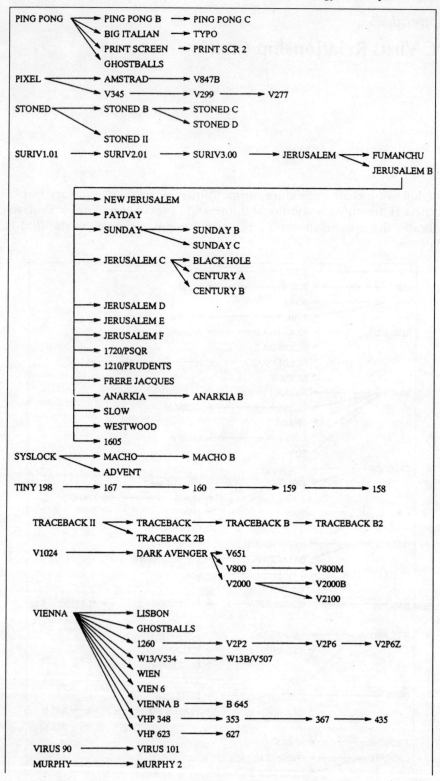

Macintosh Virus Relationship Chart

The following chart indicates the relationship between viruses on the Apple Macintosh platform.

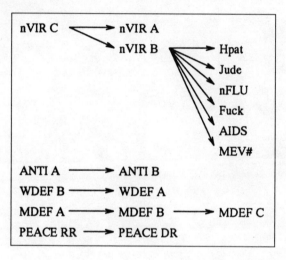

PC Boot Sequence

The following diagram indicates the components of the IBM PC boot sequence.
Square boxes indicate an individual software component within the sequence,
whose inter-relationship is indicated by interconnected arrows. The behaviour
of each boot component is modified by one or more configuration files,
indicated as filenames (not boxed) linked to their interpreting component by an
arrow.

IBM PC BOOT SEQUENCE

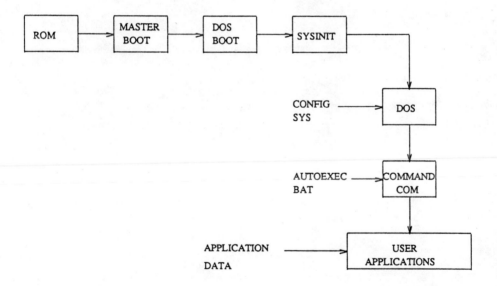

AIDS Trojan: Accompanying Licence

AIDS Information: Introductory Diskette

Please find enclosed a computer diskette containing health information on the disease AIDS. The information is provided in the form of an interactive computer program. It is easy to use. Here is how it works:

The program provides you with information about AIDS and asks you questions

You reply by choosing the most appropriate answer shown on the screen

The program then provides you with a confidential report on your risk of exposure to AIDS

The program provides recommendations to you, based on the life history information that you have provided, about practical steps that you can take to reduce your risk of getting AIDS

The program gives you the opportunity to make comments and ask questions that you may have about AIDS

This program is designed specially to help: members of the public who are concerned about AIDS and medical professionals

Instructions

This software is designed for use with IBM (R) PC/XT tm microcomputers and with all other truly compatible microcomputers. Your computer must have a hard disk drive C, MS-DOS (R) version 2.0 or higher, and a minimum of 256K RAM. First read and assent to the limited warranty and to the license agreement on the reverse. [If you use this diskette, you will have to pay the mandatory software leasing fee(s).] Then do the following:

Step 1: Start your computer (with diskette drive A empty).

Step 2: Once the computer is running, insert the Introductory Diskette into drive A.

Step 3: At the C prompt of your root directory type: A:INSTALL and then press ENTER. Installation proceeds automatically from that point. It takes only a few minutes.

Step 4: When the installation is completed, you will be given easy-to-follow messages by the computer. Respond accordingly.

Step 5: When you want to use the program, type the word AIDS at the C prompt in the root directory, and press ENTER.

On the reverse side of the blue paper it has:

Limited Warranty

If the diskette containing the programs is defective, PC Cyborg Corporation will replace it at no charge. This remedy is your sole remedy. These programs and documentation are provided "as is" without warranty of any kind, either express or implied, including but not limited to the implied warranties of merchantability and fitness for a particular purpose. The entire risk as to the quality and performance of the programs is with you. Should the programs prove defective, you (and not PC Cyborg Corporation or its dealers) assume the entire cost of any servicing, repair or correction. In no event will PC Cyborg Corporation be liable for any damages, including loss of profits, loss of savings, business interruption, loss of business information or other incidental, consequential, or special damages arising out of the use of or inability to use these programs, even if PC Cyborg Corporation has been advised of the possibility of such damages, or for any claim by any other party.

License Agreement

Read this license agreement carefully. If you do not agree with the terms and conditions stated below, do not use this software, and do not break the seal (if any) on the software diskette. PC Cyborg Corporation retains the title and ownership of these programs and documentation but grants a license to you under the following conditions: You may use the programs on microcomputers, and you may copy the programs for archival purposes and for purposes specified in the programs themselves. However, you may not decompile, disassemble, or reverse engineer these programs or modify them in any way without consent from PC Cyborg Corporation. These programs are provided for your use as described above on a leased basis to you; they are not sold. You may choose one of the following types of lease (a) a lease for 365 user applications or (b) a lease for the lifetime of your hard disk drive or 60 years, whichever is the lesser. PC Cyborg Corporation may include mechanisms in the programs to limit or inhibit copying and to ensure that you abide by the terms of the license agreement and to the terms of the lease duration. There is a mandatory leasing fee for the use of these programs; they are not provided to you free of charge. The prices for "lease a" and "lease b" mentioned above are US$189 and US$378, respectively (subject to change without notice). If you install these programs on a microcomputer (by the install program or by the share program option or by any other means), then under the terms of this license you thereby agree to pay PC Cyborg Corporation in full for the cost of leasing these programs. In the case of your breach of this license agreement, PC Cyborg Corporation reserves the right to take any legal action necessary to recover any outstanding debts payable to PC Cyborg Corporation and to use program mechanisms to ensure termination of your use of the programs. These program mechanisms will adversely affect other program applications on microcomputers. You are hereby advised of the most serious consequences of your failure to abide by the terms of this license agreement; your conscience may haunt you for the rest of your life; you will owe compensation and possible damages to PC Cyborg Corporation; and your microcomputer will stop functioning normally. Warning: Do not use these programs unless you are prepared to pay for them. You are strictly prohibited from sharing these programs with others, unless: the programs are accompanied by all program documentation including this license agreement; you fully inform the recipient of the terms of this agreement; and the recipient assents to the terms of the agreement, including the mandatory payments to PC Cyborg Corporation. PC Cyborg Corporation does not authorize you to distribute or use these programs in the United States of America. If you have any doubts about your willingness or ability to meet the terms of this license agreement or if you are not prepared to pay all amounts due to PC Cyborg Corporation, then do not use these programs. No modification to this agreement shall be binding unless specifically agreed upon in writing by PC Cyborg Corporation.

Programs (c) copyright PC Cyborg Corporation, 1989,

Compiler runtime module (c) copyright Microsoft Corporation, 1982–1987

All Rights Reserved

IBM (R) is a registered trademark of International Business Machines Corporation. PC/XT TM is a trademark of International Business Machines Corporation. Microsoft (R) and MS-DOS (R) are registered trademarks of Microsoft Corporation.

Software Infected at Source

This appendix is based on the memorandum for record: ASQNC-TWS-RA (380-380a) from Chris MacDonald, entitled "Viral infections in commercial/ government software", together with additional material from the Virus-l mailing list archives.

Software	Reporting location	Date	Virus
MSDOS			
Northern Computer (shipping infected systems)	Iceland	Mar 90	Disk Killer
Bureau of the Census	Government printing	Jan 90	Jerusalem-B
Desktop Fractal Design System	Various	Jan 90	Jerusalem-B
Unlock Masterkey	Kennedy Space Centre	Oct 89	Vienna
SARGON III	Iceland	Sep 89	Cascade 1704
ASYST RTDEMO02.EXE	Fort Belvoir	Aug 89	Jerusalem-B
Macintosh			
FreeHand	Various	Mar 88	MacMag
QLTECH MegaROM	Various	Oct 88	nVIR
MS Word 4	Various	Oct 88	nVIR
STELLA 2.0	EARN	Oct 88	nVIR
CMS Hardrive utilities 3.4	Nov 88	Scores	
NoteWriter	Colgate College	Sep 89	Scores & nVIR
Brady Hypercard 1.2.2	Sep 89	nVIR A	
Grammitik	Various	Jan 90	WDEF A
Chessmate 2100/Cribgin	Various	Apr 90	WDEF
Atari ST			
WordUp2.0	Various	Sep 89	Key
Amiga			
Sama Software Inc (infected disk distributed in *Amiga Times*)	Leonard Fetterhoff	1988	Byte Bandit

Nomenclature

Each group of workers in the computer virus field has developed its own unique naming conventions for each class of virus. This appendix attempts to offer a cross-referenced listing of terms adopted. In certain cases it is impossible to offer a direct translation for a term. In these cases, a brief explanation is given.

10.1 Types of Virus

10.1.1 Master Boot Sector Viruses

- *Virus Bulletin*, CVIA: master boot sector infector
- University of Hamburg: system virus
- S & S International Ltd.: partition record virus (PRV)

10.1.2 DOS Boot Sector Viruses

- *Virus Bulletin*, CVIA: boot virus
- University of Hamburg: system virus
- S & S International Ltd., Fridrik Skulason: boot sector virus (BSV)
- Rich Levin: boot sector infector (BSI)

10.1.3 Executable COM/EXE Viruses

- *Virus Bulletin* and CVIA: parasitic virus

- University of Hamburg: program or link virus
- S & S International Ltd., Fridrik Skulason: file virus
- Rich Levin: general purpose infector (GPI). Specialist variants include a command processor infector (CPI) which infects the COMMAND.COM and file specific infectors (FSI)
- *Computer Virus Handbook*: executable program infector

10.1.4 Memory Resident Viruses

- *Virus Bulletin*, CVIA, Fridrik Skulason, University of Hamburg: resident virus
- S & S International Ltd.: indirect action (non-resident viruses are referred to as direct action)
- Rich Levin: memory resident infector (MRI)

10.1.5 Overwriting Viruses

- *Virus Bulletin*, CVIA, Fridrik Skulason, University of Hamburg: overwriting virus
- Gene Spafford: injective virus

10.1.6 Prepending Viruses

- University of Hamburg: prefix virus

10.1.7 Appending Viruses

- University of Hamburg: postfix virus

10.2 Generations of Virus

The following generations of IBM PC virus have been identified by Jim Bates:

1. Basic: early 1986, the original PC computer viruses such as Jerusalem.
2. Camouflage: the trend for viruses to attempt to camouflage their presence within the system environment using encryption techniques, the earliest example being the Cascade virus detected in Autumn 1987.
3. Stealth: the technique of providing a shell around the user which completely hides the alterations made by the virus (e.g. by intercepting all directory and file reads). This was first used in the 4096 virus discovered in January 1990.
4. Armour: the use of extensive debug detection and interference code to prevent disassembly and delay analysis. The first example may be the Whale virus discovered in July 1990.

The fourth generation viruses are large (9K in the case of the Whale virus) and often unwieldy, and it has therefore been suggested that this level of complexity is too much for current system memory and disk capacities (in that the virus can be detected by its impact on system performance, rather than directly by observation of file alterations). Indications are therefore that third generation (referred to as second stage by the CVIA) viruses will probably still represent the limit of successful virus technology.

10.3 Classes of Anti-virus Product

The lack of consistent terminology extends to types of anti-virus software. Possibly the most extensive classification is the University of Hamburg system which identifies five categories of product, namely:

- Category 1: Monitor, software which detects attempted changes in files (type 1.1), system vectors (type 1.2) or system areas such as boot blocks (type 1.3)
- Category 2: Alteration detection, a program which detects changes of given files – checksumming techniques
- Category 3: Eradication, programs which erase viruses from files or RAM
- Category 4: Vaccine, programs which alter files in such a manner that viruses will regard them as already infected
- Category 5: Hardware methods, to detect or prevent alteration or infection of files, vectors or system areas

The classification used by Ted Shapin in his review of IBM protection programs is different, and includes three classes of product:

- Class 1: Alteration detectors, detecting changes after the fact such as checksum checkers
- Class 2: Terminate and stay resident monitors attempting to block undesirable activity
- Class 3: Combination programs which have both a checksum and monitoring component

Appendix 11

UNIX Boot Sequence

The following diagram outlines the boot sequence for a 4.3 Berkeley Software
Distribution (BSD) UNIX system, indicating each software component in the
boot sequence and the configuration files which may modify the behaviour of
the component.

UNIX BSD 4.3 BOOT SEQUENCE

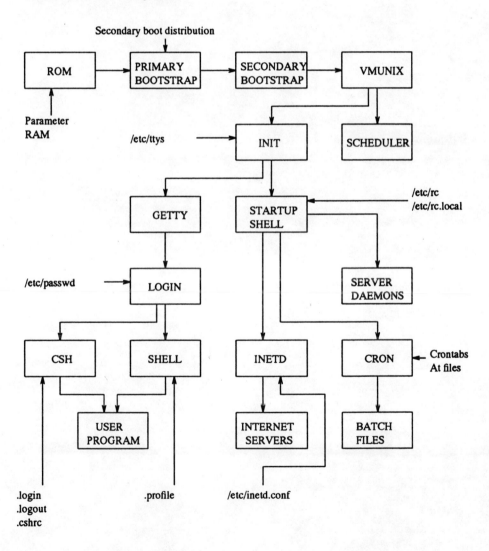

CERT Press Release

DARPA Established Computer Emergency Response Team

The Defense Advanced Research Projects Agency (DARPA) announced today that it has established a Computer Emergency Response Team (CERT) to address computer security concerns of research users of the Internet, which includes ARPANET. The Coordination Center for the CERT is located at the Software Engineering Institute (SEI), Carnegie Mellon University, Pittsburgh, PA.

In providing direct service to the Internet community, the CERT will focus on the special needs of the research community and serve as a prototype for similar operations in other computer communities. The National Computer Security Center and the National Institute of Standards and Technology will have a leading role in coordinating the creation of these emergency response activities.

The CERT is intended to respond to computer security threats such as the recent self-replicating computer program ("computer virus") that invaded many defense and research computers.

The CERT will assist the research network communities in responding to emergency situations. It will have the capability to rapidly establish communications with experts working to solve the problems, with the affected computer users and with government authorities as appropriate. Specific responses will be taken in accordance with DARPA policies.

It will also serve as a focal point for the research community for identification and repair of security vulnerabilities, informal assessment of existing systems in the research community, improvement to emergency response capability, and user security awareness. An important element of this function is the development of a network of key points of contact, including technical experts, site managers, government action officers, industry contacts, executive-level decision makers and investigative agencies, where appropriate.

Because of the many network, computer, and systems architectures and their associated vulnerabilities, no single organization can be expected to maintain an in-house expertise to respond on its own to computer security threats, particularly those that arise in the research community. As with biological viruses, the solutions must come from an organized community response of experts. The role of the CERT Coordination Center at the SEI is to provide the supporting mechanisms and to coordinate the activities of experts in DARPA and associated communities.

The SEI has close ties to the Department of Defense, to defense and commercial industry, and to the research community. These ties place the SEI in a unique position to provide coordination support to the software experts in research laboratories and in industry who will be responding in emergencies and to the communities of potentially affected users.

The SEI is a federally-funded research and development center, operating under DARPA sponsorship with the Air Force Systems Command (Electronic Systems Division) serving as executive agent. Its goal is to accelerate the transition of software technology to defense systems. Computer security is primarily a software problem, and the presence of CERT at the SEI will enhance the technology transfer mission of the SEI in security-related areas.

Appendix 13
CERT/CIAC Advisories

The Computer Emergency Response Team has issued 16 advisories concerning the security of mainframe and mini computers from its inception in December 1988 to its second anniversary.

These advisories are available by anonymous FTP from the Internet site cert.sei.cmu.edu (128.237.253.5), or by email from "cert@cert.sei.cmu.edu". The CERT organisation can be contacted on +1 412-268-7090 and is based at:

Computer Emergency Response Team
Software Engineering Institute
Carnegie-Mellon University
Pittsburgh, PA 15213-3890

List of CERT advisories issued to December 1990:

Number	Title	Date of Issue
8801	Ftpd vulnerability	12 Dec 88
8901	Passwd hole	Jan 89
8902	Sun restore hole	26 Jul 89
8903	Telnet Breakin warning	16 Aug 89
8904	WANK worm on SPAN network	17 Oct 89
8905	DEC/Ultrix 3.0 systems	17 Oct 89
8906	DEC/Ultrix 3.0 systems (update)	18 Oct 89
8907	Sun RCP vulnerability	26 Oct 89
9001	Sun Sendmail vulnerability	29 Jan 90
9002	Internet intruder warning	19 Mar 90
9003	UNISYS U5000 /etc/passwd problem	7 May 90
9004	Apollo Domain/OS suid_exec problem	27 Jul 90
9005	SunView selection_svc vulnerability	14 Aug 90
9006	NeXT's system software	2 Oct 90
9007	VMS analyse/process_dump	25 Oct 90
9008	IRIX 3.3 & 3.31 /usr/sbin/Mail	31 Oct 90
9009	VAX/VMS break ins	8 Nov 90
9010	Rumour of alleged attack	16 Nov 90
9011	Security probes from Italy	10 Dec 90

The Computer Incident Advisory Capability (CIAC) was established by the US Department of Energy and has a broader (although similar) remit to CERT, encompassing all aspects of computer security and integrity including that of personal computers. Thus CIAC have supplied a wider range of advisories covering incidents such as the Columbus Day (Datacrime) virus infection.

CIAC is based at the Lawrence Livermore laboratory in the USA. CIAC advisories can be obtained by anonymous ftp from toger.llnl.gov, or by email from ciac@tiger.llnl.gov.

List of CIAC warnings issued to December 1990:

	Authentication bypass in Sun 386i machines	Undated
	Notice of vulnerability affecting Mac/IBM running Telnet	Undated
	Notice of trojan horse affecting internet Telnet	Undated
	nVIR virus information	Undated
	Notice of availability of Sun patch for RCP & Rdist	Undated
	Announcement of vulnerability in SunOS restore	Undated
	Security holes in UNIX systems	Undated
	Availability of patch for rwalld/wall	Undated
	DecWindows under ULTRIX vulnerability	Apr 14 1989
	Jerusalem virus incidents	Jun 5 1989
	Notice of Columbus day virus	Sep 9 1989
	Information about Columbus day virus	Sep 22 1989
A1	Internet hacker attack	Oct 9 1989
A2	The W.COM worm affecting VAX VMS systems	Oct 16 1989
A3	Tools available to check the spread of the WANK worm	Oct 20 1989
A4	Information about a new version of the WANK worm	Oct 30 1989
A5	Information about a new vulnerability in the SUN rcp utility	Nov 1 1989
A6	Information about a trojan horse in Norton utilities for IBM PCs and clones	Nov 7 1989
A7	UNICOS Vulnerability	
A8	Information about a UNICOS problem	Nov 29 1989
A9	Information about the WDEF virus	Dec 18 1989
A10	Information about the PC CYBORG (AIDS) trojan horse	Dec 19 1989
A11	Problem in the Texas instruments D3 process control system	Jan 4 1990
A12	DECNET hacker attack alert	Jan 18 1990
A13	Vulnerability in DECODE alias	Jan 19 1990
A14	Additional information on the vulnerability in the UNIX decode alias	Jan 23 1990
A15	Virus information update	
A16	Vulnerability in SUN sendmail program	Jan 29 1990
A17	Eradicating WDEF using Disinfectant 1.5 or 1.6	Feb 2 1990
A18	Patch for SmarTerm 240	
A19	Internet attack advisory	Feb 23 1990
A20	Twelve tricks trojan horse	
A21	Additional information on current UNIX internet attacks	Mar 16 1990
A22	Logon messages and hacker/cracker attacks	Mar 16 1990
A23	New internet attacks	Apr 11 1990

A24	Password problems with UNISYS U5000	May 8 1990
A25	MDEF of Garfield virus on Mac computers	May 23 1990
A26	A new Macintosh trojan horse threat - Steroid	Jun 7 1990
A27	The disk killer (Ogre) virus on MS DOS computers	Jun 28 1990
A28	The Stoned virus on MS DOS computers	Jul 12 1990
A29	The 4096 virus on MS DOS computers	Jul 18 1990
A30	Apollo domain/OS suid exec problem	Jul 30 1990
A32	Sunview/Suntools selection_svc vulnerability	Aug 23 1990
A33	Virus propagation in Novelle and other networks	Sep 21 1990
A34	End of FY90 update	Sep 23 1990
B1	Security problem on NeXT operating system	Oct 5 1990
B2	UNIX security problem with Silicon Graphics Mail	Oct 12 1990

A number of other CERT centres exist which are members of the international CERT structure, including the DDN security co- ordination centre, SPAN security centre and various vendor specific security centres.

Contact Points

This appendix details the contact points for organisations with an interest in malicious software control.

Emergency Electronic Mail Contacts

Computer Emergency Response Team	cert@cert.sei.cmu.edu
Computer Incident Advisory Capability	ciac@tiger.llnl.gov
US Department of Defense Security Co-ordination Center	scc@nic.ddn.mil
Virus alert list	valert-l@ibm1.cc.lehigh.edu
Zardoz security alert list	security-emergency@uninet.cpd.com
UK UNIX security list	uk-unix- security@doc.ic.ac.uk

Administrative Electronic Mail Contacts

CERT tools list	cert-tools- request@cert.sei.cmu.edu
Virus-l mailing list	listserv@ibm1.cc.lehigh.edu
UK Virus-l mailing list	virus-l- request@cs.hw.ac.uk
Virus alert mailing list	listserv@ibm1.cc.lehigh.edu
Zardoz security list	security- request@uninet.cpd.com

Emergency Telephone and Fax Contacts

Computer Emergency Response Team:	Tel. +1 412 268 7090
Computer Incident Advisory Capability:	Tel. +1 415 423 9878 Fax +1 415 423 0913
DoD Security Co-ordination Centre:	Tel. +1 800 235 3155

UK Computer Crime Unit:	Tel. +44 71 725 2409
Federation Against Software Theft:	Tel. +44 71 240 6756
Virus Bulletin:	Tel. +44 235 555139
	Fax +44 235 559935
Virus News International:	Tel. +44 494 791900
	Fax +44 494 791602
University of Hamburg catalog project:	Tel. +40 4123 4158
Computer Fraud and Security Bulletin:	Tel. +44 865 512242
Bates Associates:	Tel. +44 533 883490
Grey Matter Ltd.:	Tel. +44 364 53499
Information Systems Integrity and Security:	Tel. +44 831 223120
	Fax +44 31 660 6839
International Computer Virus Institute:	Tel. +1 503 488 3237
International Data Security:	Tel. +44 631 0548
	Fax +44 580 1466
McAfee Associates:	Tel. +1 408 988 3832
	Fax +1 408 970 9727
Newcastle Computer Services:	Tel. +44 661 25515
PC Security:	Tel. +44 628 890390
	Fax +44 628 890116
Park Guardian:	Tel. +44 71 720 8715
	Fax +44 71 622 4706
Price Waterhouse:	Tel. +44 378 7200
SA Software:	Tel. +44 81 998 2351
S & S International Ltd.:	Tel. +44 442 877877
	Fax +44 442 877882
Sophos:	Tel. +44 235 559933
	Fax +44 235 559935
Symantec (UK) Ltd.:	Tel. +44 628 776343
	Fax +44 628 776775
Sypro:	Tel. +44 452 370144
	Fax +44 452 613135
Walsham Contracts:	Tel. +44 273 597115
	Fax +44 273 870020
Zortech:	Tel. +44 81 316 7777

A list of anti-virus software manufacturers is included in *Computer Viruses and Anti-virus Warfare* by Jan Hruska. The above list is only a sample of the UK firms.

Abbreviations

The following list gives the meaning of all abbreviations used within this work
(including appendices):

ACL	Access control list
ACM	American Association for Computer Machinery
ADS	Storage "standard" for virus after logical EOF
BAT	Batch file format (IBM PC)
BBN	Bolt, Beranek and Newman
BBS	Bulletin board system
BCVRC	British Computer Virus Research Centre
BFE	Blacker front end (DISNET)
BFV	Batch file virus
BIOS	Basic input/output subsystem (IBM PC)
BPB	BIOS parameter block (IBM PC)
BSD	Berkeley Software Distribution (UNIX)
BSI	Boot sector infector
BSV	Boot sector virus
CCC	Chaos Computer Club
CCITT	International telegraph telephone consultative committee
CCU	Computer Crime Unit
CDEF	Control definition resource (MAC)
CERT	Computer Emergency Response Team
CESG	Communications/Electronic Security Group
CFG	Control flow graph
CIAC	Computer Incident Advisory Capability
CIC	Coordination and Information Center
CODE	Executable code resource (MAC)
COFF	Common object file format (UNIX)
COM	Object file format (IBM PC)
CoTRA	Computer Threat Research Association
CPI	*Corrupted Programming International*
CPSR	Computer Professionals for Social Responsibility
CRC	Cyclic redundancy check
CREN	Corporation for Research and Education Networking
CVCM	Computer virus counter measures

CVIA	Computer Virus Industry Association
CPL	Current privilege level (80386)
DAC	Discretionary access control
DAFV	Direct action file virus
DARPA	Defense Advanced Research Projects Agency
DDN	Defense Date Network
DEA	Data encryption algorithm
DES	Data encryption standard
DISNET	Defense Integrated Secure Network
DNA	Deoxyribonucleic acid
DoD	Department of Defense
DOS	Disk operating system (IBM PC)
DPL	Descriptor privilege level (80386)
E3	End-to-end encryption
EARN	European Academic Research Network
EAROM	Electronically alterable ROM
ECM	Electronic counter measure
EEROM	Electronically erasable ROM
EICVR	European Institute for Computer Virus Research
EOF	End of file
EST	Eastern standard time
EXE	Object file format (IBM PC)
FAST	Federation Against Software Theft
FAT	File allocation table (IBM PC)
FCB	File control block (IBM PC)
FSI	File specific infector
GCHQ	Government Communications Headquarters
GDT	Global descriptor table (80386)
GPI	General purpose infector
HEPNET	High Energy Physics Network
HFS	Hierarchical file system (MAC)
IAB	Internet activities board
IAFV	Indirect action file virus
ICE	In-circuit emulator
ICMP	Internet control message protocol
ICO	International CERT Organisation
IEE	Institute of Electrical Engineers
IEEE	Institute of Electronic and Electrical Engineers
IETF	Internet Engineering Task Force
IFS	Inter-field separator
IMP	Interface message processor (TCP/IP)
INIT	Initialisation resource (MAC)
IO	Input/output
IOPL	I/O privilege level
IP	Internet protocol

IPC	Inter-process communication
IRTF	Internet Research Task Force
ISN	Initial sequence number (TCP/IP)
ISO	International Standards Organisation
ITSEC	Information Technology Security Evaluation Criteria
JANET	Joint Academic Network
JUNET	Japanese Academic Network
LAN	Local area network
LDT	Local descriptor table (80386)
LFSR	Linear feedback shift register
MAC	Mandatory access control
MBR	Master boot record (IBM PC)
MCB	Memory control block (IBM PC)
MD4	Message digest algorithm 4, RFC 1186
MFS	Mac file system (MAC)
MIT	Massachusetts Institute of Technology
MMU	Memory management unit
MRI	Memory resident infector
MS-DOS	Microsoft DOS (IBM PC)
NASA	National Aeronautics and Space Administration
NCSC	National Computer Security Centre
NFS	Network filing system (TCP/IP)
NIFTP	Network independent file transfer protocols
NIST	National Institute of Standards and Technology
NSA	National Security Agency
NSFNET	National Science Foundation Network
OSI	Open systems interconnection, ISO standard
OVL	Executable overlay format (IBM PC)
PDSOFT	Lancaster public domain software project
PFM	Program flow monitor
PRAM	Parameter RAM
PRV	Partition record virus
PSP	Program segment prefix (IBM PC)
PTE	Page table entry
QoS	Quality of service
RCR	Remote copy request
ROM	Read-only memory
ROvr	ROM over-ride resource (MAC)
RFC	Request for comments
RPC	Remote procedure call (TCP/IP)
RSA	Rivest, Shamir and Adleman public key cryptosystem
RTVM	Run time validation mechanism
R/W	Read/write
SBIR	Small Business Innovative Research
SCA	Swiss Cracker's Association

SIB	Startup information block (MAC)
SIPB	Student Information Processing Board
SMIB	Security Management Information Board
SNEFRU	XEROX secure hash function
SPANET	Space Physics Analysis Network
TCB	Trusted computer base
TCP	Transmission control protocol (TCP/IP)
TCSEC	Trusted computer security evaluation criteria
TNI	Trusted network interpretation
TSR	Terminate and stay resident (IBM PC)
UDP	User datagram protocol (TCP/IP)
UEV	Undecidable evolutionary virus
U/S	User/supervisor
Valert-l	BITNET virus alert email list
Virus-l	BITNET virus discussion email list
WDEF	Window definition resource (MAC)
WORM	Write-once, read-many device
XOR	Exclusive or operation

Further Reading

Many of the following references are only available in electronic mail or news format. These references can be obtained from one or more of the major archive sites accessible via the DARPA Internet. The cert.sei.cmu.edu archive site at the Software Engineering Institute at Carnegie-Mellon University can provide copies of the majority of these items.

Information on emergent standards for computer security can be obtained from the UK Department of Trade and Industry (Green and White Books), US Department of Defense and the National Computer Security Center (Orange Books), the UK Government Communications Headquarters (Red Books) and the International Organisation for Standardisation (OSI standards).

Internet Worm Incident

Eugene Spafford, The Internet worm program: an analysis. Purdue Technical Report, CSD-TR-823, Department of Computer Science, Purdue University, West Lafayette

US General Accounting Office, Computer security – virus highlights need for improved Internet management. Report to the chairman, subcommittee on telecommunications and finance, committee on energy and commerce, House of Representatives, GAO/IMTEC-89-57

Donn Seeley, A tour of the worm. Department of computer science, University of Utah (Electronic media: cert.sei.cmu.edu archives)

The computer worm – a report to the provost of Cornell University on an investigation conducted by the commission of preliminary enquiry. Cornell University, February 1989

Bob Page, A report on the Internet worm. University of Lowell, November 1988

Mark Eichin, Jon Rochlis, With microscope and tweezers: an analysis of the Internet virus of November 1988. Massachusetts Institute of Technology, February 1989

DECNET Christmas Worm Incident

US Department of Defense Network Information Center, Defense data network management bulletin 50, December 1988 (Electronic media: nic.ddn.mil archives)

Pat Sisson, Space Analysis Physics Network (SPAN) report, SPAN-027. NASA Goddard Space Flight Center, February 1989

DECNET Wank Worm Incident

SPAN Management Office, Security guidelines to be followed in latest worm attack. Inter-network memorandum, October 1989 (Electronic media: cert.sei.cmu.edu archives)

SPAN Management Office, Information regarding the DECNET worm and protection measures. Inter-network memorandum, October 1989 (Electronic media: cert.sei.cmu.edu archives)

Kevin Oberman, Report on the W.COM worm. Engineering Department, Lawrence Livermore National Laboratory, October 1989 (Electronic media: cert.sei.cmu.edu archives)

IBM Christmas Chain Letter Incidents

Valdis Kletnieks, Bitnet worm spotted. Valert-l electronic mailing list, October 1990

Ralf Burger, Computer viruses – a high-tech disease. Abacus Software, 1988 (ISBN 1-55755-043-3)

AIDS Trojan Horse Incident

Jim Bates, Report on the AIDS disk. Virus Bulletin (Available from Virus Bulletin Ltd, 21 The Quadrant, Abingdon Science Park, Abingdon, Oxfordshire)

OSI Security Standards

International Organisation for Standardisation (ISO), Guide to open system security. ISO/IEC JTC 1/SC 21 N5049, July 1990

International Organisation for Standardisation (ISO), Information processing systems – open systems interconnection – basic reference model. Part 2: security architecture. ISO 7498-2, 1989

International Organisation for Standardisation (ISO), Lower layers security model. ISO/IEC JTC 1/SC 6, November 1989

International Organisation for Standardisation (ISO), Security frameworks overview. ISO/IEC JTC 1/SC 18 N2606, August 1990 (Includes associated frameworks for access control, authentication and data integrity)

General Mainframe and Network Security Warnings

Computer Incident Advisory Capability (CIAC) bulletins, various dates. US Department of Energy (Electronic media: cert.sei.cmu.edu archives)

Computer Emergency Response Team (CERT) advisories, various dates. CERT, Software Engineering Institute, Carnegie-Mellon University (Electronic media: cert.sei.cmu.edu archives)

US Department of Defense Security Co-ordination Center security bulletins, various dates. Defence Communications Agency (Electronic media: nic.ddn.mil archives)

S. Bellovin, Security problems in the TCP/IP protocol suite. ACM Computer Communication Review 19(2) April 1989

Defence data network security architecture. ACM Computer Communication Review 20(2) April 1990

Richard D. Pethia, Kenneth R. Van Wyk, Computer emergency response, an international problem. CERT, Software Engineering Institute, Carnegie-Mellon University

Early Worm Experiments and References

John Shoch, Jon Hupp, The worm programs – early experience with a distributed computation. Communications of the ACM 25(3) March 1982

Department of Defense Orange Book Standards

US Department of Defense, Trusted computer system evaluation criteria (Orange Book). DOD 5200.28-STD, December 1985

US National Computer Security Center, A guide to understanding discretionary access control in trusted systems. NCSC-TG-003, September 1987

US Department of Defense, Technical rationale behind CSC-STD-003-85 (Yellow Book). CSC-STD-OO4-85, June 1985

US Department of Defense, Trusted network interpretation (Red Book). NCSC-TG-005, July 1987

US Department of Defense, Password management guideline (Green Book). CSC-STD-002-85, April 1985

US National Computer Security Center, Audit in trusted systems. NCSC-TG-001, June 1988

UK DTI Green and GCHQ Red Book Standards

UK Department of Trade and Industry, Evaluation levels manual, V22-version 3.0. February 1989

UK Government communications headquarters, UK systems security confidence levels. CESG computer security memorandum no. 3, February 1989

Harmonised European Standards

Information Technology Security Evaluation Criteria (ITSEC), Harmonised criteria of France, Germany, Netherlands, United Kingdom, Draft 1, May 1990 (Available from UK Department of Trade and Industry, computer security branch)

UNIX Operating System Security

Sun Microsystems, Security features guide, Part number 800-1735-10, 1987
Patrick Wood, Stephen Kochan, UNIX system security. Hayden Books, 1985 (ISBN
    0-810-46267-2)
Rik Farrow, UNIX system security. Addison-Wesley (ISBN 0-201- 57030-0)
Russell Brand, Coping with the threat of computer security incidents – a primer from
    prevention through recovery. Lawrence Livermore National Laboratory, June 1990
    (Electronic media: cert.sei.cmu.edu archives)
Network Working Group of the Internet Engineering Task Force, Site security policy
    handbook, Draft, October 1990 (Electronic media: cert.sei.cmu.edu archives)
Samuel Leffler, Marshall McKusick, Mike Karels, John Quarterman, The design and
    implementation of the 4.3 BSD UNIX operating system. Addison-Wesley, 1989 (ISBN
    0-201-06196-1)
X/OPEN Group, X-Open security guide. Prentice-Hall, 1989 (ISBN 0-139-72142-8)
Clifford Stoll, The cuckoo's egg – tracking a spy through the maze of computer
    espionage. Doubleday, 1989
Simson Garfinkel, Gene Spafford, Practical UNIX security. O'Reilly and Associates,
    1991 (ISBN 0-937-17572-2)

Encryption Techniques and Digest Ciphers

Dominic Welsh, Codes and cryptography. Oxford Science Publications, 1988 (ISBN
    0-198-53287-3)
R. Rivest, MD4 message digest algorithm, request for comments 1186 (Electronic media:
    uunet.uu.net archives)
Ralph Merkle, A software one way hash function. Xerox Corporation (Snefru algorithm)

Project Athena

Jennifer G. Steiner, Clifford Neuman, Jeffrey Schiller, Kerberos: an authentication
    service for open network systems, Massachusetts Institute of Technology, January
    1988 (Electronic media: uunet.uu.net archives)

Apple Macintosh Virus Internals

David Ferbrache, Known apple Macintosh viruses. Virus Bulletin, October 1990, pp 6–7
David Ferbrache, INIT 29 infectious, but your data is safe. Virus Bulletin, December
    1989, pp 6–7
David Ferbrache, nVIR and its clones. Virus Bulletin, October 1989, pp 13–14
John Norstad, Disinfectant 2.1 anti-virus software documentation. May 1991 (Electronic
    media: rascal.ics.utexas.edu archives)
Joe McMahon, Anti-viral documentation stack, Hypercard. NASA Goddard Space
    Flight Center, 1989 (Electronic media: rascal.ics.utexas.edu archives)
L. Brown, Anatomy of a Macintosh nVIR virus. Australian Defence Force Academy, CS
    88/29, December 1988

Danny Schwendener, Anti virus. ETH-Zentrum, Switzerland (Electronic media: rascal.ics.utexas.edu archives)

Thomas Bond, The eleventh word: an investigation into the 712 byte RINIT 29S Mac virus. Mac Consultant (Electronic media: rascal.ics.utexas.edu archives)

Apple Macintosh System Operation

Apple Computers Inc., Inside Mac, vols 1, 2 & 3. Addison-Wesley, 1985 (ISBN 0-201-17737-4)

Apple Computers Inc, Inside Mac, vol 4. Addison-Wesley, 1986 (ISBN 0-201-05409-4)

Apple Computers Inc, Inside Mac, vol 5. Addison-Wesley, 1988 (ISBN 0-201-17719-6)

Federal Information Processing Standards: Information Protection

US National Institute of Standards and Technology (NIST), Executive guide to protection of information resources. Federal Information Processing Standard (FIPS) 169

US National Institute of Standards and Technology (NIST), Management guide to the protection of information resources. Federal Information Processing Standard (FIPS) 170

US National Institute of Standards and Technology (NIST), Computer user's guide to the protection of information resources. Federal Information Processing Standard (FIPS) 171

US National Computer Security Center, Personal computer security considerations. NCSC-WA-002-85, December 1985

IBM PC Virus Internals

4K – a warning of data corruption. Virus Bulletin, November 1990, pp 5–6

Fridrik Skulason, Virus encryption techniques. Virus Bulletin November 1990, pp 13–16

Jim Bates, Whale – a dinosaur heading for extinction. Virus Bulletin, November 1990, pp 17–19

Jim Bates, From Brain to Whale – the story so far. Virus Bulletin, October 1990, pp 12–14

Fridrik Skulason, The Bulgarian computer viruses – the virus factory. Virus Bulletin, June 1990, pp 6–9

How does an IBM PC virus infect a computer? Virus Bulletin, April 1990, pp 11–13

Fridrik Skulason, IBM PC viruses: the new generation. Virus Bulletin, March 1990, pp 10–11

Joe Hirst, Jerusalem virus – the early days. Virus Bulletin, August 1989, pp 10–12

Virus infected media and routes of infiltration. Virus Bulletin, May 1990, pp 3–5

Patricia Hoffman, Virus information summary list, October 1990 (Electronic media)

University of Hamburg Virus Test Centre, Computer virus catalog, July 1990 (Electronic media: cert.sei.cmu.edu archives)

George Woodside, Virus 101 – an elementary course in virus technology (Electronic media: cert.sei.cmu.edu archives)

Brad Stubbs, Lance Hoffman, Mapping the virus battlefield – an overview of personal computer vulnerabilities to virus attack. GWU-IIST-89-23, George Washington University, August 1989

Joe Hirst, Fighting infections on PCs. Tech PC User, December 1988

IBM PC Internal System Operation

Terry Dettman, DOS programmers reference. Que Corporation, 1989 (ISBN 0-88022-458-4)

IBM PC Virus Protection and Precautions

Steve White, David Chess, Coping with computer viruses and related problems. IBM Thomas J. Watson Research Centre, research report RC 14405, January 1989

Raymond Glath, Computer viruses: a rational view. RG Software Systems Inc., April 1988 (Electronic media)

David Stodolsky, Net hormones, infection control assuming co-operation amongst computers, 1989 (Electronic media)

Interpath Corporation, Anti-virus measures (Electronic media)

Stephen Kiel, Raymond Lee, The infection of PC compatible computers. Georgia Institute of Technology, summer 1988

Eugene Spafford, Kathleen Heaphy, David Ferbrache, Computer viruses – dealing with electronic vandalism and programmed threats. ADAPSO

IBM, Good security practices for personal computers. G320-9280-0, March 1984

Computer virus handbook. Price Waterhouse/Auerbach, 1989

John Wack, Lisa Carnahan, Computer viruses and related threats: a management guide. US National Institute of Standards and Technology

Harold Highland (ed.) Computer virus handbook. Elsevier Advanced Technology, 1990 (ISBN 0-946395-46-2)

Philip Fites, Peter Johnson, Martin Kratz, The computer virus crisis. Chapman and Hall, 1989 (ISBN 0-442-28532-9)

Ralf Burger, Computer viruses – a high tech disease. Abacus Software, 1988 (ISBN 1-55755-043-3)

Richard Levin, The computer virus handbook. Osborne/McGraw-Hill, 1990 (ISBN 0-078-81647-5)

Jan Hruska, Computer viruses and anti-virus warfare. Ellis Horwood, 1990 (ISBN 0-131-71067-2)

Myron Cramer, Stephen Pratt, Computer virus countermeasures. Defence Electronics, October 1989

Stanley Kurzban, Viruses and worms – what can you do? ACM SIGSAC 1987, IBM Systems Research Educational Centre, 1987

Tim Sanakary, Developing virus identification products. Homebase bulletin board (Electronic media: cert.sei.cmu.edu archives)

Hardware and Cryptographic Anti-virus Techniques

Maria Pozzo, Terence Gray, An approach to containing computer viruses. Computers and Security 6(4) 1987

George Davida, Yvo Desmedt, Brian J. Matt, Defending systems against viruses through cryptographic authentication. IEEE symposium on computer security and privacy, 1989

Virus Infection of Commercial Software

Chris MacDonald, Viral infections in commercial/government software. Memorandum for record, ASQNC-TWS-RA (380-380a), US Army, April 1990

Legal Issues of Computer Misuse

Anne Branscomb, Rogue computer programs and computer rogues: tailoring the punishment to fit the crime. Rutger's Computer and Technology Law Journal 16(1) 1990

General License GTDA, Technical data available to all destinations. CREN information centre, May 1990 (US cryptographic export regulations)

Colin Tapper, Computer Law, 4th edn. Longman, 1989 (ISBN 0-582-02481-1)

Criminal law – computer misuse. Law Commission report 186, HMSO, October 1989

Computer misuse. Law Commission working paper 110, HMSO, 1988

Report on computer crime. Scottish Law Commission report 106, HMSO, 1987

Computer Misuse Act 1990. HMSO

Theory of Viruses

Ken Thompson, Reflections on trusting trust. Communications of the ACM 27(8) August 1984

Harold Thimbleby, Bugs, viruses and liveware. University of Stirling, UK, 1989

Computer viruses, theory and experiments. 7th DOD/NBS security conference, September 1984

Leonard Adleman, An abstract theory of computer viruses. Lecture Notes in Computer Science vol 403, Springer-Verlag, 1990

Fred Cohen, Computational aspects of computer viruses. Computers and Security 8(4) 1989

Winfried Gleissner, A mathematical theory for the spread of computer viruses. Computers and Security 8(1) 1989

Fred Cohen, On the implications of computer viruses and methods of defence. Computers and Security

Biological Analogies to Computer Viruses

William H. Murray, The application of epidemiology to computer viruses. Computers and Security

Daniel Guinier, Biological versus computer viruses. ACM SIGSAC 1989, IBM Systems Research Educational Centre, 1989

Codes of Ethics

Dianne Martin, David Martin, Professional codes of conduct and computer ethics education. Social Sciences Computer Review 8(1) spring 1990

Corporation for Research and Educational Networking (CREN), Acceptable use policy.
    CREN Information Center, Washington, October 1990
British Computer Society, Code of conduct, handbook no. 5, 1985
High Energy Physics Network, Acceptable use statement, draft 2, June 1989 (Electronic
    media)
Richard D. Pethia, Steve Crocker, Internet security policy, working draft, October 1990
    (Electronic media: uunet.uu.net archives)
Interim NSFNET acceptable use policy (Electronic media: uunet.uu.net archives)

Social Issues and General Commentary

Harold Thimbleby, Ian Witten, The worm that turned: a social use of computer viruses.
    University of Stirling, UK, September 1989

Artificial Life

Eugene Spafford, Computer viruses – a form of artificial life, Purdue Technical Report,
    CSD-TR-985, Department of Computer Science, Purdue University, West Lafayette,
    June 1990

Virus-l Archive Sites

The following sites carry archives of anti-viral software and information as part
of the Virus-l archive system:

cs.hw.ac.uk

Maintained by David Ferbrache
Based at Heriot-Watt University, Edinburgh, this archive carries information
on general security, Amiga, Atari, IBM PC, Apple II and Apple Macintosh
shareware anti-virus software.

The archive is accessible by an email info-server on address "info-
server@cs.hw.ac.uk".

ms.uky.edu

Maintained by Sean Casey
An Internet FTP based archive of Amiga anti-virus software (stored in the
directory /pub/amiga/Antivirus).

pdsoft.lancs.ac.uk

Maintained by Steve Jenkins
This is the UK public domain software archive and is accessible by email info-
server on address "archive- server@lancs.pdsoft", and by direct dialup on the
following numbers: +44 524 63414, +44 524 67671, +44 524 67754, +44 524
62423, and +44 524 381819.

This archive is also accessible using UK JANET guest network independent
file transfer protocols (NIFTP). The archive contains Amiga, Atari, IBM PC and
Apple Macintosh software.

ux1.cso.uiuc.edu

Maintained by Mark Zinzow
An Internet FTP based archive of Amiga and IBM PC software (stored in the
directories /amiga/virus and /pc/virus).

brownvm.bitnet

Maintained by Chris Chung
The Apple 2 listserver archive which is accessible via the BITNET listserver
address "listserv@brownvm.bitnet".

cert.sei.cmu.edu

Maintained by Kenneth Van Wyk
The CERT Virus-l archives carrying back issues of Virus-l together with general information on virus prevention. This is an Internet FTP based archive stored in the directory /pub/virus-l.

csrc.ncsl.nist.gov

Maintained by John Wack
This is the NIST archive of security bulletins issued by NIST, CERT, NASA SPAN, DDN and LLNL-CIAC. It is accessible via Internet FTP.

mibsrv.mib.eng.ua.edu

Maintained by James Ford
An Internet FTP based archive of IBM PC software (stored in the directory /pub/msdos/AntVirus).

vega.hut.fi

Maintained by Timo Kiravuo
This Finnish Internet FTP archive contains IBM anti-virus software stored in the directory /pub/pc/virus.

wsmr-simtel20.army.mil

Maintained by Keith Peterson
This is the largest IBM PC public and shareware software archive in the world, and is accessible by Internet FTP or by email via the Trickle servers "listserv@ndsuvm1.bitnet" and "listserv@rpiecs.bitnet". PC anti-virus software is stored in the directory "PD1:<MSDOS.TROJAN-PRO>".

A Macintosh archive is maintained by Rober Thum, and stored in the directory "PD3:<MACINTOSH.VIRUS>".

rascal.ics.utexas.edu

Maintained by Werner Uhrig
An Internet FTP based archive of Apple Macintosh software (stored in the directory mac/virus-tools).

wuarchive.wustl.edu

Maintained by Chris Myers
An Internet FTP based archive of Apple Macintosh and IBM PC software which mirrors the INFO-MAC archive at SUMEX and the Simtel MSDOS archive.

Relative Frequencies of IBM Viruses

The table below presents the estimates of three researchers in the IBM PC virus field of the relative frequencies of each virus. The figures are based on articles by David Chess, Fridrik Skulason and Morton Swimmer in Virus-l, and they reflect, respectively:

1. The relative frequencies of viruses reported to IBM (informal) over the last few years.
2. The relative frequencies of viruses in Iceland estimated at mid-1990.
3. The relative frequencies of viruses in Germany estimated at mid-1990.

Virus strain	US frequency	Icelandic frequency	German frequency
Italian	26%	30%	10%
Cascade	23%	55%	25%
Jersualem	21%	5%	15%
New Zealand	9%	2%	10%
Vienna	7%	-	10%
Brain	7%	2%	-
Vacsina	-	-	5%
Dark Avenger	-	-	2%
Disk Killer	<1%	2%	5%
Yale	1%	-	-
Macho	-	-	1%
Yankee Doodle	<1%	-	-
765	<1%	-	-
Lehigh	<1%	-	-
Sunday	<1%	-	-
Sylvia	<1%	-	-
Advent	-	-	<1%
5120	-	-	<1%
Icelandic	-	3%	-
Ghostballs	-	1%	-

Rough estimates were also provided by Fridrik Skulason in September 1989, and John McAfee (based on Viruscan software reports). These point estimates provide an interesting comparison with the 1990 mid-year statistics:

Virus strain	US frequency	Icelandic frequency
Jerusalem	62%	-
Cascade	17%	60%
Italian	9%	30%
New Zealand	8%	-
Brain	not quoted	5%
Icelandic	not quoted	5%
Others	4%	-

Recent indications are that the Stoned/New Zealand virus is spreading rapidly together with a number of 4096/Stealth virus incidents. Cascade maintains a high profile (approximately 25 per cent of infection) although it has been reported less frequently during the late-1990 period. This spread can be attributed to the absence (since outside the activation window) of the characteristic display which had previously permitted easy detection of the virus. Jerusalem now appears to be in decline, due possibly to the widespread publicity the virus has received.

Interestingly, the Vienna strain (and variants) have been reported as becoming considerably more common. This can be related to the widespread availability of disassemblies for this virus.

Subject Index